THE COMMONWEALTH EXPERIENCE

Volume One: The Durham Report to the Anglo–Irish Treaty

THE COMMONWEALTH EXPERIENCE

Volume One

The Durham Report to the Anglo–Irish Treaty

Nicholas Mansergh, F.B.A.

*Emeritus Smuts Professor of
the History of the British
Commonwealth and Fellow of
St John's College, Cambridge*

First edition published as one volume
by Weidenfeld & Nicolson *1969*

Second edition published as two volumes 1982 by
THE MACMILLAN PRESS LTD
London and Basingstoke
Companies and representatives
throughout the world

ISBN 0 333 33158 3 (hardcover)
ISBN 0 333 33159 1 (paperback)
ISBN 0 333 33168 0 (hardcover two-volume set)

Printed and bound in Great Britain
at The Pitman Press, Bath

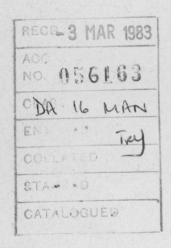

To
The Master and Fellows
of
St John's College, Cambridge

'There was a time when we might have stood alone as the United Kingdom of England, Scotland and Ireland. That time has passed. We conquered and peopled Canada, we took possession of the whole of Australia, Van Diemen's Land and New Zealand. We have annexed India to the Crown. There is no going back.

Tu regere imperio populos, Romane, memento'
JOHN, EARL RUSSELL, 1870

'*Suivez, suivez Seigneur, le ciel qui vous inspire:*
Votre gloire redouble à mépriser l'empire;
Et vous serez fameux chez la postérité
Moins pour l'avoir conquis que pour l'avoir quitté.'

Maxime to César Auguste
Corneille, *Cinna*

'Our historic Commonwealth which comprises one-fourth of the world's population . . . has the unique quality of embracing nations and peoples from every continent.'

DECLARATION BY COMMONWEALTH PRIME MINISTERS,
12 JANUARY 1951

Contents

Contents of Volume Two: From British to Multiracial Commonwealth

Preface to the First Edition

'Mr Deakin actually contended' wrote John Morley, secretary of state for India, complaining of some remarks made by the Australian prime minister at the Colonial Conference of 1907, 'that India had no right to a place at the conference table, because not self-governing. I dealt faithfully with him on the point. I laugh when I think of a man who blows the imperial trumpet louder than other people, and yet would banish India which is the most stupendous part of the Empire – our best customer among other trifles – into the imperial back-kitchen.'* This book, however, is written on the assumption that not Morley but Deakin had the clearer grasp of essentials – that there was a difference in kind between states that were self-governing and even the greatest of imperial dependencies and that these differences could not be papered over, merely by the nomination by the imperial power of representatives for that dependency. That was also the view, despite India's equivocal position, of Colonial and Imperial Conferences in the past and of Prime Ministers' and Commonwealth Heads of State Meetings in our own time, so much so that, by agreement, admission as of right to such gatherings became the accepted test of independence within the Commonwealth. Or, to put the point in another way, Empire, its government, organisation, administration and ideas is one thing; relations between autonomous polities within a community of states another. Both are deserving of study but it is the second, which in British history superseded the first, that provides the theme of this enquiry.

This book, then, is about the Commonwealth – about its origins, its development, its pattern and concepts of inter-state relations, its experience in peace and war. That Commonwealth was the heir of Empire, and imperial influences bore closely upon its earlier growth. But it developed a life and made a contribution to political thought and relations, not only distinct and distinguishable from

_____

* Lord Morley to Lord Minto, 2 May 1907. India Office Library. MSS Eur. D. 573/2.

those of Empire, but in many respects inherently opposed to them. It is that contribution, broadly conceived, which is studied in this book. The object is not detailed narrative but interpretation and analysis against a chronological background. The approach is historical, but then so in essence was the experience. The Commonwealth was not the product of political abstractions, but of a succession of historical developments.

A work that ranges so widely in time and space must rely greatly on specialist studies by other historians, and I have sought to make clear my indebtedness in this respect in footnotes and in the concluding bibliography. But I have also, at critical phases in Commonwealth evolution, sought to examine or re-examine the first-hand sources of evidence myself. I have quoted freely (though I hope not excessively) from such sources so as to convey something of the sense of occasion or the temper of debate at such times.

I have many acknowledgments to make. In respect of official records I am much indebted for their help and courtesy to the staff of the Public Record Office, and of the Commonwealth and India Office libraries in London; of the Archives of Cape Colony, in Cape Town; of the National Archives of the Republic of South Africa, in Pretoria; of the Indian National Archives, in New Delhi; while with regard to libraries I would like to express my thanks to the staff of the University and Seeley libraries in Cambridge, and also to the staff of the libraries of the University of Cape Town, of Duke University, North Carolina and of the Indian School of International Studies, New Delhi. I have to thank the Trustees of the British Museum for permission to use the papers of Sir Henry Campbell-Bannerman, and Mr C. A. Gladstone for giving me leave to consult the papers of W. E. Gladstone in the British Museum. The late Viscount Bruce of Melbourne showed me the personal records which he kept of meetings between the dominion high commissioners and the secretary of state for dominion affairs during the second world war, but from which I have not felt free to quote directly; Mr John Duncan allowed me to go through the papers of his father, Sir Patrick Duncan; the Indian National Archives, Calcutta, by courtesy of Sarvasri A. N. Sapru, P. N. Sapru and T. N. Sapru, made available to me transcripts from the papers of Sir Tej Bahadur Sapru; the Public Library in Cape Town enabled me to study the papers of J. X. Merriman; the Canadian National Archives in Ottawa, to whom an expression of special appreciation for their arrangements, both for week-end and (for the indefatigable) all-night study, is fitting, gave me permission to examine the papers of Sir Wilfrid Laurier, Sir Robert Borden and

William Lyon Mackenzie King (down to 1922). Three extracts from
the diary of the Right Hon. Vincent Massey are reprinted from
What's Past is Prologue by kind permission of Messrs Macmillan. I
am indebted to the editors of *The Economist*, the *International
Journal*, Toronto, and the *India Quarterly*; to the Duke University
Press and to Radio Éireann for permission to make use of material
first published by them as articles or, in the last instance, delivered
as lectures in the Thomas Davis series. Nor would I wish to leave
unrecorded my appreciation of the patience and care with which
the University Typewriting Office in Cambridge copied an often
difficult manuscript. Finally it is my pleasant duty to acknowledge
with gratitude a grant from the Smuts Memorial Fund at Cambridge for research and travel for the production of this book.

My greatest debt is to my wife, who accompanied me on my
travels and has not only checked facts and references throughout
the book, but has made criticisms, comments and enquiries on
every chapter and also many suggestions for additions from her
own reading and research which have much enriched the work.

Nicholas Mansergh
St John's College, Cambridge   March 1968

Preface to the Second Edition

In the decade that has elapsed since the first publication of *The
Commonwealth Experience* there have been significant additions to
our knowledge and to our understanding of Commonwealth
development and history. The opening of the official archives of
the principal Commonwealth governments under a thirty year, or
similar, rule, together with the publication in selected series of
official documents on important topics – e.g. by the Australian
Government on *Australian Foreign Policy* since 1937 and by the
British on *The Transfer of Power* in India 1942–47, has contributed
notably to the widening of our knowledge, while understanding
has been enhanced by studies both of a revisionist and a pioneering
character – the former weighted towards earlier and still controversial events or personalities, the latter including detailed analyses
of Anglo-dominion relations in more recent years. On the personal
side the period has seen the rounding out of biographical studies of
leading Commonwealth statesmen or personalities and the publication (in part) of two diaries of outstanding interest, those of Tom

Jones on Cabinet treaty-making with Ireland and of Mackenzie King in his later years. Within the limits of space and relevance to theme, account of these additions is taken in this revised edition, with appropriate references in notes and an expanded bibliography.

The decade since first publication has further witnessed developments, some still unfolding, which, so it seems, at this slight vantage point in time, must necessarily add to the Commonwealth experience. They include Britain's accession to the Common Market, changes in membership of the Commonwealth, what might be thought of as the climax of the process of decolonisation, the hardly-won resolution of the Rhodesia–Zimbabwe question, with the goal of independent status and international recognition attained by way of prior retreat from a unilaterally declared independence to colonial status – a classic example of the longest road round proving to be the shortest way home and, with echoes of earlier times, an improbable confrontation of Prime Minister with Governor-General in Australia and the 'patriation' of the constitution of the oldest dominion. These and other more general developments, notably the enhanced significance of economic factors, are considered, so far as may be in the longer perspective of history, in the concluding chapters.

I am indebted to the Jawaharlal Nehru University for an invitation to serve as a visiting professor at the School of International Studies, January to April 1980, to the British Academy for a grant to pursue research in India, and to the Leverhulme Trustees for an Emeritus Fellowship for further study of Anglo–Irish relations within the period.

An extract from Lord Soames' article in *International Affairs*, vol. 56, no. 3 (1980) entitled 'From Zimbabwe to Rhodesia' is reprinted with the kind permission of author and editor.

I would like to thank Mrs Audrey Tester for the retyping of the revised text and its alignment with the old – no easy assignment but most helpfully discharged.

My wife helped me greatly with my research, not least while in India, checked and commented on the new text, prepared the indices for both volumes and most of all sustained me with her encouragement.

December 1981   N. M.

PART ONE

The Foundation Members and the Nature of their Association

Free States, like all others, may possess dependencies, acquired either by conquest or by colonisation; and our own is the greatest instance of the kind in modern history. It is a most important question how such dependencies ought to be governed.'

JOHN STUART MILL
REPRESENTATIVE GOVERNMENT

Mr Haldane: 'The mother of Parliaments does not coerce her children.'
An Irish member: 'We do not accept that statement.'

HOUSE OF COMMONS DEBATES, 14 MAY 1900,
ON THE COMMONWEALTH
OF AUSTRALIA BILL

1 The Commonwealth in History

In the gardens at Peshawar, with the Himalayas towering high behind them, there is a statue to a Colonel Mackeson of the Bengal Army and commissioner of Peshawar, who in 1853, at the age of forty-six, was murdered by a religious fanatic. 'The defiles of the Khyber and the peaks of the Black Mountains alike witnessed his exploits . . .' begins an inscription, to which is appended a tribute from the governor-general, Lord Dalhousie. 'His value,' it reads, 'as a political servant of the state is known to none better than the governor-general himself, who in difficult and eventful times had cause to mark his great ability, and the admirable prudence, discretion and temper which added tenfold value to the high, soldierly qualities of his public character.' At the southerly tip of another continent in the gardens of Cape Town below Table Mountain there is another statue, not to a soldier of prudence and discretion but to an empire builder not famed for either, one of whose sayings, 'Take all . . . ask afterwards', impressed itself only too well upon the mind of his friend, Dr Jameson. The statue is that of Cecil John Rhodes, in his familiar loose-fitting clothes, with the outstretched hand pointing northward and the inscription below: 'Your hinterland is there'.

On the outposts of an Empire that has passed with others into history, these memorials and many besides for the moment remain. Some are to men little perhaps, but honourably known, and still remembered in the districts where they served; others to men cast in a larger, more controversial mould, whose past actions still press upon the unfolding events of later days. But unremembered or too well remembered, loyal and discreet executors of policies shaped by other hands than theirs, or themselves determining some part of the pattern of history, here were the prototypes of the men who sustained or enlarged the Second British Empire, which was the precursor of the British Commonwealth of Nations. Many more should be added, missionary and bishop, sailor and merchant seaman, administrator and clerk, trader, financier and entrepreneur, pastoralist and settler, and the engineers, military and civil, who planned and developed the lines of communication on which a worldwide empire depended, and who pioneered the railways which, as the young Winston Churchill reflected on his East African travels, provided 'a sure, swift road along which the white man and all that he brings with him ... may penetrate into the heart of Africa as easily and safely as he may travel from London to Vienna' and without which 'it is only wasting time and money to try to govern, or still more to develop, a great African possession'.[1] And, in a different category, there was the ubiquitous younger son. But for the time being the two commemorated in the gardens at Peshawar and Cape Town will suffice. Dutiful soldier and imperial 'colossus', they were of the essence of nineteenth-century Empire. The Empire which they helped to sustain and enlarge was refashioned into a Commonwealth. Without the one there would not – could not – have been the other. Yet what have they to do with Commonwealth?

One answer, which has at least the attraction of simplicity, is 'nothing'. Yet it invites an equally simple retort. If the soldier-administrator – the two rôles were not infrequently combined – had not been there to discharge his responsibilities on an advancing frontier, the frontier would not have advanced. Had it not advanced, as in fact it did, the area of the subsequent Commonwealth in Asia would have been to that extent diminished. Had Rhodes never looked and journeyed northward, it is at the least unlikely that the later Commonwealth in Africa would have had either the same geographical contours or the same political preoccupations. Both, indeed, it may be thought, would have been less. But the important point is that they would have been different. Even, therefore, at this surface level the answer 'nothing' may not stand.

There is, however, a more fashionable and at first sight more convincing reply. It is set out explicitly in commentaries or by implication in collections – some of them officially inspired – of selected extracts from speeches and documents, usually dating from the middle of the eighteenth century and designed to show that through the British Empire one increasing purpose ran.[2] That purpose was the enlargement of freedom and independence under the British flag, leading onward and upward to a Commonwealth of free nations. Those who did not further it had the misfortune to be on the wrong side of history and might be discounted or even disregarded. Burke and Durham, Elgin and Grey, Campbell-Bannerman, Balfour, Attlee with the Indian Independence Act and Macmillan with the African wind of change, are apt to figure well in such works or anthologies. So (and very justly) do some of the greater Indian administrators who, before and after Thomas Babington Macaulay's famous speech in the House of Commons on 10 July 1833, and in nearly identical terms, hopefully reflected with him that 'the public mind of India may expand under our system till it has outgrown that system; that by good government we may educate our subjects into a capacity for better government; that, having become instructed in European knowledge, they may, in some future age, demand European institutions',[3] and with him imaginatively concluded that should such a day ever come 'it will be the proudest day in English history'. The last of the viceroys, Lord Mountbatten, who was in Delhi in 1947 to satisfy that Indian demand, and did so with a splendid sense of historic occasion, has his niche. But perhaps the most famous of them all, Lord Curzon, the symbol of Empire in its noon-tide splendour, is firmly excluded. He believed in the British Raj, not as a passing stage and necessary preparation, but as a final state and absolute good. The ever watchful guardian of awful responsibilities decreed by providence, he had the soldiers' favourite hymn removed from the Order of Service at the Delhi Durbar of 1902 because of undesirable allusions to the passing of earthly empires. 'Of course,' he wrote, 'all the soldiers think about is a good tune . . . but we cannot possibly have "Onward Christian Soldiers" at the Delhi Service, because there is a verse in it that runs:

> Crowns and thrones may perish,
> Kingdoms rise and wane.'[4]

And as for self-government for India on the white colonial model, that would have meant, in Curzon's opinion, 'ruin to India and treason to our trust'.

Such contrasts are by no means confined to India. While Gladstone is assured of an honoured place in anthologies of Commonwealth, not least by reason of his peroration on Home Rule, and while Lloyd George may slip in, a trifle fortunately, with his speech on the Anglo–Irish Treaty, the voices of statesmen who with Curzon believed in Empire as a British *imperium* over subject peoples are rarely recorded. There are unlikely to be extracts from Disraeli's Crystal Palace speech of June 1872 on imperialism, or from that eloquent passage in the House of Lords on 8 April 1878 in which he spoke of all the communities that were agreed in recognising 'the commanding spirit of these Islands that has formed and fashioned . . . so great a portion of the globe' and

exulted in a dominion of very remarkable character, without
example known to him in ancient or modern history and more
peculiar than any over which a 'Caesar or Charlemagne ever
presided.'[5] Neither will there appear Salisbury's caustic allusions to
the unfitness of the Irish, Hottentots and even Hindus for
self-government,[6] nor any of the utterances of Joseph Chamberlain tinctured with notions of race superiority, nor yet of Balfour's
outraged reactions to the restoration of self-government to the
Boers. Where is Churchill on the Government of India Bill? These
men may qualify on other occasions but not on these. And as for
Cecil John Rhodes, he never qualifies at all! He was, surmised Olive
Schreiner, though later she had doubts even about this, too big a
man to pass through the gates of hell. And he has assuredly proved
too disturbing a figure to allow on to the pages of Commonwealth
anthologies. And yet was J. X. Merriman far from the truth when
on New Year's Day 1907 he wrote from Stellenbosch to his ageing
friend, Goldwin Smith, former Regius Professor of History at
Oxford and long since established in Toronto, that if any man
could have said, ' *"l'Empire, c'est moi"*, it was Rhodes'.[7] Republican
France may repudiate – though even this is questionable – but it
certainly does not neglect Louis XIV. Can the Commonwealth
neglect the 'Sun-king' of the British Empire in Africa? 'Know ye not
that there is a prince and a great man fallen this day in Israel', was
the text the archbishop chose for his address at Rhodes's funeral
service on 3 April 1902 in Cape Town Cathedral.[8] But Commonwealth historians prefer neither to know nor to inquire if this was
so.[9]

   There is, despite this selectiveness, much of the truth (though
still far from the whole truth) in the progressive view of imperial-
commonwealth history. There *was*, wherever British rule was
established and accepted, a *Pax Britannica*. There *was* the establishment of the rule of law. On these foundations there *was* a
broadening down from precedent to precedent of colonial and
later of dominion liberties. A unitary Empire *was* transformed into
a Commonwealth of free nations. The men who pierced the
shadows of the future to foresee that end, like those who in faith
proclaimed that such should be the goal, deserve to have their
foresight – or their insight – marked. Historically that is no less
than just. But others, some of them more important in their day,
had other designs or other visions. If these are not also recorded
the outcome will not be history but a distortion of history, the more
seductive and not the less corrupting because it appeals to the heart
and the mind of a later generation.

Commonwealth history, leaving aside for the moment a precise interpretation of the terms, would no doubt have been a more edifying, as it certainly would have been a less complex affair had all the signposts pointed that way. But they never did. There was at no time an ordered and general progression. If, in politico-constitutional terms in the late nineteenth and early twentieth centuries there were Canada, Australia, New Zealand and at the last even South Africa in respect of its dominant European cultures travelling the well-marked road, there was also Ireland – always Ireland – as it seemed excluded from it. And when there was no longer nationalist Ireland, there was Cyprus, and when there was no longer Cyprus there was Rhodesia. And when Rhodesia, after an interlude of unilaterally declared independence culminating in turbulent hyphenated existence, re-emerged as the internationally recognised independent state of Zimbabwe, what did that signify? That imperial history had been 'fulfilled' in the terminology of Commonwealth transcendentalists, so lightheartedly adopted by politicians and even historians? Or that with dominant purpose something of life had departed from the Commonwealth?

The selectivity, like the semantics, of many Commonwealth commentaries will find – are finding – their own correctives. But behind them lies something more substantial: the liberal interpretation of Imperial-Commonwealth history. It was by no means an exclusively British phenomenon. In exposition as well as in origin it owed as much to overseas (especially to Canadian) as to British writers. In essence it may be thought to have weathered well the test of time. True, it tended to discount the importance of 'illiberal' imperialist forces as well as words. In terms of subsequent Irish relations with the Commonwealth the question was rarely, if ever, asked whether it was not more important that Joseph Chamberlain should have 'killed' Home Rule, than that Gladstone should have proposed it; or, in terms of South Africa's Commonwealth membership, whether Milner and Chamberlain's predisposition to war in 1899 were not of more lasting consequence than Campbell-Bannerman's restoration of self-government to the Transvaal and the Orange Free State in 1906–7? In the same way there was too much emphasis on the 'idealist' element in liberal solutions. When they were finally adopted, reasons of state, reinforced by the wish of politicians and administrators to be rid of troublesome problems, played a greater part in that decentralisation of British imperial authority which made possible the transformation of Empire into Commonwealth than such interpretations are commonly apt to allow. These are things, however, which may be thought matters of balance rather than of substance. And it is not, indeed, in terms of the broad themes of imperial policy that the liberal interpretation is most likely to be misleading or deficient; it is rather in its failure, from essentially middle ground, to embrace, or indeed wholly to comprehend, those parts of the Commonwealth heritage that derived from imperialism on the one hand and nationalism on the other.

In respect of imperialism the point may be sufficiently illustrated by the posing of a single question. What was the rôle of force in the shaping of Commonwealth? This is something nowadays little weighed by British imperial historians and even less, and most reluctantly, by Commonwealth historians.[10] '*Rome est dessous vos lois par le droit de la guerre*', said Corneille's Cinna to Augustus Caesar. But the extent to which this was also true of the British Empire was rarely examined with detachment. Indeed it came to be thought of as something reprehensible and best forgotten. Yet the Roman occupation of a Britain conquered by the legions is accounted beneficial and civilising on the pages of most English histories and the Norman Conquest accepted as harsh but providential. There was also a period when in its turn British pride in forceful imperial expansion was proclaimed. Sir Richard Cox in his *Hibernia Anglicana: or, the history of Ireland from the conquest thereof to the present time*, published in 1689, commended his work in a dedication as an history 'from the Conquest' for which the Irish people 'is beholden to God'. But the disposition to such sanctimonious reflections departed with the assurance that had first prompted them. Indicative of the inhibitions constraining later historians of empire was Professor A. P. Newton's criticism of Sir John Seeley's 1881 Cambridge lectures on *The Expansion of England*, for the reason that historically they 'dealt in the main with the great wars of the eighteenth century and this gave the false impression that the British Empire has been founded largely by war and conquest, an idea that was unfortunately planted firmly in the public mind, not only in Great Britain, but also in foreign countries'.[11] It may or may not have been unfortunate, but historically what mattered was the extent to which it was true or false.

That is an important question – and not merely in respect of the eighteenth century. It is also a difficult one to answer with finality. It has been remarked that of the territories constituting the Commonwealth at its greatest extent those acquired in war and by conquest greatly exceeded in area and population those peacefully, or comparatively peacefully, occupied or settled, any semblance of balance between the two that might have come into existence disappearing with the loss of the American colonies. This would seem to be substantially true. But is it sufficiently precise? Colonies, after all, were acquired in ways other than settlement or conquest. Some were ceded, others were annexed, others claimed by right of discovery. Nor, as an eminent legal expert, Sir Kenneth Roberts-Wray, has underlined, is the distinction between them, always clear. It is *not* invariably easy to determine conclusively whether for example a colony was acquired by conquest or by cession. Many of the islands in the Caribbean changed hands in the eighteenth century and during and after the Napoleonic wars. Were they acquired by conquest, or by cession under the terms of a peace treaty? Sometimes the one literally preceded the other but it was not always so. A territory might be exchanged as a part of a general settlement. And how, to take an instance posing other queries, was New Zealand acquired? Was it by settlement or by cession or by right of discovery? Certainly there were settlers before there was cession. Their presence was indeed the cause of it. But the Maori chiefs, some five hundred in number, who signed the Treaty of Waitangi on 6 February 1840 and ceded sovereignty to Queen Victoria in return for assurances and protection, were at most entitled to act on behalf of the Maoris on the North Island and – more important – could not be regarded as possessing international personality. The treaty was not, therefore, one of international law and on this ground it has been argued that its terms did not amount to cession to the Crown. British sovereignty over the North Island was, however, proclaimed on 21 May 1840 by virtue of cession under the treaty and on the same day over the South Island, to which the treaty could not be deemed to apply, by right of discovery. New Zealand, while spoken of in general terms as a colony of settlement, was, then, acquired on the British view by cession and right of discovery. On any reckoning it can hardly be placed neatly in a single category. And what of Cape Colony? It was first acquired by the British by conquest in the French revolutionary wars. It was restored to the Dutch by the Treaty of Amiens in 1802 and finally ceded to the British as part of the general peace settlement in 1815. Was it a colony acquired by conquest or by cession? Since it was taken by force in the first instance, in 1795, the most appropriate answer would seem to be by conquest. More intractable problems were raised by the acquisition of Cyprus, a Disraelian addition to Empire, to be discounted by Gladstone as 'a valueless encumbrance', the annexation of which he denounced, with a characteristically involuted oratorical flourish, as 'a gross and open breach or rather a gross and manifest breach of the public law of Europe'. In more precise and more prosaic terms, the island was assigned under the terms of the Anglo–Turkish Convention, 1878, by the sultan of Turkey to be occupied and administered by England. There was, however, no transfer of sovereignty. In November 1914, it was annexed by Britain as a result of Turkey's coming into the war on the side of the Central Powers. There was no force employed, the island being already in British occupation. In 1923 the Treaty of Lausanne recognised the 1914 annexation. Was Cyprus then acquired by conquest in 1914, by annexation in 1914 or by cession in 1923? Similar problems arise in many African territories acquired piecemeal, part by settlement, part by annexation, part by treaty and part by cession and are graphically indicated in all their seemingly splendid inconsequence in the mosaic of provinces and Princely States that was the map of the British Empire in India, with provinces the fruits of conquest or annexation directly ruled and a multitude of Princely States, associated with the Crown through unequal treaties, which in the words of the ruler of the greatest of Indian States the Nizam of Hyderabad, the 'Faithful Ally' of the British, guaranteed to them protection, together with 'high position and privileges under the benign rule of His Majesty The King-Emperor', in return for rights surrendered to a Power recognised as Paramount, whose controlling interest was promoted and safeguarded by a Political Department, with officers in the States responsible to the Crown Representative, which came to be thought of by Indian nationalists as exercising a sinister, divisive influence on relations between Princely States and Provinces, but unkindly alleged by a later-day Viceroy to be staffed by 'soldiers who do not want to fight and civilians who do not want to work'.[12]

Cumulatively the variety of historical circumstances and subsequent legal interpretations of the manner of acquisition serve as a cautionary reminder of the risks of generalisation about Commonwealth territorial origins, beyond what was self-evidently fundamental and common to them all: namely an outward expansionist pressure from Britain, exploratory, military, commercial, demographic, missionary or some combination of these as the case might be, applying the means best suited to particular circumstances to achieve its ends. But even if the manner of acquisition in each individual instance is accordingly to be thought of as a secondary, or even superficial manifestation of an underlying historical process, it retains its own particular importance. Indigenous peoples rarely overlooked how it was they came under imperial rule or passed from the dominion of one imperial power to that of another. For them the distinctions between settlement, annexation, cession and conquest, while of terminological indifference, were apt to remain, possibly for generations, matters deep in individual and group consciousness. This was a factor of varying but often of profound significance for Empire and for the shaping of the later Commonwealth and one that is by no means always adequately conveyed in imperial historical writings with their brief, passing allusions to the negotiation of treaties, the establishment of protectorates, forays on the frontier and the native wars which pushed outward the boundaries of Empire. No doubt that is partly because, viewed in the wide context of imperial policy as a whole, these were small affairs. But things looked and are remembered differently on the other side of the hill. There, if and when it came to the final test of force, indigenous peoples had sometimes numbers but rarely weapons. The possession of the maxim gun, as Belloc noted with brutal irony in simple verse, made all the difference. Of that the battle of Omdurman, fought in 1898 near the confluence of the Blue and White Nile, provided the classic example. The British lacked numbers, just over 8000 men against the Khalifa's 50,000, but by rail and river they brought their armaments, 44 maxim guns, most formidable among them, and by their aid, with minimal loss, won what Churchill extolled as 'the most signal triumph ever gained by the arms of science over barbarians' and so reconquered the Sudan.[13] But the 'arms of science' made all the difference not only to the outcome of the struggle but to the way in which it was then and later regarded. The possessor of the maxim gun, and his historians, could afford to take a casual view of an episode in colonial history; the victims of it, on the other hand, were more likely to be decimated, dismayed or psychologically overwhelmed in the face of new and unknown instruments of power. Often, indeed, mere knowledge of the existence or evidence of the power of Europeans' formidable weapons of war sufficed to decide the issue with humanity, if without morality. Then there followed cession or protection. Yet if in one sense the end was the same, the importance of the means employed usually remained.

A familiar story may serve to illustrate this distinction. It is briefly told in the South African volume of the *Cambridge History of the British Empire:*

Though a British protectorate over the Pondoland coast had been proclaimed in 1885, Pondoland itself remained independent for a season; but disturbances on the frontiers and internal anarchy made it an awkward neighbour. For some time there was a question whether it should be annexed to Natal or the Cape, but Rhodes's view prevailed and with the consent of the Pondo chiefs it became Cape territory in 1894.[14]

The *Cambridge History* does not refer to the reason why the Pondo of the eastern Cape consented. To that Mrs S. G. Millin has supplied the answer – and with no lack of telling graphic detail.

> Rhodes [she wrote] travelled down to Pondoland in a coach and eight cream-coloured horses, some machine-guns and eight policemen, announced that he proposed to annex Pondoland, and sent for Sigcau [the paramount chief of the eastern Pondos] . . . He then offered to show Sigcau what would happen to him and his tribe if there was any further unpleasantness, took him to where the machine-guns were trained on a mealie-field, opened fire on the mealies, and brought down the mealie crop.

Sigcau noted the lesson and ceded his country. There was no bloodshed – imperialism on this occasion and in accord with Rhodes's tradition of avoiding force whenever possible achieved its end by demonstration rather than by use of superior power. That had some lasting importance, as may be judged by the testimony of a distinguished South African anthropologist.

The Bantu, noted Professor Monica Hunter, first encountered the European as a conqueror who had defeated him by superior arms. Of necessity he submitted, but impressed by the European's material culture he was anxious to obtain Europeans' goods, and the trade in blankets and guns expanded rapidly. The generation of the Xhosa who had fought the Europeans was slow to forget that the Europeans were enemies and conquerors. But, proceeds Professor Hunter, 'the Fingos who were protected by and became the allies of the British, and later the Pondo, were prepared to make the best of the domination by a stronger power' and turned towards the government 'the attitude of a people towards a superior chief. The personal prefix U is used before government and it is still thought of in remote districts of Pondoland as a person, an old man with a white beard. The people were prepared to be loyal to their new chief but in return expected to receive benefits from him.'[15]

It is also to be remembered that irrespective of the reaction of the indigenous people, submission to force or to the threat of it was by no means always without recompense. It usually brought peace and had, therefore, a reward which they were often the first to recognise. Here the northern plains of India, as well as a tribal area of southern Africa, may supply examples.

The villagers were, to begin with, frightened of the new conquerors [records Prakash Tandon of the first days of British rule in the Punjab], but fear soon gave way to curiosity and then to controversy . . . Their manners were strange but kindly and considerate, seldom hectoring or bullying. In their dress, manner or speech there was nothing of the rulers, as we were used to, and yet it was soon obvious that there was no authority lacking and that they had a peppery temper.

I think what impressed our elders most, and what they still spoke about when I was young, was that in the past there had been rulers who were virtuous and mindful of the rayats welfare, but never a whole system of government that was bent to the public good, with no apparent personal benefit to its officers. These and many other things at first intrigued the people and later pleased them.[16]

The judgment, it will be noted, was comparative – the Punjab had had much experience of conquest and for a time Punjabis were prepared to count the blessings of peace brought by a just, albeit still alien administration.

In Africa, the lives of Africans from time immemorial had been determined by force and in many cases overshadowed by fear. Africans accepted the arbitrament of the sword – or of the maxim gun. They were long inured to the judgment of arms. Professor Low goes so far as to argue that Rhodes and the British South Africa Company succeeded Lobengula in the 1890s 'as the paramount authority between the Limpopo and the Zambesi'.

In two wars – the Ndebele [Matabele] war of 1893 and the Ndebele rebellion of 1896 – the Ndebele were severely defeated, and their traditional political authorities destroyed. The royal salute of the Ndebele was the cry 'Bayete, Bayete'. When in 1902 Rhodes was buried in the Matopo Hills in southern Rhodesia, his body was carried to its hilltop tomb by Ndebele warriors crying 'Bayete, Bayete'; Rhodes was given, that is, the Ndebele royal salute. The last paramount chief of the Ndebele was thus, . . . in a very real sense, not Lobengula, but Rhodes; and in the thinking of the Ndebele it seems to have been this white man who, for all that he had done to them, had succeeded by right of conquest (a

right the Ndebele themselves fully recognized, for they had
often profited from it themselves) to political authority over
them.[17]

'Right of conquest' – the very phrase is alien to the idea of
Commonwealth. Yet even with the term conquest limited to its
precise meaning it is the case that a considerable part of the Empire
that preceded Commonwealth came within its confines by virtue of
conquest. Nor was this in any way an Asian or an African
phenomenon. The Irish, the French–Canadians, the Boers, each
in turn and likewise, at one time or another were subdued in war.
At the preliminary peace discussions at Pretoria in April 1902, the
British commander-in-chief, General Sir Herbert Kitchener, advised the Boers to accept the British flag and then to try to bargain
for the best possible terms in respect of self-government. President
Steyn of the Orange Free State asked him whether that self-
government would be similar to that of the Cape Colony, to which
Kitchener replied, 'Yes, precisely so'. President Steyn retorted that
the situation in the republics, where the colonists had never lost
their freedom, was not analogous to that in the Cape. And he is
reported to have continued, 'The Afrikanders in the two republics
were an independent people. And if that independence were taken
away from them they would immediately feel themselves de-
graded, and a grievance would arise which would necessarily lead
to a condition of things similar to that in Ireland. The conditions in
Ireland had arisen mainly from the fact that Ireland was a
conquered country'.[18] Conquest indeed, with the qualified exception of the hitherto thinly populated colonies of British settlement,
was the background for most member states to the free association
of Commonwealth. It was not the only background – had it been
there would have been no Commonwealth. But that neither alters
the fact that the frontiers of Empire were widely extended by force;
nor that the maintenance of Empire, in part at least, was conditional upon the existence of force, even if only in reserve. This
was most in evidence in the more nationally self-conscious countries within its confines.

On 28 December 1883, Sir William Harcourt warned Gladstone
that when full expression was given to Irish opinion with the
forthcoming extension of the franchise, almost every seat would go
to the Nationalists, and 'there will be declared to the world in larger
print what we all know to be the case that we hold Ireland by *force
and by force alone* as much as in the days of Cromwell. . . . We never
have governed and we never shall govern Ireland by the good will

of its people'.[19] And to move to another people and another continent at a later period, *The Times*, commenting upon the argument of the Indian National Congress that because the inhabitants of India were British citizens they were entitled to all the political rights and privileges of Englishmen, observed 'the contention has no more root in history or in law than it has in common sense. We have won India by the sword, and in the last resort, hold it by the sword.' Liberals were taken aback. John Morley at the India Office privately protested to the viceroy, Lord Minto, that it was not so. But for most Liberals, and especially for those who were avowed or unavowed Liberal imperialists, it was not so because it should not be so. In temper they were at one with Morley, when he wrote to Minto, 'Reforms may not save the *Raj*, but if they don't, nothing else will'; and they were far removed from Minto, when he replied, ' . . . when you say that "if reforms do not save the *Raj* nothing else will" I am afraid I must utterly disagree. The *Raj* will not disappear in India as long as the British race remains what it is, because we shall fight for the *Raj* as hard as we have ever fought, if it comes to fighting, and we shall win as we have always won.'[20] Liberals were shocked by assertions such as those of Minto and of *The Times* – more shocked, indeed, than many of those forcibly incorporated within the confines of Empire. Yet they hesitated to press the direct question whether, in the last resort India was held by force and await a factual answer, insofar as one could be given. And why? Surely because any affirmative, or partially affirmative answer would have exposed the inconsistency of their liberal with their imperial convictions and so have confronted them with a painful choice between one or the other.

The sanction of force and indeed the element of compulsion are alien to the idea of Commonwealth, but virtually to exclude from the pages of Commonwealth history consideration of the part these factors have played and of the importance at one remove of power in the making of the Commonwealth diminishes, and has diminished, understanding of many of the political and psychological problems that have beset it. The Commonwealth came into being in revulsion against Empire, but historically it could not escape being, among other things, the heir to Empire. It was not alone among the heirs of the privileged and wealthy in sensing that not all of the riches it enjoyed were 'well-gotten'. In the capital of the former metropolitan power it was easy to gloss over or even to forget how dominion was acquired or extended; it was not so easy in Delhi or Dublin, Rangoon or Pretoria, Lusaka or Lagos. Therein lay the principal psychological liability of Empire for Commonwealth.

The bearing of past experiences of conquest and subjection upon the emergence or revival of national sentiment is variable and debatable. At times it is exaggerated to the point of suggesting that colonial nationalisms were derivative and in essence no more than negative reactions to imperial rule. But on any assessment, defeat or experience of subjection – especially when possessing an element of actual or imagined humiliation – were in nearly all cases both corrosive and explosive in their long-term effects. This was something that the imperial power, both its agents at the time and subsequently even its historians, found hard to comprehend. For example how differently, even where there is a sustained and sympathetic attempt at understanding, are the happenings at Jallianwala Bagh in April 1919 set out and interpreted in English and Indian recollections and records. On both sides the actual circumstances and sequence of events – the mounting Indian violence in a traditionally unruly province; British fears of another 1857; the banning of processions and meetings; the gathering despite this of some twenty thousand persons in the public park at Amritsar, surrounded by high walls on three sides; the order to disperse by troops under General Dyer who, conceivably unknowingly, blocked the only exit; the shooting in which, according to the official report of the Hunter Commission of Enquiry, three hundred and seventy-nine were killed; the subsequent imposition of martial law; the public whippings and the order to Indians to crawl past the place where a woman missionary had been assaulted – all these events are generally accepted and in retrospect deemed disastrously, tragically mistaken.[21] Yet to Indians Jallianwala Bagh came to represent something more.

General Dyer, who had no doubt about the rightness of his action and was heard boasting loudly of it later that year by the young Jawaharlal Nehru on the night train from Amritsar to Delhi, was disavowed by the government of India and dismissed from the army. But debates in Parliament showed he had substantial minority Conservative support in the Commons, overwhelming backing in the Lords (a Chamber wielding a malign influence on Anglo–Indian, as on Anglo–Irish, relations at decisive moments), and sufficient sympathy in the country to ensure a presentation to him of nearly thirty thousand pounds. In India however where, as in Ireland after 1916, reactions were delayed, the longer-term impact was at a deep, dangerous and lasting psychological level. The 'frightfulness' of Jallianwala Bagh and the 'Crawling Lane' of Amritsar, attributed by Jawaharlal Nehru in his *Autobiography* to 'a sudden fear' on the part of India's imperial rulers, became 'symbols and bywords'. They were events that were annually commemorated, and when the Congress met again in the Punjab at Lahore in 1929, delegates' minds, so Nehru recalled, 'leapt over that decade and went back to the events of 1919 – Jallianwala Bagh, martial law with all its humiliations . . .'[22] Nearly thirty years later, in 1965–6, in the period of the Indo–British tension that followed the Indo–Pakistan hostilities of the autumn of 1965, in the press and in periodicals resentful Indian memories of 1919 surfaced once again. All this was part of the legacy of Empire to Commonwealth. It was no more than a part, but none the less it was a burden, not always to be borne as lightly as complacent constitutional commentators, diligently marking progress Report by Report, Act by Act, along the road to independence, were apt to suppose.

In the last stages of the transition from Empire to Commonwealth, that of rapid constitutional advance conceded by the imperial authority uniting with nationalist pressure for independence, liberals and nationalists found their meeting place – but again not necessarily in mutual comprehension. The liberal-nationalist revolutions of nineteenth-century Europe encouraged a facile identification of liberal and nationalist forces; publicists and historians of a liberal cast of mind were apt to assume that overseas nationalists struggling to free themselves from British imperial rule were necessarily also liberal at heart. But historically no such presumption was justified. They might equally well be – and in some cases were – conservative or reactionary. The political outlook and practice of each emergent nationality was determined by its own social system, the homogeneous or heterogeneous composition of its population, its own pattern of interest and security, even the nature of its economy, and might accordingly qualify or not qualify as 'liberal' by some partly artificial external standard. Whether it did so or not had no necessary correlation with its sentiment of nationality. The liberal 'act of faith' in South Africa did not make the Boers liberal; no sensible person, on reflection, could have found social or historical reasons for supposing it would. But English liberal dismay and chagrin remained none the less intense when it did not. When some half a century later African states achieved independence, there was again, despite much experience to the contrary from the past, the confident expectation that the triumph of nationalism would be accompanied by the adoption of liberal democratic processes of law, government and cultural or ethnic relations. When reality in Ghana, Nigeria, Uganda, Lesotho or Malawi belied expectation, there was at first a pronounced predisposition to reject the reality. Yet here was no isolated or transient phenomenon. There was and is a conflict between the creation of a united, self-conscious, purposeful national movement based upon cultural or ethnic unity, deriving inspiration from past cultural or warlike achievement and the bringing into existence of a liberal-democratic society in which individual rights and individual liberties and all the diversity which they imply are fundamental. The conflict is not resolved with the attainment of national independence; it may indeed then enter upon its more acute phase. Its outcome in each case depends upon a variety of factors, the strength of which can be assessed only in relation to each particular situation. This was the complexity for which the liberal interpretation of Commonwealth history most of all failed to allow. It was of significance, because in the last resort it was not liberalism but nationalism that emerged as the dominant factor in the modern Commonwealth. Yet nationalism in its varying manifestations, as much as imperialism, was among the forces that liberalism, with its pronounced, internationalist affinities, was little equipped to comprehend and much disposed to discount.

While nationalism proved to be the most important factor in the later development and subsequent eclipse of the Commonwealth, the actual concept of Commonwealth remained essentially liberal. That explains at once the extent and the limits of its comprehensiveness. The concept of Commonwealth repudiated explicitly the concept of Empire; in fact it was, as has been noted, in no small measure inspired by reaction against it and Rhodes was too much a part of Empire to be acceptable to Commonwealth. The soldier-administrator at Peshawar, it is true, *might* be absorbed into Commonwealth thinking and tradition, as a precursor of Commonwealth as well as a servant of Empire though such indeed was not ordinarily the lot of soldiers more renowned in the story of Empire. Jawaharlal Nehru, while confined in the Ahmadnagar Fort Prison Camp during the second world war, recalled[23] with indignation how the statue of General Nicholson, who was mortally wounded leading his men to the relief of the Indian capital in September 1857, 'with a drawn sword still threatens old Delhi' and, after independence, no doubt with due regard to his views, the menacing figure was duly removed, only the plinth on which the statue rested remaining to recall where it had stood in the gardens beyond the Kashmir Gate. But while the concept of Commonwealth comprehended such nationalist repudiation of the heroic figures symbolic of Empire, it remained unreceptive to though not uninfluenced by the more extreme exponents of nationalism.

Eamon de Valera, if at this stage one may further enlarge the
gallery of symbolic personalities, was excluded in so far as it was
possible from the conventional records of an evolving Commonwealth, as Rhodes was, though for precisely opposite reasons.
Neither Rhodes on the one side nor de Valera on the other were, in
Commonwealth terms, *reasonable* men; they were both in their very
different ways men of purpose or conviction too intense for
discussion. Rhodes, advancing across Africa with the railway as his
right hand and the telegraph as his mouthpiece, was not prepared
to debate whether painting the map of Africa red was a good thing
or not. He was concerned to do it. Nor was de Valera, proclaiming
the indefeasible rights of the Irish people to national sovereignty
outside Empire and Commonwealth, ready to argue why they were
rights or what made them indefeasible. He was resolved to assert
them. Such men did not fit into the recognised pattern of
Commonwealth. They were however the catalysts of changes which
bore heavily upon its origins in the one case and upon its later
development in the other. For this reason it is not enough to take
the short step of including the symbolic soldier-administrator as
being among the men who helped to shape the British Commonwealth of Nations; the larger step must needs also be taken of
acknowledging that others, and not least the imperialist-adven-
turer and the ideological nationalist, have also their own significant
places in the story.

But who, to continue for the moment to think in terms of
personalities, was at the heart of the story? Whose statue might be
thought symbolic of it? Hardly one whose contribution was only in
the council chamber, for conflict was an essential ingredient in the
fashioning of Commonwealth; not a theoretician, for in essence the
Commonwealth was not an essay in political theory but in political
pragmatism; not an imperialist, for the Commonwealth had roots
struck deep in anti-imperialist soil; not a nationalist in a narrower
sense, for the Commonwealth, though composed of nations,
aspired also in some measure to transcend nationality. Where then
is such a representative figure to be found? In Canada, the oldest
dominion? Nationally that would seem right. Mackenzie King,
perhaps, the man who to his own great satisfaction was prime
minister longer than any man in British history? The credentials
are also right. Mackenzie King distrusted Empire and imperialists
to the very depths of his complex being; he prided himself on being
the grandson of a rebel, William Lyon Mackenzie, who could be
termed [though by some stretch of historical realities] a nationalist.
But if the credentials are right, the man was not; symbolic figures

require a touch of imaginative greatness and that was a gift with
which Mackenzie King was not endowed. So while recognising that
King represents an important, even indispensable, part of the
Commonwealth tradition one must look elsewhere. In past years
one would have looked with some confidence to South Africa –
have pointed perhaps to that statue standing alone on the lawns
below the government buildings in Pretoria of General Botha in
the uniform of commandant-general of the Boer forces in the
South African war, and drawn attention to the six panels round the
base depicting successively Botha as a young farmer, as commandant-general of the republican forces with commandos riding
into action before him, as prime minister of the Transvaal
1907–10, at the National Convention, on the steps of the Union
Buildings in Pretoria as prime minister of South Africa, in the Hall
of Mirrors at Versailles with Smuts standing beside him and
President Wilson, Lloyd George and Clemenceau seated behind, as
a member of the British Empire delegation. Botha had fought
bravely against the Empire, he had helped to bring into being a new
dominion, he had served as its first prime minister, he had become
a statesman of Commonwealth, a champion of decentralisation and
liberty as the surest foundations of unity. Or if not to Botha, then to
Smuts, his partner alike in war and politics, his heir in domestic
politics and in Commonwealth purposes, the only dominion
statesman to be a member of the imperial war cabinet of the first
world war and to take part in the meetings of Commonwealth
prime ministers in the second, the only dominion statesman also to
have his statue in Parliament Square, Westminster. Yet however
great the appropriateness in an earlier historical context it would
seem ironical now to look only towards Pretoria. In these days of
multi-racial Commonwealth it seems more fitting to turn one's gaze
towards Delhi, to where the River Jumna flows beyond the walls of
the Red Fort of the Emperor Shah Jehan and to the place where,
some little distance apart, are the memorials of Mahatma Gandhi
and Jawaharlal Nehru. Nehru too had known conflict, had
experienced long years of imprisonment and emerged as a
defender of Commonwealth, the architect of its Asian membership, and finally the most respected of its elder statesmen. Along
the walls of the study of his official residence as prime minister
hang pictures of him as the young Brahmin, the Cambridge
graduate, the barrister, the prisoner, the Congress leader and
friend of Gandhi, and the prime minister of India when the
appointed day, 'the day appointed by destiny', had come round at
last. Liberal, nationalist, internationalist, he was the very archetypal

figure of those later days. Surely here history can have no ironic surprises to spring?

But it is time to turn from the personalities of Commonwealth to the history of it. That it is entangled with the history of empire is apparent and that judicious disentanglement is a major task of the historian of Commonwealth may perhaps be allowed. At the very outset the question must be faced: how and when did the Commonwealth story begin? A name may suffice for the starting point to an answer. General Smuts was the first to attribute the term 'British Commonwealth of Nations' to the group of self-governing states within the British Empire on an imperial occasion. But he did not coin the phrase. The credit for that would seem to belong to Lord Rosebery who on a hot and humid afternoon in Adelaide in January 1884 inquired of his Australian audience: 'Does this fact of your being a nation . . . imply separation from the Empire? God forbid! There is no need for any nation, however great, leaving the Empire, because the Empire is a commonwealth of nations.' The phrase was reproduced without capitals by Lord Rosebery's biographer,[24] suggesting, almost certainly correctly, that its author had used it in a purely descriptive sense. It was a description well grounded in English history – had not Lord Rosebery himself made an elegant excursion into Cromwellian studies?[25] – and one to which contemporary relevance had been restored by the urge within Australia towards a federation of states in one Commonwealth, so that for the first time in history, there would be a continent for a nation and a nation for a continent. But its use in a wider imperial setting was inspired by a prophetic sense of things to come.

For this notion of a commonwealth of nations, the closing decades of the nineteenth century were inhospitable years and Lord Rosebery, chief among Liberal-imperialists, might have later entertained reservations about some of the possible implications of the phrase had he thought about it again – of which there is no evidence. But in the reaction against the exuberant, popular, thrustful imperialism of the *fin de siècle*, the description, usually either with limited application or in abbreviated form, gained currency. On 2 May 1900 at a dinner at the National Liberal Club in honour of the Australians visiting London for the enactment of the Commonwealth of Australia Bill, Sir Henry Campbell-Bannerman was reported as saying:

The proverb ran that there was no rose without a thorn, and there was one thorn in the rose offered by their honoured guests.

It lay in the title of 'Australian Commonwealth'. Where could they find a word more exactly indicating the intent and purpose of that great aggregated community of which we are all proud to be citizens, and which included all the dominions of Her Majesty? In that great creation of the energy of our people in the past and in the present we sought only the welfare and prosperity of all and to make the commonwealth shared by all for the use of all. That was the ideal of our Australian friends, and how could it be better expressed than by the homely native phrase the 'British Commonwealth'? But we had been too late. These enterprising kinsmen of ours from the other end of the world had appropriated the word, and he confessed he owed them a grudge for it.[26]

Radicals, and more especially Fabians, liked the term 'Commonwealth' and were not seemingly discouraged in its use by Australian adoption of it. Mrs Sidney Webb wrote of a socialist Commonwealth in Britain; George Bernard Shaw, as editor of a pamphlet on *Fabianism and the Empire* published in 1900, wrote variously of 'a Commonwealth of the communities flying the British flag', 'the British Commonwealth' and 'a Commonwealth'. In a footnote, which has the air of an afterthought to repair an obvious omission, he dismissed the words 'Empire, Imperial, Imperialist' as 'pure claptrap' used 'by the educated people merely to avoid dictionary quibbles, and by the uneducated people in ignorance of their ancient meaning', and continued, 'What the colonies are driving at is a Commonwealth; and that is what the English citizen means, too, by the Empire when he means anything at all.'[27] But the use of Commonwealth or British Commonwealth in the singular, of which there are a number of examples,[28] was something different from the use of British Commonwealth of Nations in which the singular was balanced by the plural and in which the unit, which alone was implicit in the first, was matched by the national diversity explicitly acknowledged in the second part of the phrase. A unitary Empire transformed into a unitary Commonwealth was a characteristically Fabian purpose; but it was not something to be confused with, nor necessarily in line with, a transformation into a Commonwealth in which the nationalities provided a counterpoise, or more than a counterpoise, to the centre. What mattered was not the use of a word, of which too much is not infrequently made, but the idea behind the usage.

Early in the twentieth century the colonies of settlement came to be known as dominions and often to be spoken of at imperial gatherings as sister-nations. 'The British Empire,' declared Sir Wilfrid Laurier in 1902, was 'a galaxy of independent nations'.[29] This separate nationhood was underlined at successive Colonial and Imperial Conferences. In the capital of Empire their prime ministers assembled, explained their interests and expounded their views. These views were the views of separate states if questionably yet of separate nations, despite Sir Wilfrid Laurier and many others. In replying to messages of congratulation from the governments of Australia and New Zealand on the successful completion of the work of the National Convention for a Union of South Africa, Chief Justice de Villiers, the president of the convention cabled: 'We thank Commonwealth Australia (New Zealand) for its good wishes and sincerely hope the result may strengthen the wider commonwealth of states within the British Empire.'[30] This was a more exact description. The dominions in 1909 are justly spoken of as comprising a Commonwealth of states within the British Empire.

During the first world war a growing sense of national identity on the part of the dominions, stimulated by their individual contributions and sacrifices in a common cause, rendered not untimely the revival of the term British Commonwealth of Nations. The dominions were states that were in the process of becoming nations. There was apparently at the time no sense of conscious debt to Lord Rosebery or to those who had used earlier variants of the Commonwealth designation. Lionel Curtis, the 'prophet' among that group of young men who served with Lord Milner in South Africa and came to be known collectively as the Milner 'Kindergarten' prompted by Professor Hancock[31] recalled how and something of why it came to be revived. More and more, explained Curtis, he had become convinced that the British Empire stood not for Kipling's 'dominion over palm and pine' but for the promotion of the government of men by themselves, and as a result he felt that the term Empire was a misnomer.

Then hunting about for a good Saxon word to express the kind of state for which it stood, I naturally lit on the word 'Commonwealth'. I developed the theme that while the Greeks had achieved the city-commonwealth, England had made an immense advance in achieving a national commonwealth; but this was by no means the end of the process of development. The next step in the history of mankind must be the creation of an international commonwealth.

Curtis accordingly gave to a work published in 1914 as *The Project of a Commonwealth* the new title *A Commonwealth of Nations*, and these terms came into current use in *The Round Table* which was founded by Curtis and his friends of South African days to promote the cause of imperial federation.

The designation reappeared in a variety of forms in succeeding years. In April 1917 the Imperial War Conference resolved that after the war 'the readjustment of the constitutional relations of the component parts of the Empire . . . should be based upon a full recognition of the dominions as autonomous nations of an imperial Commonwealth'.[32] In speaking to the resolution the prime minister of Canada, Sir Robert Borden, echoed the phrase 'Imperial Commonwealth' and voiced a belief that 'the dominions fully realise the ideal of an Imperial Commonwealth of United Nations'.[33] General Smuts spoke of the dominions as 'equal Nations of the Empire' and their governments as 'equal Governments of the King in the British Commonwealth'. He was at some pains to let it be known that his use of the term in no way implied his conversion to imperial federation. 'The circumstances of the Empire', he said, 'entirely preclude the federal solution . . . and to attempt to run even the common concerns of that group of nations by means of a central parliament and a central executive is to my mind absolutely to court disaster.'[34] But the term British Commonwealth of Nations admitted of a quite different interpretation. Emphasis might be placed as much upon the *Nations* as upon the *Commonwealth*; upon the many comprising the whole, as upon the whole they comprised and this seems to have been the direction of General Smuts' thoughts.

> The British Empire [he said on 15 May 1917, addressing members of both Houses of Parliament at a banquet in his honour] is much more than a state. I think the very expression 'Empire' is misleading, because it makes people think as if we are one single entity, one unity, to which that term 'Empire' can be applied. We are not an Empire. Germany is an empire, so was Rome, and so is India, but we are a system of nations, a community of States and of nations far greater than any empire which has ever existed . . .[35]

Apparently Smuts did not feel that the term British Commonwealth of Nations sufficed to describe so remarkable a political phenomenon as the grouping of Britain and the dominions, for he went on to observe:

... we come to the so called dominions, a number of nations and states almost sovereign, almost independent, who govern themselves ... and who all belong to this group, to this community of nations, which I prefer to call the British Commonwealth of Nations. Now, you see that no political ideas that we evolved in the past, no nomenclature will apply to this world which is comprised in the British Empire ... The man who would discover the real appropriate name for this vast system of entities would be doing a great service not only to this country, but to constitutional theory

But there were others who felt that he had himself given the widest currency to the most appropriate designation and indeed he himself again used the phrase at a meeting of the Imperial War Conference on 12 June 1918.[36] In Article iv of the Anglo–Irish Treaty of 1921 it acquired its official cachet and in the Balfour Report of 1926 the vindication of the ideas it was intended to express. But the notion at the heart of the Curtis Commonwealth concept, of an organic federal unity, which had been expressly repudiated by Smuts, was progressively discounted by these developments. 'Tonight', wrote Lord Harcourt a former secretary of state for the colonies, after Smuts' speech of 15 May 1917, 'was the funeral of *The Round Table*.'[37] In respect of its primary federal purpose, he was not far wrong.

Can it then be said with some assurance that the history of the British Commonwealth of Nations began in 1917, when it was so named by General Smuts? It would be tempting but disingenuous to give an unqualified affirmative. General Smuts did not say that he was naming something which had just come to birth but rather that he was seeking to identify something which already existed. 'We are not an Empire. What are we?' It was a political fact that prompted the search for an appropriate designation; not the discovery of a designation that originated the political fact. There was, therefore, if this line of reasoning be accepted, a Commonwealth of Nations before it was so described. When can it be said to have come into being? To this the answer may be sought in the extension to territories overseas of traditional British concepts of representative and responsible government, coupled with the existence of a relationship between such states or nations within the framework of one political system.

Here at least the line of descent in idea may be clearly traced. It goes back to Lord Durham's famous Report on Canada, itself derivative in its principal recommendations, though not in its overall formulation of them and to the enactment of the British North America Act, bringing to birth the first dominion in 1867. The Report provided the necessary content of political ideas: the Act the successful application of some of them on a national, or potentially national, scale twenty-eight years later, the degree to which the latter was consequential upon the former remaining a matter of historical debate. However the emphasis may be placed it is self-evident that neither an idea, acceptance of which was by no means easily won, nor an Act, with limited territorial application, created a community of nations. They did however in conjunction bring into existence a form of government in Canada and a developing relationship between Britain and Canada which might, and did, supply a model from which a novel system of inter-state relations might be – and was – fashioned. British statesmen, Australian, New Zealand, South African, Irish, Indian and finally African leaders were in greater or lesser degree conscious of the Anglo–Canadian origins of the Commonwealth. To that extent it is in accord with the historical record and subsequent political understanding to think of the period 1839–67 as the seed time of Commonwealth.

Commonwealth history from that time is not to be thought of as synonymous or coterminous with imperial history. It is a part, a distinct and in some measure distinguishable part of a larger whole. In so far as the concept of Commonwealth derives from British notions of government, it was the more readily accepted and applied in colonies of British settlement overseas. 'The Mother of Parliaments,' as Haldane rightly remarked during the passage of the Commonwealth of Australia Bill, 'does not coerce her children.' But she was for many years to come still prepared to coerce those who were not. Whether it was appropriate therefore or, more important, in accord with British interests that self-government should be extended to phlegmatic and disaffected Calvinist Boers, to volatile but equally disaffected Roman Catholic Irishmen, to Indians, to Cypriots, to Africans, were matters of extended argument or open conflict of view. Increasingly however argument and conflict were apt to end one way. English historians attributed this to English enlightenment; others chiefly to the pressures of indigenous nationalisms and of changes in the patterns of world trade and power. But as important as any was probably the fact that there had been an experiment in Canada which was deemed successful. There followed other experiments in Australia and New Zealand; they too were deemed successful. There followed yet another experiment in an altogether more intractable and complex situation in South Africa; paradoxical as it was to seem to a later generation it was deemed outstandingly successful. Each experiment was carried out with an awareness, especially on the British side, of earlier experiments. Gladstone, in drafting the first Home Rule Bill, had assembled for him copies of the constitutions of the self-governing colonies, and to judge by his underscoring of phrases in the Preamble and certain sections, notably section 91 on the Powers of Parliament, he paid close attention to the British North America Act, 1867;[38] the architects of the Australian Commonwealth closely studied the same Canadian model before deciding to depart from it in important respects; Campbell-Bannerman, who thought of Canada as 'the greatest triumph' of British imperial statesmanship, and 'of broad liberal views and nobly instructed imagination', when contemplating the restoration of self-government to the Transvaal wrote out in annotated form the lessons to be drawn from Canadian precedents, for South African application.[39] 'The Canadian Constitution,' wrote Smuts to J. X. Merriman (the prime minister of Cape Colony) in January 1908 'supplies some very useful ideas for us in South Africa'; in March Merriman replied setting forth in detail how the way was prepared in Canada for the drafting and subsequent enactment by the Imperial Parliament of the British North America Act 1867, while in October representatives of the South African colonial governments, meeting in National Convention in Durban to devise a form of unification, had circulated to them commentaries upon the working of the Canadian and also of the Australian constitutions.[40] In its turn the South African example influenced British thinking (not least that of the Unionist leader, Austen Chamberlain) favourably towards an Irish dominion settlement, while the status of Ireland in the 1921 treaty was expressly linked to that of Canada, the senior dominion. Something of that story was repeated in respect of non-European peoples. Early in the century Lord Curzon had spoken in spacious Oxonian terms of a place for India at the High Table of the Empire. When in rather more than the fullness of time that place came to be allotted in a Commonwealth which in fact by then constituted the High Table of Empire, it was again with particular allusion to the success of earlier experiments, Clement Attlee as Lord Privy Seal in February 1942, noting in the War Cabinet Paper, which at an official level was the first foreshadowing of the Cripps Mission: 'Lord Durham saved Canada to the British Empire. We need a man to do in India what Durham did in Canada' – and in 1947, as Prime Minister, commending the great departure from an exclusively European

Commonwealth to the House of Commons with special reference to South African experience.[41] In politics as in other affairs of men few things succeed like success.

The unfolding pattern meant a Commonwealth by stages. It did not spring into being fully armed like Pallas Athene from the head of Zeus. There was accordingly, if one accepts the years 1839–67 as the starting-point of Commonwealth, an extended period in which in fact, though not in name, Empire and Commonwealth existed side by side. In the nineteenth century there is no doubt that Empire was the predominant partner. To the young Disraeli the colonies of settlement, the future dominions, were 'wretched millstones'. To the older and wiser Beaconsfield, the colonial still came a poor second to the Indian connection. Rosebery and Salisbury, would have agreed with this order of priorities though not without some reservations. Chamberlain would not have agreed at all. He was, complained Curzon, 'Colony mad'.[42] He believed that it was the colonies of settlement, the embryonic dominions of the early twentieth century that mattered and in this he was not mistaken. They were, so to speak, in the ascendant; they were first the daughter-nations, then the sister-nations and finally the equal, autonomous dominions of the Balfour Report. They were within the Empire but they were not of it. Even to Hobsonian critics in the aftermath of the South African war and in the full tide of the anti-imperialist reaction, there was little to condemn and much to commend in the association of young, vigorous, democratic overseas societies with Great Britain. By the mere fact of their existence, these societies made at once acceptable and almost predictable (given the character of British political institutions) the emergence of a Commonwealth. If it be asked why it was that no other European empire was transmuted into a Commonwealth, the answer is that all other western empires lacked the necessary popular foundation for commonwealth. Their peoples, with the qualified exceptions of the Spanish in South America and the French in North America, had not migrated in sufficient numbers or over a long enough period of time to form settler communities overseas which would develop in the fullness of time into nations. The British had. They were a seafaring, migrant people. From the sixteenth century overseas migration had been a constant and significant element in their social history. In the century between the end of the Napoleonic and the outbreak of the first world war it reached its phenomenal climax. More than twenty millions sailed from the British Isles in those years to destinations outside Europe and, while thirteen million of them, including the great bulk of the tragic Irish exodus of little short of two millions in the famine and post-famine years of 1846–55, went to the United States, four millions went to Canada and one and a half millions to Australia and New Zealand.[43] In their going lay the exceptional and indispensable legacy of the British Isles to the British Commonwealth, for it was these settlers and their descendants who, impatient of imperial rule yet cherishing notions of imperial partnership, pioneered a road along which a metropolitan power of itself would assuredly never have travelled.

The dichotomy of Empire and Commonwealth was implicit in the later nineteenth and early twentieth century; it became explicit in 1917. Therein lies the significance of General Smuts' essay in semantics. It was outward and audible evidence that an element existed within the British Empire, deriving from empire yet alien to the very concept of it, and that it was gathering political strength. This was the moment of transition. Thereafter the predominance of Empire gave way to the predominance of Commonwealth. The Empire which in its late nineteenth century expansionist phase had seemed the portent of a future in which by natural process of political selection the fittest alone survived in ever declining number and in correspondingly greater territorial magnitude to govern the earth, was already well on the way to becoming the relic of a heady and repented past. The great powers were becoming even greater, the small powers counting for less and less, remarked Lord Salisbury with evident satisfaction at the turn of the century. But seventeen years later as the first world war approached its climacteric, the terrible consequences that might flow from concentration of power in the hands of the few seemed all to evident on the blood-stained battle-fields of Europe. Within the British Empire, the response was a new emphasis on decentralisation and a break down of unitary control. The many were more likely to be restrained and balanced and even just than the one. In place of the politics of power the British Empire in its new guise must set an example to the world of the politics of egalitarian cooperation. That, it seemed in the sanguine post-war years, was the hope of the future and the contribution which a British Commonwealth, and a British Commonwealth alone, might make to the world.

The balance of interest and forces had therefore moved. But the conflict between Empire and Commonwealth was by no means ended. It continued, as it had been before 1917, as essentially a conflict of ideas. The concept of Commonwealth was sharpened by its critics, imperialist mostly at first, unreconciled nationalists later. Evidence of that conflict was reflected in continuing ambiguities of nomenclature, which had their origins in the speeches at the Imperial War Conference, not least in those of General Smuts. When Sir Robert Borden referred to the dominions as 'autonomous nations of an Imperial Commonwealth' the context suggested he was thinking of them as part of a whole. But General Smuts used the term British Commonwealth in direct association with the governments of the dominions as equal governments of the king. Did they then alone comprise a British Commonwealth within a British Empire? Or was their existence, the existence, as Smuts said in his speech of 15 May 1917, of 'the so-called dominions, a number of nations and states almost sovereign, almost independent . . . who all belong to this group, to this community of nations which I prefer to call the British Commonwealth of Nations' within the Empire, the justification for renaming the whole? Phrases could be quoted to support either view. All that was certain was that the existence of the dominions seemed to Smuts, and to others, to outdate the word Empire as a description embracing the British-dominion relationship.

In its limited meaning, the phrase 'British Commonwealth' passed into departmental usage and a paper prepared by the Colonial Office for the Cabinet on *A Common Imperial Policy in Foreign Affairs*[44] in March 1921 referred to the dominions as members of the British Commonwealth. But, again, did they alone comprise it? Certainly such was the reasonable inference, but it was no more than that.

Neither the Anglo–Irish Treaty of 1921 nor even the Balfour Report of 1926 removed these ambiguities. The Balfour Report described the dominions as being 'freely associated as members of the British Commonwealth of Nations' and 'within the British Empire'. L. S. Amery, the theoretician of Empire (the phrase was A. J. P. Taylor's), who was first secretary of state for dominion affairs, later explicitly confirmed that the implication of a self-governing circle of states comprising a Commonwealth within an Empire retaining its structural unity, was deliberate.[45] Though his interpretation carried only ministerial, as distinct from collective conference authority, it remains of weight. The principal objection to it, that is to say to the distinction between Commonwealth and Empire, was that it suggested, especially perhaps to those with little taste for the future extension of the practice of national self-government implicit in the idea of Commonwealth, a clear division between the self-governing territories on the one hand and dependencies on the other, which might in itself prove restricting, whereas by contrast might not 'British Commonwealth of Nations' used as an alternative to 'British Empire' suggest a continuing sense of movement towards an overall Commonwealth goal? Such was the drift of one strand of debate, with the more precise connotation being felt to presume limitation at a time when no non-European people had been admitted to the circle of the self-governing elect, the more comprehensive one implicitly endorsing notions of continuing expansion. But there was another strand. It was maintained, notably in Canada, that to apply or extend the term Commonwealth with or without qualification to territories that were still dependent was a misuse of or abuse of language. In so far as the argument was about words it was of negligible importance: in so far as it was about political intention there was only one answer. The example of the dominions had about it a compulsive attraction for still dependent peoples and if, as Professor Hancock observed on precisely this point, 'Life within the Empire was flowing too vigorously to let itself be congealed in two separate seas',[46] the chief reason was their resolve that the status of dominion should not remain a privilege limited to European settler communities.

The Preamble to the Statute of Westminster 1931, did not significantly clarify the semantic ambiguities. It further and most closely associated the dominions, which were there listed by name, with the British Commonwealth of Nations but equally it neither stated nor necessarily implied that they alone composed it. During the second world war Winston Churchill sought to cut his way out of the verbal thicket with the comprehensive title 'British Commonwealth and Empire'. It had its appeal to all sections of opinion without, however, being satisfactory to any of them or indeed being satisfactory in itself. When the barrier of colour was broken with the admission after the war of Asian self-governing states, the term British Commonwealth of Nations was foreshortened by the discarding, in practice, under pressures of nationalisms that were not British, not only (as was logical) of the adjective British, but also, by general consent, of the concluding national counter-balance to Commonwealth. But even then there was neither a new uniformity nor even a new precision. The London Declaration of April 1949 spoke of the government of India having informed 'the other governments of the Commonwealth' of the intention of the Indian people to adopt a republican constitution and also referred to 'the governments of the other countries of the Commonwealth'. There was in these phrases the implication that collectively those countries with their own autonomous governments alone comprised the Commonwealth, though the former legal adviser to the Commonwealth Relations and Colonial Offices has argued that this implication was not strong and that it would be reasonable to interpret the document as if the phrases 'other governments' or 'other countries' were qualified by a phrase such as 'by whom this declaration is made'.[47] Political pronouncements also were less rather than more conclusive. In matters of nomenclature freedom of choice became a matter of principle. 'All constitutional developments in the Commonwealth, the British Commonwealth, or the British Empire – I use the three terms deliberately – have been the subject of consultation between His Majesty's governments, and there has been no agreement to adopt or to exclude the use of any one of these terms . . .' So the British prime minister, Clement Attlee, told the House of Commons in May 1949, adding the judicious comment that since opinions on this differed 'in different parts of the British Empire and Commonwealth', it was 'better to allow people to use the expression they like best'. This was another way of saying that at that time the Commonwealth meant different things to different people and in different places and that its nature for that reason was likely to elude those seeking for the uniform attitude, which assent to one common appellation would presume.[48] It also suggested the terms were interchangeable. This was not uniformly accepted in the Commonwealth overseas. On the Canadian view, already alluded to, only with the completion of the process of decolonisation would it be correct to apply the term *Commonwealth* to all the territories within this political association. But in general practice by the later 1960s, with the process of decolonisation nearly completed, the Commonwealth had become the accepted and acceptable designation other than in Australia and New Zealand where British Commonwealth of Nations continued to be preferred.

Names are symbols, symbols of aspiration and intention, as well as of political realities. In general it was because this was so that General Smuts attached much importance in 1917 to a new name for a system of states, to which history could furnish no parallel; that traditionalists were reassured in 1926 with the retention of British Empire in the Balfour Report, while reformers rejoiced at the inclusion of the British Commonwealth of Nations; and that the London Declaration of April 1949, by which republican India was enabled to remain a full member, gave the sanction of governments to the shorter designation of Commonwealth without, however, finally discarding older forms. To the historian of the Commonwealth such variations suggest not refinements of little meaning but essentially conflicts of purpose and aspirations which while not always of lasting significance usually indicated the pattern of

contemporary thinking, and as such mattered in their day and are
of importance as a guide to the likely developments of succeeding
days. To those however whose interests are less specialised they
may suggest that the Commonwealth, as Hazlitt condescendingly
remarked of the universe, if good for nothing else, was at least a
fine subject for speculation.

2 Commonwealth Origins, 1839–67 English Thinking and the Canadian Experiment

LORD DURHAM AND HIS REPORT

British North America was deemed an important, but by no means necessarily the most important, of British overseas possessions in that second British Empire which came into being with the secession of the American colonies. But among the colonies of settlement, as distinct from colonies of conquest or administration such as the West Indies or even India – nominally under the control of the East India Company until the mutiny in 1857 – those in British North America occupied a preeminent position. This was as much by virtue of their geographical position, their extent and their comparatively long period of colonisation as by any immediate strategic or economic significance. In a very particular sense they were a test case. First settled by the French in the early sixteenth century, they became British under the terms of the Treaty of Paris in 1763. Some two decades later the St Lawrence and lake region settlements, designated the province of Upper Canada in 1791, became a principal (though by no means the only) refuge of United Empire loyalists – in 1783 some ten thousand had also arrived in the St John's district on the bay of Fundy, mostly military personnel with their wives and children; separating from Nova Scotia they formed in 1784 the province of New Brunswick – men resolved to escape from the claims of republican allegiance. The nationalism of the United States, Professor Lower had observed, 'is founded on violent repulsion from England, that of Canada originally rested on repulsion from the United States'. But even for the United Empire loyalists and their descendants, the force of example and the draw of environment remained. As the United States advanced in wealth, power and numbers could or would the loyalties of English settlers north of the frontier remain indefinitely unimpaired? And what of the French? In the fullness of time an obelisk was placed on the plains of Abraham just above the ramparts of Quebec, to Wolfe and Montcalm, to the youthful victor and the more seasoned vanquished, in the colonial war which decided that the future of North America should be Anglo–Saxon. *Mortem virtus communem Famam. Historia Monumentum Posteritas Dedit*, reads the Latin inscription with the name of Wolfe inscribed on the left and that of Montcalm on the right. It is a monument rare in commemorative sculpture[1] and one displaying an honourable magnanimity. But the fact remained (as Alexis de Tocqueville and his friend Gustave de Beaumont who sketched it were little disposed to overlook on their visit to Quebec in August 1831)[2] that it was the French who had been defeated. Others might forget; the inhabitants of Quebec did not. Who was to say when and in what circumstances they would seek to turn back the page of history?

By the third decade of the nineteenth century there had been more than one example in the Americas of successful revolt against imperial rule. If British statesmen were shadowed in their imperial thinking by memories of the Stamp Act and the Boston Tea Party, they were stimulated in their international attitudes by more recent and more exhilarating recollections of George Canning's calling of a New World into being to redress the balance of the Old. Few could doubt that when it came to empires other than their own the British were anti-imperialist. As champions of successful revolution in Latin America they had derived satisfaction not only from their liberal rôle but from the opening up successively of former Spanish and Portuguese colonies to world and – more especially – to British commerce and enterprise. In conjunction, North and South American revolutions strengthened the widely held conviction that as far as the Americas were concerned the days of political Empire were numbered and that being so, wisdom, combined with commercial self-interest, counselled a peaceful parting from settler-subjects.

In 1837 rebellions in Upper and Lower Canada suggested to receptive home opinion that the time of final severance was approaching. As Lord John Russell put it to the House of Commons on 16 January 1838, 'I repeat that I am not prepared to give immediate independence [but] this I will say, that if the time were come at which such an important change might be safely and advantageously made I should by no means be indisposed to give the fourteen hundred thousand of our present fellow-subjects who are living in the provinces of North America a participation in the perfect freedom enjoyed by our mother country.'[3] 'If we are wise,' said the radical, J. A. Roebuck, fearful most of all of the absorption of British North America into the United States – 'a nation that has now dominion from Florida to the lakes of Canada' – 'we shall see and arrange all matters in Canada and in our other North American possessions so as to prepare them for when a separation shall come, as come it must, to be an independent nation.'[4] But while William Lyon Mackenzie's revolt in Upper Canada, provoked by the lack of responsibility of colonial governments to colonial peoples and strongly reinforced by incipient, indigenous radicalism,[5] had certainly sought to advance the cause of Canadian freedom on a United States republican model, that of the eloquent and impassioned Louis-Joseph Papineau in Lower Canada, stirred by particular French-Canadian resentments and backed by underlying separatist or nationalist sentiment, fell into another category.[6] In this second case, animosity was directed not so much against a distant and detached imperial authority as against the proximate and purposeful British settlers. Alexis de Tocqueville and Gustave de Beaumont had already sensed the existence of this deep-seated antipathy on their visit to Quebec in 1831 and had reflected – not without a certain satisfaction – on the prospect of a French rebellion and even, fleetingly, on the possibility of the restoration of a French Empire in North America.[7]

The 1837 rebellions in Upper and Lower Canada seemed politically portentous. But what did they portend? The end of Empire or something less, protest against the governance of that Empire? The history of the eighteenth century suggested the former; the insignificance of the rebellion in Upper Canada, by reason of the loyalty of the great majority of colonists, the latter. In either case and, more particularly in the second, there was occasion for enquiry. That there was antagonism between Crown and colonists was hardly in question, but if indeed that derived at root from political frustration, caused by patterns of government no longer suited to the needs or conformable to the aspirations of colonists, these were matters that might be remedied. It was the purpose of Lord Durham's enquiry into the affairs of British North America to recommend how best that might be done.

The choice of Lord Durham as Governor-in-chief and High Commissioner charged with this critical mission commended itself to the Colonial Reformers and to the Prime Minister, Lord Melbourne, but for very different reasons. To the Reformers 'Radical Jack' was one of themselves, a reformer at home where he had played a notable part in mustering support in the House for the passing of the Great Reform Bill and one to be relied upon to approach problems of administration overseas with reforming zeal; to Lord Melbourne Durham was an uncomfortable colleague, whom he was well pleased to see depart for distant places. In the Canadas news of the appointment aroused expectation and, among the more conservative, a certain apprehension little allayed either by 'the jaunty confidence with which Canadian Radicals tried to appropriate him'[8] or by the reputation of some members of the staff Durham was bringing with him. But whether in hope or with reserve, few doubted that the man and the enterprise were of high moment for the future of British North America.

In 1838 – Durham arrived at Quebec on 29 May that year – representative government was the most advanced form of government in British colonies. It ensured in theory and often in practice a tight measure of imperial control. The governor was appointed by the Crown and was responsible to the government of the United Kingdom. In turn he nominated his executive advisers and they were responsible to him. Over against the Executive, thus constituted, stood a Legislature comprised of two Houses, one nominated and the other elected. The Lower House of the Legislature represented (in so far as it was then represented) popular opinion. Members of that House might discuss and debate; and by discussion and debate thus might, and sometimes did, influence executive action. But – and here was the rub – they could not control it. In his Report Lord Durham concisely summarised some of the consequences:

A governor, arriving in a colony in which he almost invariably has had no previous acquaintance with the state of parties or the character of individuals is compelled to throw himself almost entirely upon those whom he finds placed in the position of his official advisers. His first acts must necessarily be performed and his first appointments made at their suggestion. And as these first acts and appointments give a character to his policy, he is generally brought thereby into immediate collision with the other parties in the country and thrown into more complete dependence upon the official party and its friends. Thus, a governor of Lower Canada has almost always been brought into collision with the Assembly, which his advisers regard as their enemy.[9]

What was it, then, that was wrong with a system which produced such consequences? Lord Durham was clear and emphatic in his answer: it was the entire separation of legislative and executive powers – the natural error, as he remarked, of governments desiring to be free of the check of representative institutions.

> It was impossible [he wrote] to observe the great similarity of the constitutions established in all our North American Provinces and the striking tendency of all to terminate in pretty nearly the same result without entertaining a belief that some defect in the form of government and some erroneous principle of adminis-tration have been common to all . . . It may fairly be said that the natural state of government in all these colonies is that of collision between the executive and the representative body. In all of them the administration of public affairs is habitually confided to those who do not cooperate harmoniously with the popular branch of the legislature; and the government is constantly proposing measures which the majority of the Assem-bly reject and refusing its assent to bills which that body has passed.[10]

Such disharmony indicated deviation from sound constitutional principles or practice. No representative body composed of men of experience and standing would be content to act as a mere law-giving and tax-raising assembly while entrusting the direction of policy to an irresponsible clique of officials. In British North America least of all were they likely to acquiesce in so subordinate a rôle when, as Lord Durham noted, they could see men endowed with no greater capacity for the conduct of affairs than at least some among them filling the highest positions of political responsibility in the United States.

Diagnosis of defective principles of government was followed by Lord Durham's enunciation of his sovereign remedy. It was responsible government[11] – a phrase which itself was to become a part of Commonwealth history. Every purpose of popular control, he argued, might be combined with every advantage of vesting the immediate choice of advisers in the Crown, were the colonial governor to be instructed to secure the cooperation of the Assembly in his policy by entrusting its administration to such men as could command the support of a majority there. The authority of the Crown would remain wholly unimpaired but the governor, in Lord Durham's view,[12] should be given to understand that he need count on no aid from home in the event of his having any differences with the Assembly not directly involving relations between the mother country and the colony. This implied a necessary distinction between domestic and imperial affairs. How was this distinction to be drawn? Lord Durham proposed quite simply by the reservation to the imperial government of matters of imperial concern. He identified these concerns as any constitutional amendment of the form of government, the regulation of foreign relations and trade with the mother country, the other British Colonies and foreign nations, and the disposal of public lands. In so doing Durham made clear how 'very few' in his opinion were the imperial interests at stake in day-to-day colonial administration. Indeed, so certain did he feel on this point that he devoted no more than three sentences to his outline of them.[13]

Three aspects of Durham's proposals merit particular attention.[14] The first is Lord Durham's determination that British institutions were appropriate and should be developed in British North America. United States' precedents, especially with regard to an elected executive, he considered only to discard as being incompatible with monarchy. Secondly, the British constitutional practice which he desired to see extended to British North America was cabinet government applied, not as in seventeenth-century England, as had been the case hitherto in colonial territories, but as in early nineteenth-century England, with the cabinet responsible to a popularly elected House of Commons. Thirdly, this association between executive and legislature would, he maintained, not only remove the outstanding cause of friction between colonies and the mother country but would further, by giving control over domestic affairs (which ordinarily loom largest on the horizon of most citizens of all states) discourage notions of colonial separation by eliminating what had hitherto been the principal cause of them. This hopeful conclusion, little in accord with the trend of contemporary opinion, may be thought of as being in many respects the most telling feature of the whole Report.

While responsible self-government was the principal recommendation of the Durham Report, it was not the only one of importance. There was a cultural as well as a politico-constitutional cause of discontents. In Lower Canada where the rebellion, as Lord Durham noted, was the product of a 'conflict of races', no reforms, political or institutional could (as he also recognised) remove causes of conflict which derived from 'the very composition of society'.

I expected to find a contest between a government and a people: I found two nations warring in the bosom of a single state: I found a struggle not of principles but of races; and I perceived that it would be idle to attempt any amelioration of laws or institutions until we could first succeed in terminating the deadly

animosity that now separates the inhabitants of Lower Canada
into the hostile divisions of French and English.[15]

He indicated where responsibility for this situation rested with the
confident assurance of a nineteenth-century English aristocrat.
'The error', he wrote, 'to which the present contest must be
attributed, is the vain endeavour to preserve a French Canadian
nationality in the midst of Anglo–American colonies and states.'[16]
'Two nations warring in the bosom of a single state' was a phrase
which represented something very close to reality. Lord Durham's
response to the threat of a cultural conflict, which if it could not be
ended might at the least be contained and then diminished, was to
recommend union of the provinces of Upper and Lower Canada.
It was a recommendation prompted by his faith in the future of the
British race. A radical in politics, Durham was conservative and
insular in respect of culture. He believed in the great nineteenth-
century march of progress; he noted that English people were
everywhere in the vanguard of it and he concluded that the destiny
of French Canada, not least in the interests of its own people,
should lie in gradual absorption in an advancing Anglo–Saxon
society. Before he left for Canada Durham, according to Charles
Buller, had seen 'what narrow and mischievous spirit lurked at the
bottom of all the acts of the French Canadians; and while he was
prepared to do the individuals full justice, and justice with mercy,
he had made up his mind that no quarter should be shown to the
absurd pretensions of race, and that he must . . . aim at making
Canada thoroughly British'.[17] 'I entertain', he wrote in the Report
itself, 'no doubts as to the national character which must be given to
Lower Canada; it must be that of the British Empire; that of the
majority of the population of British America; that of the great race
which must, in the lapse of no long period of time, be predominant
over the whole North American continent.'[18] Accordingly it should
be henceforth 'the first and steady purpose' of the British government to establish 'an English population with English laws and
language in this province and to trust its government to none but a
decidedly English Legislature'. And accordingly also the project of
a federal union, to which Lord Durham himself had first inclined,
must needs be discarded in favour of union of the two provinces of
Upper and Lower Canada which would ensure in terms of
population a clear English predominance in numbers; for only
when faced with such numerical preponderance could the French
be expected to abandon 'their vain hopes of nationality'.
There was some irony in contemporary French Canadian esteem

for Durham. He had been received with awe when he arrived at Quebec. No governor hitherto had come with so great and – be it said – so liberal a political reputation – and one which he enhanced when, on the Queen's Coronation Day 28 June, in an act of 'prodigal clemency', which shocked Conservatives in Upper Canada, he authorised by a Royal Proclamation, the terms of which were questionably within the discretionary powers conferred upon him, the release of the great majority of political prisoners in Lower Canada, exiling the remainder to Bermuda – and none assuredly with greater display of magnificence. Quebec's historian writes of the splendours of the festivities and of the quasi-regal reception accorded to one who as high commissioner was deemed to be of even higher status than that of governor-general.[19] His baggage took two days to land; it included his sporting trophies and the horses he was later to race on the plains of Abraham. Finally, on 29 May 1838, clothed in brilliant uniform, wearing the collar of the Bath, Durham himself rode up amid cheering crowds on a white horse from the banks of the St Lawrence to what remained of the Château St Louis after the fire of 23 February 1834.[20] For more than two months Durham stayed at Quebec, while at Kingston the days and weeks went by with loyalists 'waiting for Durham'. At last on 11 July he came, satisfying expectations as he rode out once more on his white horse to inspect the docks and to meet prominent citizens.[21] But his visit to Upper Canada was brief and cursory, a fact to which critics later attributed the inadequacies of the commentary upon the affairs of the Province in his Report. Nonetheless, when following upon the disallowance by Melbourne's government of Durham's Bermuda Ordinances on the grounds that they had exceeded the powers conferred upon him, Durham decided upon an immediate return to England, the news 'was bewailed by almost everybody in the Canadas without distinction of race or class or political affiliation'.[22] Most of all was this true in the city of Quebec, where on his departure in the early afternoon of 1 November 1838, accompanied by a military escort and followed by a procession of three thousand citizens, 'the streets' as Buller noted, 'were crowded; the spectators filled every window and every house-top; and though every hat was raised as we passed a deep silence marked the general grief for Lord Durham's departure'.[23]

Yet French Canadian regard was by no means wholly misplaced. If Lord Durham thought the future of French Canada lay in absorption in a greater and more progressive Anglo–Saxon whole, he showed also much concern that this should happen equitably, gradually and by natural laws, as he conceived them, of political development. If he was resolved to bring about majority English-speaking rule, he was equally determined not to allow a minority of English settlers in Lower Canada to control the destiny of the French speaking majority. And while Durham's contempt for French–Canadian language and culture – the last not unknown among Parisians, as many French–Canadian visitors were aggrieved to discover, down to the Gaullist era – was a great blot upon the Report, its most lamentable effect being the accentuation of an already pronounced sense of Anglo–Saxon superiority, its one beneficial consequence the hardening of a resentful French-Canadian resolve to show Durham wrong, Durham's insistence that the Canada of the future must have the character of the majority, which was British, may be distinguished (as is not always done) from grandiose later Milnerite notions of demographic engineering intended to create a British majority in white South Africa where one did not exist. Indians, or Irish, or Africans had few doubts that, on the attainment of responsible government, it was essentially the character of the majority that should prevail.

In respect of union, which was introduced in a form less equitable to the French-speaking minority than Durham had contemplated, Lord Durham was at one with the outlook of his time and the spirit of the old colonial system, while in respect of responsible government he was ahead of it. In consequence of this, the latter was extracted by argumentative and frustrating stages, while Union at once commended itself to the home government and was implemented in the Union Act, 1840.[24] The Act was the first and critical step on the road to Canadian federation. And while in the history of the Commonwealth the coming into existence of the first dominion in 1867 of necessity takes pride of place, in Canadian history the order of priority may well be otherwise. It was from union in 1840, however chequered its subsequent development, that thoughts and possibilities of a trans-continental association stemmed.

Responsible government, by contrast, aroused much contemporary misgiving. There were doubts in particular about its compatibility with Empire. In March 1839 the *Quarterly Review* concluded that the 'new, and to us, incomprehensible system of "colonial connexion" . . . is absolute separation' and asserted that if 'that rank and infectious [Durham] Report does not receive the high, marked, and energetic discountenance and indignation of the Imperial Crown and Parliament, British America is lost'.[25] If this represented an extreme view, not all misgivings were either unreasonable or necessarily misplaced. Adam Smith had observed in *The Wealth of Nations* that to suggest that Great Britain should voluntarily give up all authority over her colonies would be 'to propose such a measure as never was, and never will be, adopted by any nation in the world'. True, any such intention was vigorously repudiated by Lord Durham, whose declared purpose was to consolidate Empire by timely concession and reform, not to hasten its disintegration. But – and here was the crucial issue – might not the concession of self-government in domestic affairs lead to divided authority, with the local government enlarging its powers step by step until it was in fact separate and sovereign? Lord Durham had laid down (in principle) a dividing line reserving matters of imperial concern to the imperial government, but would such an exercise in theoretic definition stand the trial of experience? Delicate issues might well arise – for example, disposal of public lands, a matter of close concern to settlers, was placed on the short list of subjects reserved to the imperial government. Might not conflicts arise here, or elsewhere, when interests and attitudes differed? 'It may happen', noted Lord John Russell in a dispatch of 11 October 1839 of such an eventuality

> ... that the governor receives at one and the same time instructions from the queen and advice from the executive council totally at variance with each other ... If he is to obey his instructions from England the parallel of constitutional responsibility entirely fails; if on the other hand he is to follow the advice of his council he is no longer a subordinate officer but an independent sovereign.[26]

The potential predicament was perceptively diagnosed, and although long and sensibly evaded by essays in 'harmonious' government, it was finally resolved only in terms of independent sovereignty. Britain, in the terminology of Adam Smith, did ultimately and for the most part voluntarily relinquish all authority over her colonies of settlement.

'A new era in the colonial policy of nations began with Lord Durham's Report: the imperishable memorial of that nobleman's courage, patriotism and enlightened liberality.' So John Stuart Mill, at once the source and principal interpreter of many of the imperial ideas of Victorian liberalism, wrote in his *Representative Government*[27] of Lord Durham's Report of 1839 upon 'the Affairs of British North America'.[28] The verdict is the more noteworthy in that Mill, subscribing to a widely entertained opinion, discounted

Lord Durham's major rôle in the writing of the Report that bears
his name, incorrectly (as is now known) attributing the chief part of
its composition to the two radical colonial reformers, Charles
Buller, who had served as his chief secretary, and Edward Gibbon
Wakefield, at the time something of a social outcast, who also
accompanied him to Canada and allowed that 'the honour' of being
the earliest champion of the new colonial policy belonged not to
Durham but 'unquestionably' to another of the Colonial Reformers, 'Mr Roebuck'. Mill was also mindful of how, at the time of his
Mission, Durham had been assailed by political foes and timid
friends in England and believed that an article which he [Mill] had
written in the *London and Westminster Review* before publication of
the *Report*, stating his conviction that Durham's 'policy was almost
exactly what mine would have been' was 'the touch which deter-
mines whether a stone, set in motion at the top of an eminence,
shall roll down on one side or the other'.[29]

Recent commentaries for the most part, however, have been
highly critical of the man, his Report and earlier assessments of its
longer term influence.[30] In so far as these criticisms are directed at
the lack of originality in the content of the Report, they are well
grounded. Not only had the claims of Roebuck and others among
the Colonial Reformers in England to be taken into account, but
also those of Canadians, Professor Creighton in 1934 remarking
that of the two basic ideas in the Report, one, that of legislative
union, derived mainly from the Canadian Tories, and the other,
the idea of local autonomy, from the Canadian reformers, leaving
Durham with the rôle, not of an original philosopher from the
mother country but 'a brilliant populariser' of colonial ideas.[31]
Popularisers, especially those with more than a touch of
flamboyance – well captured, in Durham's case, in Lawrence's well
known portrait of him – are apt to be vulnerable to the judgement
of a remoter posterity. Yet there are moments in history, when style
and manner of presentation may be of decisive importance in
effecting a breakaway from postures of profitless negation to some
enlarging prospect. Such, it may be contended, was the nature of
Durham's contribution. Certainly he was well equipped to make it
by reason both of his qualities and their defects. He had inclination
and aptitude for great affairs, but no corresponding taste or grasp
of smaller matters: he had the larger insight but not equal foresight
and was thus temperamentally predisposed to prescribe remedies
of broad and general import with a fine, aristocratic disregard for
the difficulties that stood in the way of their detailed application
and the problems that would be encountered when the attempt was

made. His contribution, then, however measured, was to be weighed in terms of psychological approach over and above that of constitutional recommendation – and Professor Creighton well conveyed this aspect of it when he wrote of 'the spirit of Lord Durham brooding over the achievement of responsible government'.[32]

The influence of that 'brooding spirit' while most directly felt in the particular geographical area, the crisis in whose affairs was the occasion of Lord Durham's Mission, was not to be confined to it but was in time to extend from the colonies of British North America through the Dominion of Canada to the British Commonwealth of Nations. The memorial Lord Durham left behind him was in that sense not less but greater than John Stuart Mill could have surmised. It rested upon the concept of responsible government. For more than a century at least no discussion of imperial or Commonwealth constitutions, based on that principle, whether for Australia or South Africa, for India or later Ceylon, for Nigeria, Kenya or the West Indies, was complete without a first reference to the seminal contribution of that moody nobleman, with his dramatic good looks and volatile, uncomfortable temperament – with his radical opinions, his aristocratic connections and his great wealth (Creevey called him 'King Jog' because he once remarked that 'he considered £40,000 a year a moderate income – such a one as a man *might jog on with*'),[33] who by a brief visit of inquiry to British North America had impressed his personality upon the politics of imperial reform as surely as his father-in-law, Earl Grey, by presiding over the passage of the first Reform Bill, had enrolled his name on the page of English domestic history. It was for that reason that a century later Clement Attlee, with a politician's sensitivity to the importance of association, proceeded by way of first reference to Durham to propose that a mission be sent to India.[34] No more reassuring precedent could have been laid before a predominantly Conservative War Cabinet with Churchill at its head. That Attlee placed it in the forefront of his argument, that as a result Cripps assumed the mantle of Durham, that like his predecessor he was mistrusted by a majority of the Cabinet, deemed to have exceeded (or to be about to exceed) the authority conferred upon him, to have his report left undiscussed by the Cabinet, his mission seemingly unproductive at the outset, provides not merely historical analogies illustrating the occupational hazards of political missionaries, but more important underlines that the influence of such enterprise is rarely to be measured by its immediate impact. Both Durham and Cripps (as Churchill was to lament) on the longer term pointed the way to the end of an old and the opening of a new relationship.

THE FAVOURABLE IMPACT OF PUBLIC OPINION AND THE COMMERCIAL REVOLUTION

It has to be allowed that in respect of timing Lord Durham's Report was doubly fortunate. In the first place by 1839 public opinion in England was predisposed (or resigned) to imperial, over and above domestic, reform;[35] while in the second place the advance towards free trade, culminating in the Repeal of the Corn Laws in 1846 and Navigation Acts in 1849, progressively diminished and finally ended the economic advantages of a centrally controlled and centrally directed imperial system.

The political liberalism of mid-nineteenth century England was compounded, in its imperial context, of reforming zeal and growing indifference. Lord Melbourne, who did not like being pressed into an active reforming rôle, told Queen Victoria that radicals had neither ability, honesty, nor numbers. Of the Colonial Reformers, radicals in domestic politics, the first was as manifestly untrue as the last was obviously correct. They never claimed numbers in the form of wide popular backing for their imperial panaceas but, in respect of ability, not least in publicising their views and pressing home their arguments, they were well equipped to leave a mark upon the thinking of their contemporaries and even more of their successors. Their immediate influence might indeed have been greater but for their eccentricities. Edward Gibbon Wakefield, who went with Durham to Canada twice eloped with an heiress and it was during a three year period of imprisonment in Newgate for abduction that he had made, in his diplomatically if misleadingly entitled *A Letter from Sydney*, his early study of the problems of colonisation. He conceived, ironically enough, the idea of the respectable middle class settler societies of South Austrialia and New Zealand, and despite an initial setback in the first instance played a critical pioneering rôle in bringing them into existence.[36] William Molesworth, closely associated with him and remembered not least for his assaults upon the Colonial Office, was sent down from Trinity College, Cambridge, after challenging his tutor to a duel. Charles Buller, a more constructive and formidable critic, created in 'Mr Mother Country'[37] the prototype of an insensitive and irresponsible bureaucrat controlling the Empire from a backroom in the Colonial Office, and modelled (but by no means fairly) on Sir James Stephen, under-secretary for the colonies, 1836–47, and subsequently Regius Professor of Modern History at Cambridge. Collectively the Colonial Reformers formulated the ideas, which, like the first draft of a memorandum submitted to a meeting, provided, despite all the criticisms levelled against them, the basis from which subsequent discussion proceeded. That was their great achievement and their lasting contribution to imperial affairs.

The Colonial Office, associated with the War Office until 1854, was a first and favourite target of the Colonial Reformers. Its range of responsibilities was wide and varied and its patronage, both military and civilian, was very considerable, so long as its dual character survived. Moreover, there was so often disturbance, grievance or even conflict in one part or other of the Empire that the office appeared to draw trouble to itself. As the Office 'at war with all the colonies' it was the play of Lord Derby's wit; but to the Colonial Reformers it was itself a source of mischief, not merely the victim of its situation and responsibilities.

> In the dark recesses of the Colonial Office [declaimed Molesworth in the debate on Canada in early 1838],[38] in those dens of peculation and plunder – it was there that the real and irresponsible rulers of the millions of inhabitants of our colonies were to be found. Men utterly unknown to fame, but for whom, he trusted, some time or other, a day of reckoning would come, when they would be dragged before the public and punished for their evil deeds. These were the men who, shielded by irresponsibility and hidden from the public gaze, continued the same system of misgovernment under every party which alternatively presided over the destinies of the Empire.

Of course there was much that was exaggerated. Who, in reading Molesworth's diatribes, would think that the affairs of the much-abused Colonial Office were administered by a man whose greatest satisfaction was to have had official responsibility for the emancipation of West Indian slaves and who has good claim to be regarded as the originator of *laissez-faire* in British dealings with colonial governments? In both respects, notes a historian of the Colonial Office,[39] Stephen 'founded traditions which are still at work in the Colonial and Commonwealth Relations Offices – that the welfare of native peoples is paramount and the autonomy of Commonwealth countries is to be continuously championed'. Yet at the time, the greater impact upon the public mind at home and still more in the colonies was made by the appearance – which sufficiently represented reality – of autocracy, remoteness and secretiveness, all of which surrounded the affairs of the Colonial Office. The Colonial Reformers, it is clear, were not voices crying in the wilderness; they were the sharp-tongued, often intolerant spokesmen of sentiments widely, though not universally, entertained by those few who were concerned with the consequences of *laissez-faire* in colonial affairs.

The purpose behind the radical reformers' campaigns against the old colonial establishment was constructive at heart and inspired by a faith which few of their fellow-countrymen shared. It was to refashion the system in terms of liberty, which, politically speaking, meant colonial self-government. In itself this was thought desirable, by Stephen within the Colonial Office among others, for were not colonists, like other people, the best judges of their own interests? But the Colonial Reformers went further. They challenged the widespread assumption that colonial freedom to pursue these interests would lead to separation. On the contrary, they argued, it would encourage a close and mutually advantageous association in liberty. The saying 'Emancipate your Colonies', according to Molesworth, meant more at that time than usually appeared. It was used, by some at least, to convey the opinion 'that a country like this would be better without colonies, and even that it would have been better for us if we had never had colonies'. And he proceeded to say to the House of Commons:

> Instead of wishing to separate from our colonies, or to avert the establishment of new ones, I would say distinguish between the evil and the good; remove the evil, but preserve the good; do not 'Emancipate your Colonies', but multiply them, and improve – reform your system of colonial government.[40]

'The experiment of keeping colonies and governing them well', Lord Durham maintained, 'ought to have a trial.' Even if it did, contrary to his own expectation, lead to separation then, at least, there would be the satisfaction of a parting in friendship and with the assurance that 'the British colonies should not be the only countries on the American continent in which the Anglo–Saxon race shall be found unfit to govern itself.'

The cause of the Colonial Reformers was advanced chiefly by circumstance. On 2 February 1848, the first responsible ministry in a British colony was formally instituted, not unfittingly in Nova Scotia, the oldest British colony in the Second Empire. But its

formation was the consequence, not of British conversion to the
concept of responsible, colonial government in the abstract, but of
British appreciation of the relevance of the idea to situations in
which they were faced with sustained and mounting pressure of
colonial demand for an administration responsive to the opinion of
elected representatives. Where Nova Scotia led others followed,
but in each instance less because of principle than because of
considerations of practical advantage. Yet it was all-important that
the idea should have been formulated by Durham in his Report
and developed by his reformist friends in argument in advance of
the days when colonial demand moved towards its climax. Concessions as a consequence, could be seen to derive from a measure of
conviction.

That conviction at this as at other times was notably assisted by
the resigned wisdom – reinforced by niggardliness and verging on
indifference – of established statesmen and parties. It was well
summed up in a private letter from Lord Grey at the Colonial
Office to Lord Elgin in Canada, written on 18 May 1849, in which
he observed:

The main object of our policy ought to be to support the hopes
and courage of the Canadians . . . but unfortunately there begins
to prevail in the House of Commons and I am sorry to say in the
highest quarters, an opinion (which I believe to be utterly
erroneous) that we have no interest in preserving our colonies
and ought therefore to make no sacrifice for that purpose. Peel,
Graham and Gladstone, if they do not avow this opinion as
openly as Cobden and his friends, yet betray very clearly that
they entertain it, nor do I find some members of the cabinet free
from it, so that I am powerless to do anything which involves
expense – it is the existence of this feeling here which is to me by
far the most serious cause of apprehension for the future.[41]

In the fastnesses of the Colonial Office, Sir James Stephen, who
never visited any colony, entertained much the same notions. 'It
remains,' he wrote, 'for the Canadians to cut the last cable which
anchors them to us . . . The same process is in progress in the
Australian colonies.' But, it is worth remarking, it was British
acquiescence in a Canadian initiative that he contemplated and
indeed thought right. Responsibility for any final break must in his
view rest with the colonists themselves. Even in respect of the
smaller colonies which he described – in a foreshadowing of a more
famous Disraelian phrase – as 'wretched burdens', responsibility

for which 'in an evil hour we assumed, we have no right to lay down again, unless relieved of the moral obligation by the initiative of the colonists themselves'. Lord Derby, with something of the underlying note of fatalism to be found in Stephen's comments, summed up prevailing opinion well in a debate in the House of Lords in 1854: 'If the North American colonies,' he said, 'increasing in wealth, in population and in importance desire to part from this country, in God's name let us part in terms of peace and friendship.'[42]

This viewpoint was indeed understandable and well-nigh predetermined by the lessons drawn from the apparently conclusive precedent of the American colonies. It was not merely that they had seceded but that in one of the best remembered of historical forecasts Turgot had declared a quarter of a century before the Declaration of Independence that 'colonies are like fruits which cling to the tree only till they ripen' and that accordingly as soon as the American colonies could take care of themselves they would do 'what Carthage did'.

> Most of the permanent under-secretaries for the colonies during the early decades of Queen Victoria's reign [wrote Professor D. G. Creighton][43] subscribed to what may be called the pomological view of colonies – the view, that is, that all colonies, like ripe apples, were destined inevitably to drop off the parent tree. They and their contemporaries showed little disposition to arrest the fall. There was scarcely a front-rank statesman in early Victorian England who was not prepared to view the departure of the colonies with cheerfulness decorously mingled with resignation.

The resignation, at least, was comprehensible. If parting was inevitable did not statesmanship demand that this time the parting should be amicable? Why resist the inevitable unravelling of an imperial-colonial relationship? Why not, instead, accede to colonial demands for responsible government as they were advanced and so bring about the withdrawal of imperial authority by stages until responsibility was finally taken over by a successor government not inexperienced in the conduct of affairs?

A widespread presumption about the probable course of events enhanced the probability of its occurence. Or so at least it has been argued by C. A. Bodelsen, on the ground that the constant talk about the necessity and desirability of separation, by exasperating and wounding colonial loyalties actually brought separation nearer. On the other hand, he has noted – and this at least is hardly

open to dispute – that the liberal policy of almost unlimited
self-government and the constant yielding to colonial demands, to
which the continuance of the connection was chiefly due, was
greatly facilitated by the conviction that the connection would not
in any case long survive. 'Paradoxically,' Bodelsen concluded,[44] 'the
Separatists may thus be said to have contributed their share
towards the continued unity of the Empire.'

Political liberalism in colonial affairs, compounded as it was of so
many attitudes, considerations and emotions, would hardly have
advanced so far or so fast had it not been paralleled by the
successful culmination of the campaign for free trade. Britain, the
industrial workshop of the world, had thereafter little or no
interest in remaining cabined and constricted within the confines
of the imperial economic system which she had herself constructed.
The world, not the Empire, was or was rapidly becoming her
market. Britain (in Professor Hancock's telling phrase),[45] 'the imperial metropolis of a far-flung polity', was becoming, 'the commercial metropolis of a farther-flung economy'. And to the
free traders, to Cobden and to Bright, the obliteration of the
economic frontier between the Empire and the world was not a
matter of accident; it was a fundamental article of faith. The world
must be opened to the trade of all nations for by trade came both
profit and peace among men.

For the Second Empire [wrote Professor Creighton in 1938] the
meaning of the new industrialism and the new political economy
was all too clear. It was not that the English had unselfishly
abandoned the urge for empire: it was simply that they had
substituted the new, divinely-inspired imperialism for the old,
simple-minded, sinful imperialism of the First Empire. They
looked beyond the limits of their stunted domination of the
world.[46]

Expanding economic interests reinforced by faith in free trade
thus demanded the final winding up of the old colonial system, and
with the repeal of the Navigation Laws in 1849 it was formally laid
to rest.

The free traders, accordingly, far from being hostile to colonial
independence tended to favour it, not least as a means of reducing
imperial expenditure.

Hawes [wrote Lord Grey from Howick to Elgin in Canada on 22
August 1849][47] received the other day a letter from Cobden

which I think it desirable you should see as there is a good deal of truth in the representation it gives of the state of public opinion here on the subject of the colonies – it is impossible to disguise from oneself that there is a growing impatience as to the amount of expense they occasion and a strong feeling that they ought during peace to pay for their own military expenditure, nor can I deny that there is some justice in this . . . To proceed as Cobden and his friends would wish would be to abandon the greater part at all events of our colonies which I am old fashioned enough to believe would be a national misfortune, and what is more a misfortune to the civilised world . . .'

Cobden would certainly have thought such sentiments old fashioned, if not deliberately perverse. But they could also be discounted, as the claims of colonial expenditure could not. For its reduction, a campaign of criticism against the cost of colonies was required and was pursued in succeeding years.

For the colonies, and especially those in British North America, the transition from the old colonial system to the new free trade era was in some instances painful. One Canadian historian, Professor Creighton, has written of the British adoption of free trade as 'a major catastrophe', followed as it was by profound, if short lived, depression in the North American colonies; he has concluded that the Empire was nearly broken on responsible government and a fiscal revolution carried through in British, not colonial, interests. It was not, he remarks in a telling paradox, the colonies that had separated from Britain, but Britain that had broken away from her own Empire.[48] This, however much it may need qualification (unless indeed the view be taken that the real bonds of Empire were all, or chiefly, economic), focuses attention on the central fact of a British imperial initiative which demanded colonial readjustment in response.

The severance of exclusive trading ties in itself rendered timely reconsideration of the purposes of Empire. In April 1851 the editors of the *Edinburgh Review* undertook the task. They noted that in former times colonies were valued as an outlet for manufactures and as sources of supply 'for needful products which we could not obtain, or could not obtain so cheaply or so well, elsewhere'. They were 'the principal and the surest channels for that commerce which we felt to be the life-blood of the nation'. They were bound to the mother country in the bonds of a strict and mutually favouring system of customs duties; 'we compelled them to trade with us exclusively, to take from us exclusively all the articles with which we could supply them; and to send us exclusively all the produce of their soil . . . our colonies were *customers who could not escape us*, and vendors who could sell to us alone.'

But all that was gone, to be replaced by a new system based upon radically different notions. All protective and discriminating tariffs had been removed and Great Britain no longer favoured colonial products and could no longer compel the colonies to favour hers. The colonies had thus become friendly trading communities, nothing more. 'The very object for which we founded, governed, defended and cherished them has been abandoned; why then should we any longer incur the cost of their maintenance?' Why indeed, when this cost had been estimated by Sir William Molesworth to amount to four million pounds a year, nearly equal to the proceeds of income tax which could, were the colonies abandoned, be repealed 'to the infinite relief of our people'.

Was the fiscal argument against Empire conclusive? Certainly there were many ardent free traders who were prepared to think so and in this they had strong support from Goldwin Smith, Regius Professor of History at Oxford. 'The time was', he observed in retrospect in 1863, 'when the universal prevalence of commercial monopoly made it worth our while to hold colonies in dependence for the sake of commanding their trade. But that time has gone. Trade is everywhere free or becoming free; and this expensive and perilous connection has entirely survived its sole legitimate cause.' This was, characteristically, an extreme statement. But it was not, it will be noted, an anti-colonial expression of view theoretically advanced; it was an argument against political Empire in a free-trade era. The distinction is not without importance. The so-called and now much questioned anti-imperialism of free trade was by no means, even on its own evaluation, necessarily anti-imperialist in absolute terms. An early and formidable critic of liberal interpretations of nineteenth-century imperial history, Professor Creighton, noted on the contrary that 'the heart of the whole movement was Manchester – Manchester, the centre of the new imperialism masquerading in a sober anti-imperialist disguise'.[49] A free trader accordingly might be and usually was anti-imperialist in the particular circumstances of mid-Victorian England because he believed that what he deemed to be the essential purposes of Empire might be promoted more effectively when freed from the entanglements of a now outdated political system. In a deeper sense, however, he might be moved by an imperialism as real as that of his predecessors and more 'arrogant' – the term is Professor Creighton's – than that of his late nineteenth-century, territorially expansionist successors. Or to put the point rather differently and more broadly (using terminology which has been given wide circulation by Professor Gallagher and Professor Robinson's frontal assault on traditional concepts of an anti-imperialist mid-Victorian and an imperialist late Victorian period in British history, and to view in one wide perspective the formal Empire over which Britain exercised political control and the informal Empire over which she maintained influence and pursued her interests by means of indirect control in some form or another) it can be persuasively argued, as they have done, that the so-called anti-imperialist and so-called imperialist phases were no more than superficial manifestations of one underlying purpose. The difference, the authors conclude, 'between formal and informal Empire has not been one of fundamental nature but of degree'.[50] The new economic enlightenment, sensible of the advantages to Britain at that time of informal economic control and anxious for Britain to be free of burdensome and expensive direct political responsibility, did not in reality, as it did in outward appearance, necessarily imply departure from – let alone transcendence of – old imperial motivations. On the contrary, the period of its unquestioned predominance coincided – and not fortuitously – with significant extensions of formal and a notable expansion of informal Empire. But despite this apparent paradox the new thinking did predispose British statesmen to contemplate more readily the advantages, both to Britain and to colonies of settlement, of promoting measures of self-government that might lead to independence. In the history of the Commonwealth this has lost none of its importance. Without such predisposition on the British side (whatever the motive that inspired it) there would not have been a Commonwealth. Relaxation of metropolitan control at a critical phase in imperial history opened the way to friendly association as against colonial secession on the earlier American model. That the British government in its so-called anti-imperialist phase should continue to acquire new territories in India and Africa was irrelevant in this context. British colonists overseas were at the most only remotely interested in general theories of imperial policy and their application. What concerned them was its direct impact upon the conduct of their affairs. And in that limited context the 'anti-imperialism' of mid-Victorian years marked a break decisive for a Commonwealth future, with the imperialism of the preceding age.

The argument of Empire was, however, conducted at the time in less abstract terms. The *Edinburgh Review*, in the same article in which it presented the case against retaining our colonies, supplied the counter balancing arguments *for* Empire. On a point of fact the cost to Great Britain of her colonial Empire, fairly calculated, by 1850 came to two million pounds a year rather than the four million alleged by Molesworth (though admittedly it had been far greater). For the rest, the arguments ran on lines which were to be familiar for a century or more. The colonies, the article noted, did not desire independence and were not therefore unwilling or troublesome dependencies. They might hate the Colonial Office; they did not hate England. England in any case was so bound to them by ties of blood and affection that even if they were independent she would, if need arose, come to their defence. They were countries with expanding populations, possessing most valuable opportunities for commercial enterprise, with whom therefore, on grounds of long-term self-interest alone, the closest ties should be maintained. Their populations were partly or largely British and with growing pressure of numbers at home it was of the greatest importance that the colonies should remain an easy, natural outlet for British overseas migration. Nor should humanitarian considerations be overlooked. There were British obligations to minorities and to peoples of other races in these colonies which it would be dishonourable to discard. In sum therefore, what the situation demanded was not – as purely fiscal considerations might suggest – the abandonment of the colonies but continued rule, exercised with forbearance and justice, leading the colonies forward to the fullest self-government where there was a sufficient infusion of British blood to warrant it. The goal should be the existence and cohesion of a vast dominion 'blest with the ... most beneficial form of liberty which the world has yet enjoyed'.

With one reservation or qualification this was the language of Commonwealth. What had been modified some seventy years later was the association, common to Lord Durham's *Report*, the *Edinburgh Review* and most nineteenth-century commentaries, of self-government with people of British origin who alone, by reason of history and aptitude in the art of government, were thought qualified to exercise its responsibilities. It was because this opinion was then so widely entertained that the settlement of British peoples overseas was felt to be at once of advantage to Britain, of most significant service to the fulfilment of the continuing purposes of Empire, and a contribution to world peace by extending the areas fitted for the highest recognised form of government. *The*

Times, on 4 February 1862, reacting sharply to one more plea from Goldwin Smith in Oxford for the dismemberment of the queen's dominions 'with as little delay as possible', rested its case for Empire not exclusively but most weightily upon the opportunities it afforded and the advantages it offered for continuing British settlement overseas. British settlements abroad, *The Times* argued, were large elements in England's mercantile greatness. Not even the conquest of India had excited more the admiration of foreign nations than the colonisation of Australia.

> Every French traveller [it continued, with mounting enthusiasm] breaks forth into raptures at the prosperity of Melbourne and regrets that the Orleans government did not assert its right to the islands of New Zealand. Yet it is but a few years since colonies of Australia were denounced as failures and philosophers of Mr Smith's school declared that the attempt to renew the experiment of America must end in ruin. Australia has grown up and now takes our manufactures by millions. The truth is that there is no wiser policy for a country like ours than to take possession of the waste places of the earth, and give our crowded populations the power of settling in them under our own laws, modified, if need be, to suit their particular exigencies.

Economists, though apt to put the case in more sober language, generally reached the same conclusion. With them demography had come to provide a strong, perhaps the strongest argument for Empire. No such generalisation can be made about the 'official mind'. In so far as there was any consensus of opinion on the settled Empire, at the Colonial Office or in Parliament, after the introduction of responsible self-government and the completion of the free trade revolution in British commercial policy, it was along the lines sketched out by Earl Grey (colonial secretary in the critical years 1848–52) in correspondence with Lord John Russell. The first was that Britain had 'no interest whatever in exercising any greater influence in the internal affairs of the colonies than is indispensable either for the purpose of preventing any one colony from adopting measures injurious to another, or to the Empire at large . . .' or for the equitable and impartial administration of colonies whose populations were too ignorant and unenlightened to manage their own affairs. And the second principle, flowing from the abandonment of all restrictive colonial trading policies and of all needless interference in colonial domestic affairs, was that Britain on her side had a right to expect that the colonies should take upon themselves 'a larger proportion than heretofore of the expenses incurred for their advantage'.[51]

THE FIRST DOMINION AND ITS CONSTITUTION

In the twenty-eight years that elapsed between the Durham Report and the passage of the British North America Act experience was gained of the working of responsible self-government and some of its little-understood implications were revealed. Of the latter one very important example may suffice. Durham had recommended that the regulation of trade should be reserved to the imperial power. Did this mean imperial control both over colonial trading relations with foreign countries and with Great Britain herself? Lord Durham certainly said so. But had not the position been changed with the coming of free trade? The old imperial tariff arrangements were dismantled. Were the colonies thereafter obliged in all circumstances to adopt and maintain free trade policies? They might require revenue from customs. They might desire to protect infant industries, a legitimate exception approved by Adam Smith. They might even, heretical though the notion might seem in the days of the new economic enlightenment, desire to establish tariffs in their own national interest.

The first question, that in respect of trade with foreign countries, received a partial answer in 1854, when the short-lived Canadian–American Reciprocity trading agreement was concluded. Evidently a self-governing colonial government could negotiate a trading agreement, even if approval by Queen and Parliament was accepted as being necessary for its ratification. But could a colony enjoying self-government further impose tariffs upon goods from other parts of the Empire, from Britain herself, as she wished? The Colonial Office thought not and on two occasions in the early 1850s asserted its opinion. But in 1859 its view was challenged. Alexander Galt, Canadian minister of finance, imposed a first Canadian tariff. It was designed to help home industry, though Galt spoke with deliberate ambiguity of 'incidental protection';[52] by which he meant tariffs levied primarily to produce revenue but also – as the phrase implied – incidentally affording protection. The colonial secretary, the duke of Newcastle, prompted by a memorial from the Sheffield Chamber of Commerce, reacted sharply, expressing in a dispatch of 13 August 1859 to the governor-general mingled reproof and regret at the Canadian action. Galt prepared his reply. In its detailed refutation of the arguments submitted by the Sheffield Chamber of Commerce and of the statistics which buttressed them it was devastating; in respect of the principle at stake it lacked nothing in force and pungency.[53] The relevant passage read:

> The government of Canada acting for its Legislature and people cannot, through those feelings of deference which they owe to the imperial authorities, in any manner waive or diminish the right of the people of Canada to decide for themselves both as to the mode and extent to which taxation shall be imposed . . . Self-government would be utterly annihilated if the views of the imperial government were to be preferred to those of the people of Canada. It is, therefore, the duty of the present government distinctly to affirm the right of the Canadian Legislature to adjust the taxation of the people in the way they deem best, even if it should unfortunately happen to meet the disapproval of the imperial ministry. Her Majesty cannot be advised to disallow such acts, unless her advisers are prepared to assume the administration of the affairs of the colony irrespective of the views of its inhabitants.

For the imperial government the sting was in the tail. They could not 'resume' the government of Canada, or any other colony, against the wishes of a people growing accustomed to the practice of self-government, without assuming virtually unlimited responsibilities and an intolerable burden, for the weight of which continuation of imperial uniformity in tariff policy would afford the most meagre compensation. The debate ended, accordingly, with a notable advance along the road to colonial autonomy.

In British North America itself the two decades following the Durham Report underlined the incompleteness of the union of the two Canadas and the insufficiencies of separate self-governing institutions in the remaining colonies. The Grand Trunk Railway started with government backing in 1854 became, with the opening of the Victoria Bridge across the St Lawrence at Montreal by the prince of Wales in 1860 which marked its formal completion, the longest railway under single management in the world and Canada 'a railway in search of a state'.[54] With the railway, the opening up of the western prairies quickened, and even if it was difficult for east and west to live together politically, it was increasingly deemed impossible for them to develop apart. And to economics was added the powerful argument of defence. Separately the colonies were indefensible, except on the assumption of imperial aid on a scale by no means always likely to be forthcoming, and the United States, or groups within it (as the Fenian raids were to demonstrate in 1866 in the period of the Civil War) was potentially an aggressive or expansionist neighbour, presenting a potential external threat of the kind needed to intensify the efforts of colonists and also of British officials to achieve unity. In sum, the combination of economic and political circumstance was such as to invite an experiment in nationhood, and agreement to initiate this great undertaking was reached by the representatives of the provinces in conference at Quebec in 1864. Yet, as so often happens, the approach to the conference and to its goal was devious and not without its surprises.

The first initiative came from the maritimes, when at a conference in Charlottetown, the capital of Prince Edward Island, the possibility of the political union of the three maritime provinces, Nova Scotia, New Brunswick and Prince Edward Island was debated by their leaders. The imperial government inclined favourably to this limited, regional union and later, in the person of the governor-general of Canada, Viscount Monck, played a more active intermediary rôle in enlarging the scope of the original conference and its purpose so as (to quote a letter of Lord Monck's of 9 July 1864 to the lieutenant-governor of Nova Scotia)' to ascertain whether the proposed union may not be made to embrace the whole of the British North American provinces'.[55] The idea, entertained in many quarters, found favour and a larger, more widely representative conference was called to consider it.

The building in which this conference assembled in Quebec, overlooking the great sweep of the St Lawrence River, was originally intended as a post office and had served as a temporary residence for the prince of Wales in 1860 and thereafter as the temporary home for the Canadian legislature, until the Parliament buildings were completed in Ottawa. Each province was represented by men of all parties but the atmosphere at the conference, enriched as it was by a sense of history in the making, was essentially conservative.[56] As to the over-riding intention of the delegates, here there could be no doubt. It was to make in Canada a strong national union. Two years later Lord Monck, writing to the secretary of state for the colonies, Lord Carnarvon, said that he was:

persuaded both from the internal evidence afforded by the resolutions which they drew up and from intimate personal knowledge of most of the able men who composed the Quebec convention, that their intention was to form out of these provinces a solid and lasting political consolidation with a supreme central authority managing all the general interests of the people of the Union, which would attract to itself the – so to speak – national sentiment and aspiration of the entire people.[57]

The Resolutions[58] which were approved by the conference at Quebec formed the basis of the British North America Act 1867. 'Let us not,' urged Alexander Galt, 'lose sight of the great advantages which Union offers because there may be some small matters which as individuals we may not like.'[59] It was an observation too evidently just to be gainsaid. Yet, as J. A. Macdonald also underlined to the Canadian Parliament when introducing the proposals agreed at Quebec for a federation of all the British North American provinces on 6 February 1865:

It must be admitted that had we not met in a spirit of conciliation and with an anxious desire to promote this union; if we had not been impressed with the idea contained in the words of the resolution – 'That the best interests and present and future prosperity of British North America would be promoted by a federal union under the Crown of Great Britain' – all our efforts might have proved to be of no avail.

Why were those efforts and so much good will required? The answers lay in the geographical spread and in the cultural variety of European settlement in British North America. The former found its political expression in the regionalism of areas with special community attachments and particularist economic preoccupations. Such regional sentiment was emerging in the as yet sparsely populated prairies lying between the lakes and forests of Upper Canada on the east and the Rockies on the West; it was already self-evident in British Columbia, cut off by the barrier of the mountains from the rest of British North America, and most pronounced in the maritimes along the eastern seaboard, warmly attached to Britain and with a distinctive outlook of their own which made them little enamoured of the idea of absorption in a polity necessarily dominated by the inhabitants of the populous St Lawrence Valley. Theirs happened to have been the initiative but they perhaps more than any others were called upon to make concessions in the interests of federation. Yet while for the maritimes this sense of the prospective submergence of a cherished identity was pronounced, it was tempered, as elsewhere in the

English-speaking provinces, by an appreciation of the destiny that might lie before a vast, united and predominantly English-speaking, self-governing dominion of the British Crown in North America. For those of another culture there was no such exciting prospect. Upper and Lower Canada, divided by language and origin, united by the great river which flowed through them, had hitherto been held in a balanced if uneasy union, symbolised by a succession of 'hyphenated' ministries, the best known of which was that of Baldwin-Lafontaine. But now in a federal state that balance was destroyed. There were to be no more such ministries. Lower Canada, Quebec, was no longer one of two but one among many. However securely the religion, the language, the social traditions of the *habitants* might be protected, the fact remained that it was by safeguards alone that the cooperation of the French-speaking minority could be obtained. At the time of confederation and for ninety years thereafter the dominant element in their political thinking was defensive. They were resolved before all else to survive. It was not so much that their situation was about to be changed in political form – but that the realities of it were to be exposed.

Some thirty-six years before Confederation, on 1 September 1831, Alexis de Tocqueville made a record of his impressions of French Canada as he steamed up the St Lawrence to Montreal. They stand the test of time. What was true in the early nineteenth century was still substantially true at the time of the confederation and even in 1967 when the centenary of confederation was celebrated. This was so because there was constancy of purpose. The French Canadians, like all cultural minorities worthy of the name, were resolved to preserve their cultural heritage for themselves and to transmit it to future generations. 'Vous serez ce que vous voulez être, c'est-à-dire maîtres de vous-mêmes ...' declared the president of the French republic, General de Gaulle, on his dramatic and disconcerting visit to Quebec in July 1967, 'votre avenir, ce qu'il doit être, un avenir français.'[60] On the longer view and in the deeper sense everything that mattered most to French Canadians was contained in those words – to remain masters of themselves in changing and often unfavourable circumstances and to ensure for Quebec a French future.

De Tocqueville's first exuberant hopes of a restored French Empire in North America soon waned and were replaced by a sobering appraisal of the prospects before the French community in Lower Canada. The instincts of the people, he noted,[61] were against the English, but 'many Canadians belonging to the upper-classes did not seem to us [de Beaumont, it will be recalled, was travelling with him] animated to the degree we believe [they should be?] by the desire to preserve intact the trace of their origin and to become a people entirely apart.' Several did not seem far from amalgamating with the English, if the latter would adopt the interests of the country.

It is therefore to be feared that with time, and above all with the immigration of the Irish Catholics, the fusion will take place, and it cannot do so except to the detriment of the race, the language and the customs of the French.

However it is certain: 1. Lower Canada (happily for the French race) forms a separate state. Now in Lower Canada the French population is to the English population in the proportion of ten to one. It is compact . . . 2. The English up to now have always kept apart . . . 3. In the towns the English and the Canadians form two societies. The English affect great luxury. There are only very limited fortunes among the Canadians. Thence small-town jealousies and vexations. 4. The English have all the foreign trade in their hands and direct all the domestic trade. Thence again, jealousy . . . 5. Finally, the English show themselves in Canada with all the traits of the national character and the Canadians have retained all the traits of French character. The odds are therefore that Lower Canada will end by becoming a people entirely French. But it will never be a numerous people. They will be a drop of water in the ocean. I am much afraid that . . . fate has in fact decided that North America will be English.'

The notes jotted down by this distinguished French historian and political philosopher express something of the spirit of French Canadian participation in Confederation a generation later. It was a spirit of resignation but by no means of despair. Fate having seemingly decreed that North America would be English it remained for the French Canadians to preserve their own identity as best they might and to ensure their own survival. Federation had self-evident advantages over a union of Upper and Lower Canada in which the will of the majority would prevail. 'In a struggle between two, one a weak and the other a strong party,' observed Georges Étienne Cartier in the Canadian confederation debates,[62] 'the weaker could not but be overcome; but if three parties were concerned the stronger would not have the same advantage; as when it was seen by the third that there was too much strength on one side, the third would club with the weaker combatant to resist the big fighter.' Cartier added that he did not entertain the slightest apprehension that Lower Canada's rights would be jeopardised by the fact that her representatives would be outnumbered in the Federal Legislature by all the others combined. None the less for French–Canadians the federal constitution must needs be fashioned first and foremost to serve essentially defensive ends.

The constitution of Canada was British in conception and design. It was by no means the first constitution modelled on the principles of government and parliament as practised at Westminster to be transplanted overseas or even to British North America itself. But it was significant that Canadian leaders, with the example of the American system of government constantly before them, should have decided so emphatically in favour of the British. They did not doubt that they should have a Parliament with two Houses, one elective the other nominated, a cabinet by convention collectively responsible to the Lower House, a governor-general at the apex as the representative of the Crown and an independent judiciary. At Quebec the assembled representatives, George Brown explained,[63] were 'earnestly deliberating how we shall best extend the blessings of British institutions'. That predisposition the French Canadians shared. The British pattern and the monarchical element seemed to offer assurances of constitutional conservatism and stability. Yet what had to be achieved was not the comparatively simple task of adapting British institutions to another continent and another political environment; but the more complicated one of adapting the parliamentary system as it had developed over centuries without a written constitution to the written form which federation demanded. The characteristics of the Canadian constitution were not individually novel; its contribution to political thought and practice lay rather in its successful association of the British parliamentary system with federalism. 'The constitution of Canada', noted André Siegfried, 'presents no original feature: it partakes at once of the English parliamentary system and of American federalism but there is nothing in any of its provisions to attract attention by reason of its novelty; its chief interest lies rather in the way in which it is applied.'[64] The note is unduly disparaging but the substance of the comment is just.

At the outset the Canadian confederation consisted of Upper and Lower Canada and the maritime provinces of Nova Scotia and New Brunswick. Manitoba joined it in 1870, British Columbia in 1871, Prince Edward Island in 1873, Alberta and Saskatchewan in 1905 and Newfoundland, after a brief, chequered interlude as a

dominion on its own, in 1949. The constitutional structure was
monarchical with the governor-general filling the rôle of the absent
monarch. In the making of this constitutional design – neither
Canadian nor British – United States experience reinforced the
claims of loyalty and conservative sentiment. 'By adhering to the
monarchical principle,' said J. A. Macdonald 'we avoid one defect
inherent in the Constitution of the United States' – namely an
elective head of state holding office for a short period of years.[65]
And with regard to the actual conduct of affairs the Canadian
founding fathers kept as close as circumstances would allow to the
British precedents which guided them. 'In the constitution,' to
quote Macdonald once more,'[66] 'we propose to continue the system
of responsible government, which has existed in this province since
1841 and which has long obtained in the mother country. This is a
feature of our constitution . . . in which, I think, we avoid one of the
great defects in the constitution of the United States.' There the
president was in great measure a despot; in Canada ministers
would at all times be responsible to the people through Parliament.
But there remained the one all important respect in which the
circumstances of Canada did not permit of the adoption of the
British system. Canada was to be, like the United States but unlike
Britain, a federal state, though even here United States' practice
was held up as a warning, not as a guide. In the British North
America Act all spheres of domestic legislative competency were
defined in Section 91. To the provinces were assigned sixteen
enumerated and exclusive subjects; to the confederation twenty-
nine, together with a field for the exercise of concurrent power
over agriculture and immigration, it being further provided that in
the event of conflict the will of the federal authority would prevail.
But while the provinces were given wide powers, including – as was
a condition of federation for Quebec – exclusive control over
education with specially guaranteed protection for denominational
schools, and were sovereign in their own sphere, ultimate residuary
authority rested with the federal government. This was the
essential element in the Canadian federal system. There were no
states, only provinces, and there was no entrenchment of provincial
rights in such a way as to give them that higher status. That would
have been altogether inconsistent with the resolve of the founding
fathers to create a strong central government. As Macdonald put it:

> We have conferred upon them [the provinces] not only speci-
> fically and in detail all the powers which are incident to
> sovereignty, but we have expressly declared that all subjects of

general interest not distinctly and exclusively conferred upon the local governments and local legislatures shall be conferred upon the General Government and Legislature. We have thus avoided the great source of weakness which has been the cause of the disruption of the United States.

The purpose of ensuring strong central government was later qualified – only the extent to which this was done remains disputable – by judgments of the judicial committee of the Privy Council in London, which was made the final court of appeal in constitutional cases. In its interpretation of federal and provincial powers notable members of the judicial committee, deliberately and of conviction, adopted at a critical time in the evolution of federation a conservative and limiting view of the extent of the central federal authority, which was deemed by many English-speaking Canadians to be in conflict if not with the letter then certainly with the spirit and intention of the constituion.[67] Yet without discounting the significance of a series of Privy Council judgments, the fact remained that the bias of the constitution towards the centre was too pronounced to be thereby fundamentally changed.

In a true federation the powers of the centre and the constituent units ought to be coordinate, neither subordinate one to the other. It has been questioned whether Canada fulfils this condition and whether therefore she can be regarded as a true federation.[68] If the letter alone counted, this question might be thought deserving of a negative answer. But inevitably this is not so, and in spirit (as indeed in practice) the government of Canada may be thought to be in essence federal. The position of Quebec ensured this for while French Candians were not satisfied in the longer run with a constitution which placed the province as one among many, all the others being predominantly English-speaking, they would assuredly at no time have been content with a form of government that was not federal at least to the extent of ensuring provincial control over matters closest to the French Canadian heart. Indeed in one respect Quebec was accorded a special (though not a privileged) position in as much as the province was allotted sixty-five seats in the House of Commons, with representation in the rest of Canada to be determined at each decennial census in the same relation to population as existed in Quebec. But while this constitutional provision was valuable by way of protective guarantee, ensuring that Quebec representation could not be reduced other than by constitutional amendment and accordingly not without the approval of the imperial Parliament at Westminster, the population and the economically strategic position of the province made it difficult if not impossible to govern Canada against Quebec, even though it was the case that in other respects the position and powers of the provinces were alike and without distinction. Generally however there is no doubt that the need to safeguard the rights of a cultural minority concentrated in one province, in effect enhanced the status of all and modified in practice the predominance the central government might otherwise have enjoyed. This was the case rather more in respect of the conventions of government than of strict constitutional provision.

Canadian prime ministers (to take one important example), in nominating members of their cabinets have in practice found it prudent to satisfy the principal regional interests by giving all of them representation in it. This was so well understood forty years after the passing of the British North America Act that William Price sent a memorandum to Sir Robert Borden from Montreal on 2 October 1911, when Borden was engaged in forming his first cabinet, stating '1. It is necessary to have three French Canadian ministers from this province. 2. It is customary that two of the ministers should be chosen from what is known as the Montreal District and one from the Quebec District'.[69] The politically 'customary' in this case, as in many others, reflected the underlying federal nature of Canadian politics and administration. But it existed and found expression within a constitutional framework created by Founding Fathers, most of whom would have preferred union, and all of whom finally agreed to establish a federation, with the balance of power weighted in favour of the centre.

The constitution of the Dominion of Canada was embodied in the British North America Act 1867[70] and subsequent amendments to it. By way chiefly of reassurance for French-Canadians, the Act made no provision for its own amendment: that remained, until the constitution was 'patriated' in 1982, the responsibility of the imperial parliament. Yet while ultimate control thus remained at Westminster, the initiative in the subsequent amendment as in the initial framing of the B.N.A. Act was Canadian. The constitution of the first, as of all later dominions, was and remained essentially home-made. It was however (unlike some of them) the product of agreement between governments without the direct popular sanction of plebiscite or referendum.

Besides its indigenous origin there was another factor of equal significance for the future. The confederation of Canada came into existence through the association of a number of neighbouring but hitherto separate British colonial territories in one political system; that too became part of a later Commonwealth pattern. Once more the initiative was local, not imperial, but the consequences were of more than local importance. The imperial power had its interest in unification both in terms of administrative economy and convenience and of the effective diminution of its own responsibilities. Where for example a number of small colonies were likely to appeal for imperial assistance in times of stress – financial or military as the case might be – a larger and stronger union would be able to rely upon its own resources. In an age dominated by Gladstonian finance and anti-militarist free traders this was a consideration which warmly commended Canadian confederation to the home government – though even that did not suffice to satisfy John Bright. He feared that even with federation there would be perpetual Canadian requests for railways or defence and speaking – as the biographer of John A. Macdonald, the chief architect of confederation, has observed with undisguised distaste – 'with that unctuous mixture of pecuniary considerations and moral values which was so characteristic of his school'[71] he concluded that it would be 'cheaper for us and less demoralising for them that they should become an independent state, and maintain their own fortresses, fight their own cause, and build up their own future without relying upon us'.[72]

Macdonald, who had talked of 'founding a great British monarchy in connection with the British Empire',[73] voiced a widespread Canadian hope that it would be named the Kingdom of Canada with a viceroy as representative of the Crown. But in the Colonial Office the designation was thought pretentious and opinion in Washington was known to be hostile. London accordingly demanded a more sober, unprovocative designation. S. L. Tilley, reading from Psalm lxxii, verse 8 – 'He shall have dominion also from sea to sea, and from the river unto the ends of the earth' – is thought to have first pointed to the appropriateness of the title, *Dominion*.[74] And so it was that as the first dominion the Confederation of Canada came into existence, on the first day of July 1867. Lord Carnarvon, the colonial secretary, had sensed much and spoken stirringly in the House of Commons of the significance of the occasion. But the Colonial Office, according to Macdonald, had treated the unification of Canada as if the British North America Act were a private bill uniting two or three parishes, while according to Macdonald's biographer the members of Parliament at Westminster could hardly conceal their 'excruciating boredom' while the measure passed through its necessary stages and when they were at last concluded turned with great relief to a debate on the desirability of introducing modification in the duty on dogs.[75] So, with inspiration and apathy nicely mingled, the first step was taken in the Mother of Parliaments on the road to Commonwealth.

3 South Africa; Races and Riches, War and Union

In South Africa it was usual to speak of Britain, Canada, Australia and New Zealand as the foundation members of the British Commonwealth of Nations; elsewhere it was customary to include South Africa itself among their number. Historically the distinction is debatable and in any case of no great importance; conceptually South Africa's place is with the founder-states. At almost every stage in the evolution of the Commonwealth, South Africa was notionally, if not actually, an integral part of it. Canadian confederation was at once preceded and succeeded by abortive attempts at South African federation; and the problems of race and colour, existing with peculiar intensity in the South African colonies, came to be accepted as belonging from the outset to the Commonwealth as a whole. Such problems might no longer exist in more than nominal form in respect of Red Indian survivors in Canada or of the aborigines in Australia; they did exist, but within manageable dimensions, in New Zealand with its indigenous Maori population. But long before a united South Africa became a dominion in 1910, they had their place in the thinking which brought the Commonwealth into existence. It was no chance, it was the logic of history that made first popular reaction against an imperialist war in South Africa and then popular (if in part misguided) enthusiasm for a magnanimous South African settlement the immediate precursors to the recognition by name of a Commonwealth, already thought of as being in embryonic existence.

South African history is too rich and varied to be forced into any particular mould. If the country has its highly significant place in the early history and in formative thinking about the Commonwealth, it has also a place possibly even more important in the history of Empire. This dual rôle derived at root from the composition of its population and the character and resources of its land. The first with its two European cultures and its majority of non-European origin was a challenge at once to humanitarian zeal

69

and to liberal principles; the second with its vast extent and its
mineral wealth, a magnet to imperialists, both of the more
simple-minded map-painting and of the more sinister Hobsonian
capitalist-exploiter variety. The existence of challenges and opportunities made of South Africa a land of divergent and often
conflicting purposes, in which the threads of motive and action are
unusually difficult to disentangle. British imperial historians have
been for the most part predisposed to interpret nineteenth- and
early twentieth-century South African history in terms of the
safeguarding of imperial strategic interests or of the achievement
of imperial economic or political ends, the latter especially too long
delayed by confusion of purpose and uncertain resolve; British
liberal historians have approached it in terms of European and
more particularly of British enlightenment, seeking, in the face of
critical settler and obstinately obscurantist Boer opinion, to assert
the principles and to introduce by stages the conditions of race
equality; South African historians have tended generally to interpret South African history in the context of settler interests,
conflicts and territorial expansion, with the English-speaking of
them dwelling especially upon the development of self-governing
institutions, first in Cape Colony and then in the Union, on an
acceptable, if limited, Westminster model and the Afrikaners
concentrating upon Boer resistance to British imperialism
throughout 'A Century of Wrong' – the title chosen by J. C. Smuts
for an essay in historical polemics produced at the onset of war,
1899 – which through defeat and near destruction, finally
triumphed in the establishment of a South African republic.
Widening perspectives are reflected in more recent studies by
liberal Africanists but for a sustained African essay in historical
interpretation we have still to wait.[1] It is easy to generalise, to say for
example that the imperial factor, as Rhodes called it, has been over
or underestimated; to argue that the growth of English institutions
or the exclusivist aspirations of Afrikanerdom have been the key
factor: to maintain that the course of South African history was
determined by the impersonal forces of world capitalism or that the
colour question has been its dominant theme. But the study of any
extended period is likely to cast doubt upon the validity of such
conceptions or preconceptions. There were so many factors which
exerted a decisive influence at a particular time but which were in
turn superseded not so much by new as by older forces, brought
once again by some shift in the seemingly unending struggle for
control into a position of power. English writers, complacently
recording the downfall and final destruction of the Boer republics

early in the century (to take one example) afford ironic and occasionally almost comic warning against any finality of judgment in a field where finality is the one thing that is lacking. The downfall of Kruger's republic presaged not (as they supposed) the end of Krugerism or of republicanism but the triumphant vindication of both in a setting much larger than the Transvaal two generations later. Yet, among all the vicissitudes of South African history in the period, one theme was constant. It was the contact and consequent relationship of European settlers with African peoples, first on a limited scale with the Hottentots at the Cape and then on the eastern frontiers of Cape Province and beyond with a native population to be numbered in its millions, a population which was in large measure subdued but never absorbed, economically, politically or least of all socially into the European controlled provinces or states into which southern Africa was divided.[2] It was this which gave to South Africa its unique place and its unique significance in Commonwealth history.

Jan van Riebeeck landed at the Cape in 1652, during the period of English and French settlement in North America. But the growth of the Dutch settlement was hampered by the restrictive policies of the Dutch East India Company. Its directors were interested not in colonisation but in trade. And in terms of trade the Cape was a refreshment station on the way to the East Indies. Settlement took place – and it was by no means exclusively Dutch. Hollanders and Flemings were reinforced, notably by emigrants from Western Germany, and after the repeal of the Edict of Nantes by Huguenot exiles from France. The Huguenots were few in number and were to lose their separate identity, their language and the original pronunciation of their names but they added nonetheless a distinctive element with a continuing influence in the settler community, as has been testified right down to our own time by the prominence of men of French or part French extraction – Malherbe, du Toit, Olivier, du Plessis, Centlivres, Joubert, Daniel François Malan – in the public and professional life of South Africa. Most remarkable, however, was the number of French names among the early Voortrekkers. Olive Schreiner once contended that it was 'in the French blood which flows in the Boer veins that we have to look for the explanation of great historical movements', on the grounds apparently that the French settlers had 'vivified the torpid mental life of the otherwise Teutonic Boer', stimulated his faculties and 'made his blood course more rapidly in his substantial veins'.[3] It may be, too, that the Huguenots lent something of the sharper edge of French logic to Dutch Calvinist doctrine. Most important for European (as distinct from later British) settlers was the lack of reinforcement from their home-lands. There was but little immigration to the Cape from Holland after the end of the seventeenth century with the result that the temper of the Europe of the seventeenth century, the century of the great religious controversies, wars and persecutions, was transplanted to another continent, to be reinterpreted there in terms of frontier conflicts and frontier psychology, and was left untouched by the enlightenment of eighteenth-century Europe. Even by the time of the first British occupation, 1795–1803, the sentimental and commerical ties with Holland were no longer supplemented by corresponding social and intellectual contacts. The long isolation of the Boer had already begun. The second and more lasting British occupation from 1806 completed it. The Boers were thereafter no longer colonists under the protective wing of a mother country; they were a people numbering only some twenty-seven thousand souls, out on their own. They were also, for the most part, pastoralists, forever seeking new ground for grazing and moving their cattle with them. In this way they spread themselves thinly over great tracts of land, where they were faced with the harsh alternatives of survival by their own endeavours or destruction as a separate group. They survived; they became a nation – the only European nation in Africa. This was not a matter of choice but of will and of necessity. The former they never lacked and the latter was always before them. They had no other home, no other country. They said so time without number. It happened to be true.

In South Africa there were other settlers; later settlers, British settlers. They came in with the new imperialism – administrators and soldiers, traders, missionaries and farmers. Some of them came on their own initiative; others, notably the 1820 settlers early in the period of British rule, under schemes of officially inspired and planned emigration. They too acquired in the process of time the settler outlook and the frontier mentality. But there was this difference between them and the Boers. The links with their mother country remained strong, secure and binding. They may not have been especially enlightened but they were familiar with the climate of early nineteenth-century opinion; they may not have been markedly humanitarian but they had felt the flowing tide of humanitarian sentiment. While they might not agree or might even sharply disagree with the home government on methods of colonial administration or the treatment of native races they understood something of the motives and forces which shaped home opinion. The Boers did not. James Bryce, writing in the closing years of the century felt that the timing of British annexations was especially unfortunate. Had they happened thirty years earlier no difficulties would have arisen, he thought, over the treatment of natives or slavery because at that time the new philanthropy had not begun to influence English opinion. Had they occurred later then quicker and more frequent ocean communication would not have left room for so much misunderstanding and as a result the errors that contributed to the alienation of the Boers might never have been committed.[4]

Government and treatment of native races in South Africa were not separable things; in the last resort they were one. That was because government there, over and above the ordinary responsibilities of nineteenth-century colonial administration, carried also the extraordinary responsibility of decisions upon the treatment of majority native races. Was this an imperial or a local matter? The home government throughout the greater part of the nineteenth century, despite moments of doubt and contemplated withdrawal, generally believed and asserted that it was an imperial responsibility. Evangelicals and humanitarians were insistent that it should be properly discharged and for the greater part of the century they were able to exert formidable pressure in Parliament. The settlers perforce acquiesced. They were dependent upon imperial protection. But their acquiescence was usually reluctant. They felt they had the knowledge and experience which imperial officials lacked. They knew the Hottentot, the Kaffir, the Bantu; they had daily contact with them. What they would have liked was imperial protection without imperial control. That meant European self-government on liberal Canadian lines, but with a white minority determining the place of the black majority in South African society. It was an end not secured till 1909. Until then there existed an uneasy balance in imperial-colonial relations. The imperial government could not, save at the price of great expenditure of money and effort, govern the colonies against the settlers; the settlers, divided as they continued to be between Boers and British, could not resist the pressure of the imperial factor beyond a certain point. The outcome was an unstable equilibrium of imperial-colonial forces. In South Africa and in South Africa alone among the colonies that were to become dominions, was there continuing conflict between liberal principles of responsible self-government and humanitarian pressure for continuing imperial protection of native races.

The history of nineteenth-century South Africa is its own. But in the context of Commonwealth there are some problems the nature of which must needs be noted. The first is government. In the second period of British rule the governor, appointed by the Crown, was until 1825 in effect an autocratic ruler. But then a new phase began. An advisory council was established, at first composed wholly of officials, but with two non-official members added in 1827. There was a more radical change in 1834 when executive and legislative councils were set up. The members of both, according to the practice of the time, were chosen by the governor. That however did not avoid friction. Settlers on these councils did not cast off their settler outlook or their settler associations. They were not representatives but they were very often representative in their opinions. Having taken the first step, experience (much of it in terms of frustration) underlined the importance of the second. It was taken in 1853. The instrument was the Cape of Good Hope Ordinance. It established representative government. The new Parliament (which met for the first time on Friday 30 June 1854 in the Goede Hoop Banqueting Hall in Cape Town and which passed as its first measure an Act – No. 1 1854 – to secure freedom of speech) was composed of two Houses, with the Upper as well as the Lower Chamber elective – a departure in British imperial history. But in the conditions of South Africa, as important as freedom of speech and more important than the structure of the legislature was the nature of the franchise. It was colour blind. There was a financial qualification, no literacy test and, all-important in the setting, no colour bar. The financial qualification for candidates, as distinct from voters, was high and while Coloured and natives qualified to vote in quite considerable numbers, no non-European was elected a member of the Cape Parliament in all the years of its existence (1854–1910).

Representative government was not responsible government. Members of the Cape Executive Council were not responsible to the colonial legislature but continued to be appointed and dismissed by the governor. That intermediate phase ended in 1872 when self-government on the Canadian model was conferred on Cape Colony. Its timing was due less to a sense of constitutional appropriateness than to a variety of economic, strategic and political considerations. Ostrich farming and the discovery of diamonds at Kimberley heralded a revolution in the economy of Cape Colony and provided a material foundation for self-government, while the opening of the Suez Canal in 1869 reduced its strategic importance to Britain. The prospect of local self-sufficiency, allied to diminishing imperial strategic significance, strongly suggested that the time had come for imperial withdrawal from direct responsibility for the domestic government of the colony. But there was a further factor. It was argued in the Colonial Office that Cape Colony, the oldest and richest of the political communities in South Africa, must become self-governing before there could be consolidation of all of them under one government. As in Canada, self-government was to be a step on the road to unification.

While British settlers first in Cape Colony and then in Natal (which became a Crown colony in 1856 and attained self-government in 1893) advanced along the road to colonial self-government, it was otherwise with the Boers. They did not like British government. It was in the first place alien government. In the second place, both in itself and in many of its actions, it was unfamiliar to the point of incomprehensibility. And thirdly, it brought in its train high-minded evangelicals, whose especial concern was the protection and care of the native peoples but whose principal preoccupation (so it seemed to the Boer farmers) was the disruption of their way of life. Since the seventeenth century they had relied partly upon slave labour and that in itself established a tradition different from any that prevailed in other British colonies of settlement, though not in other British possessions. The social pattern, thus long established, struck deep roots. It was reinforced by Calvinist emphasis upon the Old Testament. Though there were important differences between the three sections into which the Dutch Reformed Church came to be divided, the Boers throughout their history were encouraged by their pastors to liken themselves to the Children of Israel, to the chosen people of God – as was done once again by the moderator of the Nederduits Gereformeerde Church of the Cape in his oration at the state funeral in Pretoria of the assassinated prime minister of South Africa, Hendrik Verwoerd, on 10 September 1966 – a people also seeking their promised land and continually engaged in righteous war against the unbelieving Philistines first to possess and then to preserve it. It was their destiny to survive and to multiply. But, as with the Children of Israel, survival was a hard and bitter struggle – in the nineteenth century a struggle, as it seemed to the Boers, against native hordes thirsting to destroy them, against pestilence, drought and floods, and in later days against the British occupying power.

The new British factor was felt to present a threat more insidious and potentially no less destructive than older and more familiar dangers. For the British with their humanitarian ideals, their evangelical missionary zeal (typified by Dr John Philip of the London Missionary Society) appeared to aim both at confining the Boers within settled colonial frontiers and at placing them on an equality with Coloured and native freemen. Few things, for example, rankled with the Boers more than an ordinance – the nineteenth ordinance – of June 1826 which allowed a slave to give evidence in criminal cases against his master and to purchase his freedom by tendering his appraised value. Then in 1833 slavery was abolished throughout the British Empire. 1 December 1834 was the date that was finally fixed for the emancipation of the 35,742 slaves at the Cape.[5] The Cape of Good Hope Ordinance (No. 1 of 1835) read as follows:

> Enacted by the governor [Sir Benjamin D'Urban] of the Cape of Good Hope with the advice and consent of the Legislative Council thereof, – For giving due effect to the Provisions of an Act of Parliament, passed in the third and fourth years of the reign of His Majesty King William the Fourth entitled 'An Act for the abolition of slavery throughout the British Colonies . . .' Now therefore, in pursuance of the said Act of Parliament and for carrying the same into effect within the Colony of the Cape of Good Hope be it enacted by the governor of the Cape of Good Hope: with the advice and consent of the Legislative Council thereof . . . upon, from, and after the first day of December 1834 . . .

The Boers resented both the fact and still more the implication of their relations with the natives being determined by an Act of a remote and interfering imperial authority. There was, it is true, compensation for the loss of the slaves, but it was compensation in bonds which depreciated rapidly from their original stated value, so that to resentment at imperial action was added indignation at what appeared to be imperial sharp practice.

The abolition of slavery was not, as has been alleged, the cause nor even the occasion of the Great Trek. The trekkers were in fact by no means the most considerable owners of slaves and the many who came from the eastern border lands of Cape Colony were far more preoccupied with the competitive struggle for land with the Bantu than with any loss of slaves. The frontiersmen of the Cape, indeed, were accustomed to think of six thousand acres as the proper extent of a farm, and while they were comparatively few in number their sense of what was fitting in this respect was more likely to be satisfied in the unsettled north than in the settled Cape.

So it was against a growing sense of actual or potential confinement that the abolition of slavery and the circumstances of it, adding significantly to a consciousness of accumulated grievances, was rightly interpreted as evidence that the British government had its own ideas of colonial society and intended to enforce them. It was this which completed the Boer sense of alienation from the British authorities.[6] Many of the Boer farmers, nomadic pastoralists by tradition, in effect decided to recover their freedom to order their own lives and above all to determine the nature of their own relationship with native peoples. Disregarding British attempts to fix the frontier they moved across the line of the northern boundary of Cape Colony where there was least resistance to them, across the Orange and then the Vaal rivers into the lonely and largely untenanted tracts beyond. There were many starting points, many 'Voortrekker-roetes', many destinations and many leaders whose names are still cherished in the folk memory of a people – among them Louis Trichard who left from near Bedford and is buried at Lourenço Marques; A. H. Potgieter from Tarkastad in the eastern Cape, buried at Schoemansdal; J. van Rensburg who reached the valley of the Limpopo, Uys, Maritz, Piet Retief . . .[7] There were differences among leaders which led on occasion to a fatal parting of the ways, most notably in the case of Piet Retief and his followers, slaughtered by the Zulus in February 1838. And there were famous victories, chief among them that of Andries Pretorius at the Blood River on 16 December of that same year, ever since commemorated. If the Voortrekkers were exiles, their exile was self-appointed and, as their tradition records, they were moved by a sense of destiny to face certain hardships and uncertain perils, sustained in their pilgrimage by the Calvinist faith of their fathers. More than a hundred years later a memorial in dark granite was built on a hill outside Pretoria to commemorate the Trek and there inside, in bas-relief, panels were placed depicting the bearded trekkers with their families, their sheep, their cattle and their household possessions, leaving their homes in Cape Colony, their waggons moving northward or bound together in defensive laager; the disasters, the victories and at last the thanksgiving. There is much depicted there to stir the imagination and to enhance the resolution and fortitude of an isolated people; and even more, to keep alive the racial animosities of trekker times.

The outcome of the Great Trek was the foundation of two Dutch republics in the hinterland of South Africa; the Republiek Oranje-Vrijstaat, or Orange Free State, and the Zuid-Afrikaansche Republiek, or South African Republic of the Transvaal. Both were landlocked. The trekkers hoped for an independent outlet to the sea in the short-lived Republiek Natalia but Zulu power and British intervention denied it to them. In 1843 the Natal republic had perforce to submit to British control of a province, limited in its extent by British understandings with the Zulus and other neighbouring tribes. Great and justly honoured among their own people were the lasting achievements of the trekkers. But while they had travelled far beyond the bounds of British rule they had not finally escaped from dependence on a British power, by which they were still at vital points surrounded.

What action was the British government to take about the trekkers and their republics? Was it to lay claim to their allegiance and the hinterland they had occupied, thus extending imperial responsibilities far to the north? Or was it, in acquiescent dissociation from the trekkers and the consequences of their trek, to allow them to work out their own destiny? Either course, as seen from London, had evident disadvantages, the former because of the expenditure in money and men it would assuredly entail; the latter because the existence of two distinct types of settlement in southern Africa, given especially the known differences between them in respect of native policy, was equally bound to cause embarrassment at the least and might at some stage even constitute a threat to British security at the Cape. The dilemma remained, but not surprisingly reactions to it varied partly in accord with local circumstances and partly with imperial thinking about colonial possessions. The latter, especially by 1850, predisposed the Colonial Office to policies of coexistence. The independence of the South African republic in the Transvaal was accordingly recognised by the Sand River Convention in 1852 and two years later claims to effective control over the Orange Free State were abandoned. Both were deliberate and significant acts of policy. The British decided to pull out of a waste 'fit only for Springbok', and being landlocked, little likely to offer opportunities to foreign nations to disturb the power that controlled the coasts.[8] The principle of reciprocal non-interference between Britain and the republics guided them and this implied among other things – and was understood to imply – freedom on the part of the Boers to apply their own native policies.

Sir George Grey, governor of Cape Colony 1854–61, out of sympathy with Colonial Office views and with a memorable period of office in New Zealand behind him, challenged prevailing opinions. He was not impressed by supposedly conclusive arguments against expansion based on the cost and consequent liability of extending the frontiers of effective British colonial control. He urged on the contrary the need, as he also sensed the opportunity, for the federation of the two British colonies with the Trekker republics and he had at least good reason for believing that the Orange Free State was favourably inclined toward such federation. Against explicit instructions telling him to take no steps without reference to the Colonial Office, Grey continued to do so. He was rebuked by one colonial secretary in 1858 and dismissed by his successor the following year in a dispatch the plainness of whose language left nothing to be desired. 'I can but agree,' wrote the incoming secretary of state of his predecessor's written rebuke 'in its strong terms of disapproval of your conduct, not only in respect of the question of federation . . .' Sir George Grey did in fact return after a brief interlude to govern the Cape but by then the prospect of federation had departed.

To imperialists later in the century it was the lost opportunities of federation in the 1850s which had left open the way to the conflicts that followed. No words were too strong to condemn the parsimony and lack of imagination shown in London. South Africa, in their view, was one. Geography and economics predetermined it. There was therefore only one question to ask: Who was to control it, Briton or Boer? That, certainly, was political oversimplification on the grand scale. The making of a federation, as is now only too well understood, carries no assurance of its survival or of the avoidance of conflict. Indeed all that may reasonably be said is that the failure to federate in the 1850s probably increased the chances of conflict and accentuated – if only by the passage of time – the problems of future union. The Boers in the republics free from British influence established their own political institutions. Both republics had written constitutions, that of the Orange Free State being rigid, that of the Transvaal very flexible. They were democratic in one respect: the ultimate source of authority was the people. In the Transvaal there was a unicameral legislature, the Volksraad, and an elected president responsible to it. But democracy had its clearly defined colour limit. 'The people desire', so the relevant section in the Transvaal constitution reads, 'to permit no equal standing [the Dutch word is *gelijkstelling* which is generally but not exactly translated 'equality']⁹ between the coloured people and white inhabitants, either in Church or State.' This was a provision sharply at variance with the colour-blind franchise of the near-contemporary Cape of Good Hope Ordinance, and the assertion of two contradictory principles in respect of an issue that was social and economic as much as it was political in its implications and full of perplexities in itself, foreshadowed the dispute and conflict that was to come. For behind the two contrasted constitutional provisions there lay different philosophies of the right relations between men of different colour. They could be practised side by side so long as the Boers continued to live in isolation. But circumstances determined otherwise.

Catastrophe, an Afrikaner historian, F. S. Malan, has remarked, overtook the Dutch republics 'in the form of fabulous riches'. The story of their discovery began in 1866. Erasmus Jacobs, a farmer's son, caught sight of a pebble glittering in the glare of the sun near the banks of the Orange river: he carried it home in his pocket and was playing a family game with the pebble and some ordinary river stones when a neighbour, van Niekerk, arrived. The boy's mother gave it to him, believing it to be only a pebble. Van Niekerk passed it to Jack O'Reilly, a travelling trader, who showed it to Lorenzo Boyes, civil commissioner of Colesberg. He understood the importance of the find and a general examination of the district followed.[10] Other sparkling stones were found near the Orange and Vaal rivers, and then in 1869 there was the romantic discovery by a Griqua shepherd boy of the superb white diamond which later came to be known as the Star of South Africa.

> a tremendous rush ensued ... ships crews deserted to come up country ... Everything from a handcart and a chaise to the big Boer wagon joined the trek. A busy line of camps presently formed along the Vaal so that in 1870–1 ten thousand river diggers were ransacking the river soil, shaking it through cradle sieves, far too preoccupied even to notice the advent of newcomers. In moments of inattention fortunes may be lost ... A strange brotherhood it was! Like all pioneer encampments, it abounded in colourful characters.[11]

A 'big hole' was dug at Kimberley and the fortunes of Cecil John Rhodes, who later acquired control of it, were laid; and many things besides. Kimberley was in Griqualand West; the Griquas deemed themselves to be under British protection but Griqualand West was disputed territory between the British and the republics. It had now assumed a quite new importance. There were negotiations of a protracted and acrimonious nature, only concluded when President Brand of the Orange Free State came to London in 1876. He agreed that the republics' claim should be abandoned for ninety thousand pounds proferred by way of compensation. Not often has so little been paid for a title to so much.

If the discovery of diamonds at Kimberley imposed strain of one kind, the return of Lord Carnarvon to the Colonial Office in 1874 created tensions of another. Lord Carnarvon, who as earlier remarked had imaginatively and successfully piloted the British North America Act through Parliament in 1867, was neither unmindful of his contribution to that great achievement nor unaware of the possibility of applying some at least of the lessons of Canadian confederation to the very different circumstances of South Africa. But more important, this mild-mannered, erudite but fussy man, who involved Disraeli in many troublesome situations and had earned from him the soubriquet of Twitters, was an imperialist *tout simple*. He believed in Empire and was convinced that if Empire were to be sustained one condition in terms of security and defence was British control of southern Africa. He thought this might best be secured by the once deliberately discarded policy of federation. If the omens were not so favourable as in the 1850s they were at the least not unfavourable. The republics were small and impoverished, the government of President Burgers in the Transvaal being on the verge of bankruptcy: Zulu power was in the ascendant and threatening, and the time – it seemed – was approaching when the Boers in the Transvaal might be faced with the choice of annihilation or annexation. J. A. Froude, historian and adviser to Carnarvon in his South African policy, was converted to federation after extensive travels in southern Africa. Carnarvon himself resolved upon action from London with the support of the government of the Cape and the agreement of the republics if both were obtainable; but if not then without them.[12] Neither for the first nor for the last time was British policy in South Africa to be the victim of its own impetuosity.

The colonial secretary's agent was Sir Theophilus Shepstone, secretary for Native Affairs in Natal. He proceeded to Pretoria early in 1877 and was not impressed by what he found there. President Burgers was a man of ideas and some vision but of uncertain following. He wished to preserve the independence of the republic by introducing reforms. The reforms required finance and the Boers, more than most, were reluctant to pay taxes. When Shepstone arrived no salaries were being paid to civil servants and the total resources of the Treasury amounted to twelve shillings and sixpence. He was empowered, by secret instructions, to proclaim the annexation of the Transvaal providing he was satisfied in the first place that it was necessary and in the second that the majority of the inhabitants would approve of it. Shepstone exercised this power on 12 April 1877. President Burgers acquiesced in annexation on condition that he was left free to protest against it in public – Shepstone being shown the terms of the proposed protest and making no objection to them.[13] In January 1879 came the long awaited war against the Zulus, launched by Sir Bartle Frere and approved by the new colonial secretary, Sir Michael Hicks Beach. After an initial British disaster at Isandhlwana[14] there followed, with the arrival of reinforcements, decisive victory at Ulundi on 4 July. Zulu power was destroyed, Zululand broken up and the threat to the Boers removed. They had, accordingly, no longer need of British support. Nor had they received the local autonomy Shepstone had promised. Sir Bartle Frere, it is true, gave renewed assurances of self-government, but General Sir Garnet Wolseley, fresh from his victory over the Zulus, struck another note. 'The Union Jack,' he declared in a burst of soldierly eloquence, would fly over Pretoria 'as long as the sun shone and the Vaal flowed down to the sea.' The Boers became increasingly restive. They had, moreover, a particular consideration in mind. Gladstone, in opposition, had denounced annexation; he returned to power in 1880. The Boers thought, not unreasonably, that annexation would be rescinded. The British, both at home and in South Africa, assumed that what had been done could not be undone.

In the event Gladstone pursued an indeterminate middle course. He rejected the policy of federation and recalled Sir Bartle Frere, the man on the spot most closely associated with it. But he gave neither the freedom nor the disannexation he had championed out of office nor yet the long deferred self-government. The Boers revolted. The British under General Sir George Pomeroy Colley were decisively defeated at Majuba Hill on 26 February 1881. Reinforcements however were arriving in Natal; the verdict could be reversed. But was Gladstone, who had condemned annexation, now to fight for it? Or was he to concede independence after conclusive, even humiliating defeat? The dilemma was a painful one. Gladstone decided on peace after defeat. He believed he was acting on principle but the Boers gave little credence to this. They noted simply the consequences of successful revolt and in later years remembered only too well the victory of their arms in what they spoke of as the first war of independence.

The terms of peace were embodied in the Pretoria Convention of 1881. The independence of the Transvaal was recognised, being made subject in the preamble to 'the suzerainty of Her Majesty' and to a British control over foreign policy as expressly stipulated in the text. Three years later the terms of the convention were negotiated afresh and embodied in a new 1884 Convention of London. There was no mention of suzerainty and in respect of relations with foreign countries it was more narrowly stated that the South African Republic should 'conclude no treaty with any state or nation other than the Orange Free State, nor with any native tribe to the eastward or westward of the republic', without the Queen's approval. The British maintained and the Boers repudiated the notion that suzerainty still subsisted. It seems in fact that on the British side there was no deliberate renunciation but a feeling that the term itself had insufficiently precise meaning. 'Whatever suzerainty meant in the Convention of Pretoria,' Lord Derby told the House of Lords on 17 March 1884, 'the condition of things which it implied still remains.' The use of the term had been given up 'because it was not capable of legal definition, and because it seemed to be a word which was likely to lead to misconception and misunderstanding'.[15] But granting that this was the reason for its abandonment the harm was done in that uncertainty was not removed but increased. There were those in later years, eminent jurists among them, notably James Bryce on the British side and Chief Justice de Villiers on the South African, who traced the Anglo–Boer conflicts of the 1890s to the ambiguities consequent upon the omission of that one word 'suzerainty' from the text of the London Convention of 1884, without any corresponding British renunciation of their claim to exercise it. The conception of suzerainty, noted Bryce, was 'purely legal, though somewhat vague', and in practice it served to obscure Britain's obligation to treat the Transvaal with a strict regard to the recognised principles of international law as if it were a great power and regardless of the fact that the Dutch republics were no more than 'petty communities of ranchmen'.[16] Oom Paul Kruger, who as a boy had journeyed northward in the Great Trek, who was elected president of the South African Republic for the first time in 1883, and who least of all men was likely to be unmindful of British expansionist pressures, did not overlook the implications of contrasted interpretations of what might be held to subsist in terms of sovereignty after 1884.

The restored independence of the Transvaal was followed by the discovery and exploitation of new mineral wealth which made of the republic a magnet drawing speculators and adventurers from all over the world and in so doing brought that independence once again into jeopardy. 'The historian of the fall of the South African Republic,' writes Professor J. S. Marais in the opening sentence of

The Fall of Kruger's Republic, 'must take as his starting point the great gold discoveries of the 1880s in that state.' The wealth of the Witwatersrand led to a sudden chaotic influx of foreigners (or Uitlanders as they were called) many of whom were, and more of whom claimed or aspired to be British subjects. Their numbers, in the absence of any census of population, were a matter of dispute and remain uncertain, but it is likely that within a decade from 1886 the population of the Transvaal was doubled. At a census which was taken in Johannesburg in July 1896, there was a European population of 50,907 of whom 6,205 were Transvaalers and the rest aliens. Of the aliens the largest number, 16,265 came from the United Kingdom, and the next largest, 15,162, also British subjects, from the Cape Colony.[17] As the Uitlanders made their fortunes the president determined that in return they should help to sustain the finances of the republic by the payment of taxes which, while onerous, were by no means incommensurate with their newly-won riches. He was no less resolved that they should not acquire political control of the state. Taxation without representation or with inadequate representation appeared to him a trifling matter by comparison with the safeguarding of the recently regained independence of his people. The 'creators of wealth', as the Uitlanders deemed themselves to be, complained. No doubt there were some who cared about the substance of their complaints but assuredly there were more who, recking little or nothing of the much publicised hardships of Johannesburg financiers, mine-owners or millionaires, saw in them an opportunity for furthering ends on which they had set their heart. Chief among those ends was the unification of South Africa.

In the last decade of the nineteenth century South Africa suffered from a plethora of strong men. At the Cape there was Cecil John Rhodes, forever talking and dreaming about sometimes confused but always spacious imperialist designs, as – seated on his favourite wicker chair – he faced towards the close, overhanging mountains above the stoep of his Cape Town home, Groote Schuur. Against Bismarck's 'blood and iron' Rhodes consciously balanced 'peace and gold'. He possessed a certain largeness of mind and a power of attraction over men as varied in age, in outlook and in background as the elder Hofmeyr, the young Smuts and even Milner at the last. He understood (as most English statesman not least Joseph Chamberlain never did) something of the nature of Afrikaner nationalism. While he believed passionately in the British mission, he was a racialist neither in the older nor yet in the newer sense. He became prime minister of the Cape in 1890

with the support of J. H. Hofmeyr, 'Onze Jan' – a man of stature
and wisdom without political intensity and a dislike of final
commitment[18] – and the Afrikaner Bond, and he numbered W. P.
Schreiner, that early champion of native rights, among his closer
friends. He coined the phrase so expressive of the Cape tradition,
'equal rights for all civilised men'. But his insights were not
matched by equal patience or balanced judgment. Rhodes thought
that mineral wealth as great as that of the Rand lay to the north and
he based his hopes of counterbalancing the Transvaal on this
conviction. Bechuanaland accordingly was a life-line, his 'Suez
Canal to the interior'.[19] But this belief was not well founded and
when, faced with deteriorating health – he was thought by his
friends never to have been quite the same again after a fall from his
horse in 1891 – he understood that this was not so, his mind
inclined towards a quicker and more brutal solution. If the South
African Republic could not be pressed into union or confederation
by economic factors then more forceful means must needs be
employed. Rhodes continued to believe in gold; his faith in peace
was dimmed. Therein lay the tragedy of a man, to whom ends came
to justify means which good judgment alone would have firmly
repudiated.

Rhodes dominated the South African scene but in London he
had to deal, at the climax of the unfolding South African struggle
for power, with one of the strongest administrations and the most
formidable colonial secretary in modern British history. Lord
Salisbury was prime minister and foreign secretary; his nephew, A.
J. Balfour, first lord of the Treasury; Lord Lansdowne was at the
War Office and Joseph Chamberlain at the Colonial Office.
Chamberlain had travelled far since his early radical-republican
days and he knew the issue which had crystallised his latent
imperialism. It was Irish Home Rule. The 'killing' of Gladstone's
Bill in 1886 was the symbolic gesture. Thereafter he was a Unionist
but not a Tory. He thought in terms of a United Kingdom that was
strong because it remained united; of an Empire that would be
stronger if it became united. The large, elusive themes of imperial
federation, imperial defence, imperial *Zollverein* appealed to his
restless, thrustful mind. He thought but indifferently of the
Colonial Office officials he had inherited and they for their part
had their misgivings about the impulsive actions of 'pushful Joe'.
For unlike his traditionalist Tory colleagues Chamberlain was not
content with policies of imperial *laissez-faire, laissez-aller*; he wished
to develop imperial estates he deemed undeveloped, to organise
imperial power and imperial trade.

He has been [wrote A. G. Gardiner later in a brief, penetrating character sketch] the great disturber of the modern world. He has given it battle-cries and banners – never opiates or anodynes. With him the barometer has always stood at 'stormy'. Long ago, Lord Salisbury hit off his part in politics in one of his happy similes. 'The cabinet,' he said, 'is like an old Dutch weatherclock. When it is going to be fine Lord Hartington appears, and when Mr Joseph Chamberlain is seen you may look out for squalls'.

Joseph Chamberlain did not disturb for the sake of creating disturbance but because he was intent upon the attainment and exercise of power.

The charge [continued A. G. Gardiner] which history will make against Mr Chamberlain is not that he broke with his party but that he broke with his faith. He broke with it because his passion for mastery has been the governing motive of his career. He believed that he could make Toryism the instrument of his purposes. He recreated it and gave it its motive power, and then it used him for its own ends. It found in him the ally it needed . . .[20]

In 1895 Salisbury offered Chamberlain the Exchequer but he declined, asking for the Colonial Office instead. There was much surprise at his choice, the more so in that as a Liberal Unionist minority leader in a Tory cabinet he might have been expected to buttress a weak political position with a strong traditional office. But this 'modern merchant', as the German chancellor von Bülow called him,[21] sensed better than his aristocratic Tory colleagues the flowing tide of imperialist sentiment and, more substantially, the potential of Empire in a world of changing patterns of power. And last, but by no means least, Joseph Chamberlain never lacked self-confidence.

Rhodes and Chamberlain had one goal in common – the unification of South Africa. But beyond that one large purpose the differences between them were more pronounced than the area of agreement. Chamberlain was intensely 'British' in his approach. To him Crown, flag, nationality had of very necessity to be British. Rhodes entertained more flexible opinions. He was viewed with some suspicion in the Colonial Office because of an earlier contribution to Irish Home Rule funds, assuredly a gift not likely to commend him to the colonial secretary.[22] For Rhodes, winning the confidence of Afrikaners at the Cape and entering into a lasting

union with the Afrikaners of the Orange Free State were alike steps
in the fulfilment of the wider aims of persuading the Transvaalers
of the desirability of cooperation. So long as he was advancing
towards that goal he was willing, as Chamberlain was not, to
compromise about symbols on the way. Even when he had
abandoned hopes of peaceful advance Rhodes expected, in the
event of a successful revolt by the Uitlanders in Johannesburg, that
the immediate result would be 'an Anglicised and liberalised
republic', whereas on the other hand Chamberlain thought in
terms of a British colony with the British flag[23] and under the
British Crown. Even when Rhodes' emphasis on an emerging
South Africanism founded on cooperation between Briton and
Boer weakened with growing impatience, it remained something
not wholly absent from his thinking. In Chamberlain's mind it was
rarely, if ever, present. Rhodes was not a particularly sensitive man
but he had not the insensitivity of Chamberlain to the aspirations of
another and a smaller people. Then, too, Rhodes disliked and
mistrusted the imperial factor; in the all-important years Chamberlain was its physical embodiment.

In the small country town capital founded by the Voortrekker,
Andries Pretorius, where the streets were wide enough for an
oxwaggon to turn, Oom Paul Kruger presided over the destinies of
the Transvaal republic. His greatest asset, the wealth of the Rand,
was also his greatest liability. But time, contrary to Rhodes'
confident expectation, was not necessarily against him. By October
1894 the railway line to Delagoa Bay was completed, with President
Kruger travelling there on a ceremonial first journey to underline
the fact that the Transvaal at last had access, independent of British
control, to the sea. It could be used for trade and thus reduce
dependence upon the Cape railways. It could also be used, and it
was used, for the import of arms free from all British control. First
hand evidence was hard to come by, but the British Consul, Roger
Casement, later to have his own interest in German arms, observed
some consignments arriving. Having first advised Lord Salisbury
that anyone shipping goods through Delagoa Bay would be well
advised, because of the chaotic conditions at the port, to claim loss
of cargo as soon as it was landed, he later intimated that
considerable quantities of arms had entered the port destined for
the Transvaal, but that it was difficult to be precise about them,
because they were landed under the label of 'Government Goods'.
On 16 June 1896, however, he was able to report *inter alia* that 104
cases of maxim guns and 65 cases of rifles were in transit to the
republic.[24] Kruger, a patriarchal 'volk' figure of 'gnarled

magnificence' – the description was John Buchan's[25] – eccentric, even at times alarming in his personal habits, steeped in his boyhood memories of the Great Trek and ever mindful of annexation and Majuba Hill, was convinced, (not mistakenly) that Rhodes at the Cape was with tacit British support planning to undermine and then to destroy the independence of the Transvaal and was taking what seemed to him appropriate counter-measures. Caught in the web of wealth and immigration, franchise and independence, he himself, by his own policies helped to provide occasion for intervention.

The republic was enjoying unprecedented prosperity due to the gold mines owned and worked by the Uitlanders. The president took the view that he had allowed the Uitlanders to come, but having come of their own free will they must accept what laws and more especially what taxation the republic saw fit to impose. Chamberlain on the other hand, while acknowledging that the republic was free to determine its own immigration policy, was firm in his conclusion that the Uitlanders, once admitted, must be fairly treated. Since they were for the most part British subjects it was the responsibility of the Colonial Office to ensure that this was so. Colonial Office representations however made little apparent impact on the president's actions. The Uitlanders, conscious of injury and encouraged by expressions of British sympathy, plotted to revolt. Chamberlain was made aware of their intentions. He offered no discouragement; on the contrary, he proffered opinions on the most convenient time for a rising.[26] His more general reflections were summarised in a letter to Salisbury dated 26 December 1895. 'I have received private information', he recorded, 'that a rising in Johannesburg is imminent and will take place in the next few days . . . There is nothing to be done but to watch the event which we have done nothing to provoke. If the rising is successful it ought to turn to our advantage.'[27] The rising in Johannesburg did not take place. As revolutionaries, the millionaire mine owners of Johannesburg were tardy and for ever undecided. Relying upon them, it was caustically remarked, was as sensible as backing a carthorse to win the Derby.

There was, then, no rising, but there was a raid.[28] The two were planned to coincide in time, the raiders riding in from Pitsani on the Bechuanaland border in response to an appeal from British subjects in the Transvaal driven to desperate revolt by Boer oppression. But even without the revolt there was still an appeal. It had been composed some time beforehand but was released as the raiders crossed the border. It contained moving allusions to the

plight of women and children in Johannesburg and inspired
Alfred Austin, the Poet Laureate, to write:

> There are girls in the gold-reef city,
> There are mothers and children too!
> And they cry, 'Hurry up! for pity!'
> So what can a brave man do?[29]

The girls, the mothers and the children were, however, quite safe
when Dr Jameson crossed the border on 31 December 1895,
unable any longer to tolerate the perpetual postponements of the
Johannesburg rising. He had been stationed there with his force by
Rhodes. This had been made possible by the concession, after long
negotiations first with the Rosebery and then with the Salisbury
administration, of a strip of land on the Transvaal frontier to the
Chartered Company to carry the Cape Town-Kimberley line on to
Rhodesia. With control went policing rights. Did Chamberlain
know of the other purposes for which the territory and the rights
that went with it might be used? Did he have foreknowledge of a
raid to coincide with a rising? Certainly he denounced Rhodes and
the raid in unequivocal terms as 'an act of war or rather filibuster-
ing'.[30] Rhodes, ruined by his own impatience and by the rashness of
his closest friend, resigned, but Kruger was little impressed.
Indeed he did not have great reason to be. To this day, despite a
parliamentary inquiry – the Committee of no-Inquiry – which was
a model of all that a parliamentary inquiry ought not to be, and
despite critical historical investigation, uncertainty and doubt on
this point, so closely affecting the honour of the colonial secretary
and the integrity of the British government, remain. Was it the case
that the colonial secretary, who on his own admission knew all
about the rising, knew nothing about the raid? Was he unaware,
when the territory around Pitsani was transferred, of the purposes
for which it was to be used? Did he not suspect that the timing of the
Johannesburg rising was related to the question of armed assistance from across the border? It has indeed been so affirmed but the
weight of evidence and probability hardly suffices to sustain the
affirmation.[31]

Kruger, moreover, was now strongly placed. Not only had he
disposed of the raiders; he had also received commendation from
an exalted, albeit a dangerous quarter. It came in the form of a
telegram from the Kaiser Wilhelm the Second. The wording was
strong but in the circumstances of its drafting the surprise is that it
was no stronger. The kaiser presided over a council at which (if

Holstein's testimony be accepted)[32] an embarrassed chancellor and state secretary listened to some eccentric proposals for German intervention in the Transvaal. It was suggested that a Colonel Schele, 'a handsome man whose talents were generally considered very mediocre',[33] should disguise himself as a lion hunter and present himself to President Kruger with an offer of his services as chief of staff. More disturbing was the notion, also discussed, that one or two companies of German troops should be diverted from East Africa and proceed via Lourenço Marques to the Transvaal. All that was decided upon was the telegram that has gone down to history as the kaiser's telegram. It was despatched on 3 January 1896 and congratulated President Kruger on repulsing 'the armed bands' which had broken into his country, by his own and his people's energy 'without appealing for the help of friendly powers'.[34] The reaction in England was sharp. The raiders, if not absolved, were deemed misguided and overhasty rather than fundamentally mistaken. And in Anglo–German relations a turning full of danger had been taken.

'Well, it is a little history being made,' said Rhodes in a high-pitched voice, his face all fallen in, as he drove back in his Cape cart from Government House to Groote Schuur, after hearing of the capture of Jameson and his raiders, 'that is all.'[35] But it was by no means all. Between Boer and Briton confidence was gone. And the great issue still remained unresolved. Was it possible for the two Boer republics and the two British colonies to live together independently and also amicably in South Africa? Before the raid a compromise federal solution was conceivable; after the raid there were the sharp alternatives of mistrustful coexistence or war. Events had left Kruger in no mood for conciliatory gestures. He was unrepentant about the treatment of the Uitlanders. New and more oppressive laws were introduced, to be repealed only at the insistence of Chamberlain. The Transvaal armed. War material imported through Delagoa Bay rose in value from £61,903 in 1895 to £121,396 in 1896 to £256,291 in 1897. Forts were constructed at Pretoria and Johannesburg at a cost of over one and a half million pounds.[36] President Kruger, asked what the arms were for, replied on one occasion, 'Oh, kaffirs, kaffirs and such like objects.' Yet such evasions (in which the president at all times delighted) are not evidence that the arms were bought for other than defensive purposes. Nor indeed did the British government anticipate Boer aggression. What they feared was that, with increased strength would come increased recalcitrance. Kruger himself was triumphantly re-elected to the presidency in February 1898 by 12764 votes against 3716 and 1943 for his two opponents, Schalk Burger and Commandant-General Joubert, the slogan 'Beware of Rhodes and keep your power dry' being said to have decided many a waverer to support him.[37] There was also strong Boer resentment at the reassertion by Chamberlain in a dispatch of 6 December 1897 of British claims to a suzerainty which in the Boer view had lapsed with the signature of the London Convention in 1884. The Transvaal government proposed international arbitration; the colonial secretary and the high commissioner rejected all such ideas, partly on grounds of principle and prestige and partly because, in Milner's words 'the convention is *such a wretched instrument*, that even an impartial court would be likely to give such an interpretation to it as would render it perfectly worthless to us'.[38] And meanwhile there was the constant, exacerbating pressure of the Uitlanders for what they claimed to be their rights. In Alfred Milner they found a new and most formidable champion.

Milner was a product of Balliol College, Oxford, and among the most distinguished alumni of its greatest age. To his fine classical scholarship he added zeal, method and a capacity for work often attributed to his Germanic background. He came to South Africa as governor of Cape Colony and high commissioner in succession to Lord Rosmead in May 1897 and spent much of his first year in learning Afrikaans. Then he turned his mind to an analysis of the problems of South Africa. He noted that there was full equality in voting rights as between Boers and British in Cape Colony and that there was none in the Transvaal. The contrast exasperated him. He complained of the 'unprogressiveness not to say retrogressiveness of the Transvaal government'. In February 1898 he warned Chamberlain privately that 'There is no way out of the political troubles of South Africa except reform in the Transvaal or war. And at present the chances of reform in the Transvaal are worse than ever.' Kruger had returned to office 'more autocratic and reactionary than ever', and, he continued, '*looking at the question from a purely South African point of view*, I should be inclined to work up to a crisis, not indeed by looking about for causes of complaint or making a fuss about trifles but by steadily and inflexibly pressing for redress of substantial wrongs and injustices. It would not be difficult thus to work up an extremely strong *cumulative case*.'[39] From that conclusion Milner was not to depart. He became progressively less the British high commissioner and more the spokesman of the British in the Cape and in the Transvaal. He urged Chamberlain not to weaken, not to delay the time of final decision. Among the Uitlanders there was a widespread conviction that Kruger would not concede an effective franchise until he had 'looked down the cannon's mouth'. Their opinion was made known in London.[40] A British demand for Uitlander enfranchisement, on this view, would accordingly be met only if backed by the threat of force. On 4 May 1899 Milner, 'risking upon it his reputation and career', sent an official despatch, deliberately inflammatory in its phrasing, to the secretary of state endorsing the Uitlanders' complaints. 'The spectacle of thousands of British subjects kept permanently in the position of helots,' read the most provocative of its sentences, 'constantly chafing under undoubted grievances, and calling vainly to Her Majesty's government for redress, does steadily undermine the influence and reputation of Great Britain and the respect for the British government within its own dominions.'[41] The despatch was not published until 14 June and then one paragraph, emphasising the increasing military strength of the Transvaal, was omitted. In the excitable and emotional atmosphere of late nineteenth-century imperialism, especially in London, the publication of this despatch, even if not in its complete form, stirred up the strong emotional popular reaction that Milner hoped for. Chamberlain was questionably, Milner assuredly, by then convinced of the inevitability of war. And increasingly the atmosphere of impending war spread to Pretoria. The Boers thought the British intended 'to jump the Transvaal'. Sir Robert Ensor believed the cabinet was not affected by popular clamour – 'avenge Majuba' was the cry – but he added: 'If the Boers became united by the mistaken conviction that a British government wanted their blood, it was largely because they heard a British public calling for it'.[42]

On 31 May 1899, that is after the 'helots' despatch had been sent but before it was published, a conference was held at Bloemfontein. President Kruger was there and among his advisers was his youthful state attorney, J. C. Smuts.[43] So too was President Steyn of the Orange Free State. And there also was Sir Alfred Milner. It was not likely even under the most favourable circumstances that the venerable president and the purposeful high commissioner would find each other mutually comprehending; and the circumstances were far from favourable. Milner, described by his friend John Buchan as 'the last man for the task',[44] became more and more impatient. He found Kruger 'very slow'; he 'rambles fearfully', he talked continually of 'my independence', he said a vote for the Uitlanders (because of their numbers) was 'worse than annexation'; he declared it to be 'wholly against God's word to let strangers carry on the administration, seeing that they cannot serve two mas-

ters . . .'; and, again, that he was 'not ready to hand over my country
to strangers'. 'It is our country that you want', cried the old
president in an emotional climax.[45] Milner unmoved, was prepared to listen no longer. He broke off the conference on 5 June
before a telegram from Chamberlain telling him to let Kruger talk
himself out, had reached him. There were no reforms of the kind
he deemed sufficient, so he urged war. The cabinet approved an
ultimatum. But it was not delivered. It was anticipated, as was
hoped by Chamberlain and Milner, playing for time so that British
reinforcements might first reach Cape Town, as well as for political
advantage, by an ultimatum from the Boers on 9 October 1899.

It was a strange outcome. Its inherent unlikelihood has focused
historical attention on the concrete issues that divided the British
government and that of President Kruger in the spring and
summer of 1899. 'The gap which remained to be bridged at the end
of August' writes Thomas Pakenham in his history of the war that
followed 'was actually small enough . . . the underlying tragedy of
the war [was] the narrowness of the margin by which the peace was
lost.'[46] That it was lost he attributes to Kruger's rejection of the
chance of compromise, because he did not realise it existed. But did
it? That raises a larger question still.

The war could have only one outcome – the defeat of the Boers
and the British annexation of the two republics. It happened,
annexation preceding final defeat, with the Orange Free State
being annexed in May and the Transvaal in September 1900. Nor
was such annexation to be temporary: 'If we are victors,' declared
Chamberlain, ' . . . the territories of these republics must be finally
incorporated in Her Majesty's dominions.' This implied unconditional surrender. Milner, easily convinced of the impossibility of
conciliating (in his own words) 'panoplied hatred, insensate ambitions, invincible ignorance' was insistent that it should be so. And
peace, albeit with qualifications, was made on that basis at Vereeniging on 31 May 1902. Thus by force of arms the extent of the
future Commonwealth was significantly enlarged.

The war established British supremacy in South Africa. It does
not follow from this alone that the war was fought to establish it. In
1900, George Bernard Shaw surmised: 'Whether the electorate
shares President Kruger's political ideas or believes them to be as
outdated as his theology, it probably suspects that if the government had been as earnest in its efforts to stave off war as in its
efforts to stave off Old Age Pensions, there would have been no
war.'[47] This was less than the truth. The question which preoccupied the government was not whether to stave off but whether to

precipitate war. In fact they did precipitate war by adopting a posture of menace, deliberately intended to force the pace and the issue. Certainly there were other factors in the situation, from the manipulations of financiers to the still insufficiently analysed ambitions of the Boers, but they do not alter the fact that the purpose of British government policy – including in the term government, high commissioner, colonial secretary and the cabinet acting with collective responsibility – was to secure undivided British control over southern Africa by any necessary means. Milner expounded that purpose more clearly than any other and the war, accordingly, has been called by Professor Le May 'Sir Alfred Milner's War'.[48] Certainly Milner had his 'grand design' in which quick and decisive military victory in a limited war – 'an Austerlitz in the veld' – would open the way for 'a gigantic exercise in physical and social engineering' intended to ensure for the foreseeable future British supremacy in South Africa. He was too the most influential of British proconsuls in the decisive years. Yet on the other hand neither a theoretician's formulation of aims nor the undoubted reality of Milner's influence warrant any such token attribution of final responsibility. Milner was not colonial secretary; still less was he a member of the cabinet which in the last resort determined British policy in South Africa. The members of the cabinet were neither the victims of circumstances nor under the domination of Milnerism. They were acting – notably the colonial secretary despite his occasional recorded misgivings – in conformity with their own views and in accord with a vocal section of public opinion in sanctioning policies which led, as they were intended to lead, to the establishment of British supremacy. It was not, therefore, in this context Milner's war; it was a war embarked upon for reasons of state which whether subsequently thought sufficient or insufficient convinced those responsible for British policy in South Africa at the time of the need to act. On that basis, to return to the earlier question prompted by the Boer ultimatum, there was no long-term chance of compromise on the basis of an autonomous Transvaal republic.

The conduct of the war was not unrelated to its purposes. It was a war to end disputed supremacy in South Africa by destroying the Boer republics as separate political entities. 'You want to take away my independence' Kruger had complained to Milner at Bloemfontein. That was so. Divided sovereignty in South Africa was deemed too dangerous to be allowed to continue. That meant a war to establish a single sovereignty. In turn that meant, in fact and possibly of necessity, insistence upon a policy of unconditional surrender. And unconditional surrender meant, short of the quick victory that Milner understood to be near-essential for the fulfil-ment of his aims, protracted, inconclusive campaigning across the vast spaces of southern Africa and with it, what Milner so greatly deplored, a blunting of the fine edge of resolution.

The prolongation of war meant other things besides. It meant most of all the sanction by successive commanders-in-chief of measures which cast long shadows down future years: indiscrimi-nate or nearly indiscriminate burning of farms ostensibly in order to preserve law and order in the Orange Free State – 'what fool in his folly', commented Lionel Curtis, 'taught us we could prevent men from brigandage by making them homeless?' – the rounding up of women and children in concentration camps in which more than twenty thousand died of epidemics or disease, as well as threatened deportations first of large numbers of Boers – Fiji and Madagascar were in Kitchener's mind as their possible destinations provided that, in the latter case the French were agreeable – and when the cabinet rejected the policy, then selective deportation of wives, Kitchener taking the view, which once again the cabinet firmly rejected, that they were the more implacable and therefore responsible for prolonging the war. On the other hand, it is also to be recorded, as a matter of historical consequence, that 'while some of the means by which the war was prosecuted implanted feelings of bitterness and resentment among the Afrikaner volk that endured through and beyond the second world war, it was conducted among the fighting men with a chivalry that left behind in the higher ranks at least feelings of mutual esteem and respect'.[49]

Peace was imposed but not without conditions. It could hardly have been otherwise. The Boers were skilful negotiators, they knew what mattered to them most and moreover they found the military arm, in the person of Lord Kitchener, more conciliatory than the civilian. The terms of peace accordingly proved more tolerant and more tolerable than had been anticipated. But the decision to make peace was nevertheless painfully reached by the Boer leaders.

It was in May 1902 near Vereeniging in a large tent pitched by command of Kitchener that the sixty representatives of the two republics discussed the issue of peace or continued war. It had already been made clear to them that the British, however adaptable on lesser matters, were not prepared to negotiate on the basis of continuing Boer independence. The debate opened with an account of declining Boer fortunes, of shortages of horses and food in many though not in all areas, of the necessary abandon-ment of hope of foreign aid or of a rising in the Cape. 'There will be no general rising in the Cape'[50] despite much sympathy, reported Smuts. Many commanders voiced their great anxiety about the women and children and the casualty roll in the concentration camps.

> Have we not now [asked Acting State President Burger][51] arrived at that stage when we should pray: 'Thy will be done?' ... We have already effected supernatural things at which the world stands amazed. Shall we now allow a people who have sacrificed even women and children, to be exterminated? ... We were proud and despised the enemy, and is it not perhaps God's will to humble us and cast down the pride in us by allowing us to be oppressed by the English people? ... Our people do not deserve to be annihilated.

A more considerable figure, Commandant-General Botha, dwelt upon that self-same thought:

> It has been said we must fight to the bitter end, but no one tells us what that bitter end is. Is it where everyone lies in his grave or is banished? In my opinion we must not consider the time when everyone lies in his grave as the 'bitter end'. If we do so, and act upon that view, we become the cause of the death of our people. Is the bitter end not here, where the people have struggled till they can struggle no more? ... If we wish to negotiate, now is the time. If the Lord God wills it, then, however bitter, we must come to terms.[52]

General Smuts was in agreement with him. There was one thing that could not be sacrificed even for independence. That was the Afrikaner people. For their sake, for the sake of its women and children, must peace be made. But not all shared that opinion. There was also heard the voice of the romantic, unrealistic, militant nationalist.

> The war is a matter of faith [declared Chief Commandant de Wet]. If I had not been able to do so in faith, I would never have taken up arms. Let us again renew our covenant with God ... The entire war has been a miracle. ... I cannot see into the future, but this I know, that behind me it is light. What lies before me I do not know. There it is dark, but we must go on trusting God, and then, when victory comes, we shall not be proud.[53]

The realists won the day, but the voice of the romantic remained to trouble the thoughts and divide the minds of later generations.

Some among the Boers who made peace at Vereeniging were later to be numbered among the chief architects of the Common-wealth. Their insight was applauded and the road they had travelled viewed mostly in comfortable Commonwealth retrospect. Yet it was as important that they and their people had known defeat as that they – or rather some among them – should have been reconciled to Empire within a broadening Commonwealth con-cept. And history records that the impress of that defeat and the resolve that it should be undone was more enduring than that of subsequent and magnanimous reconciliation. In September 1905 J. X. Merriman, reflecting in Cape Town with some asperity about the events of the recent past, in a letter to Goldwin Smith deplored, among other things, evidence of continuing British fears of the Dutch 'and the terrible things they may do'. He remarked upon the fact that since defeat the Boers had shown great dignity and self-control, and concluded with the sobering and in the event well-justified warning that the Boer 'is a good man at a waiting game'.[54] On this occasion, however, he did not have long to wait.

The Treaty of Vereeniging decided the vexed question of sovereignty in South Africa. By compulsion of arms the Boer republics had been brought under the British flag and for the first time since the Great Trek all Europeans in South Africa owed allegiance to one ruler. It was this which opened the way to the unification of South Africa; but it did not of itself bring it about. There remained after the treaty the four separate political entities, Cape Colony and Natal enjoying responsible self-government, the Transvaal and the Orange River Colony the status only of Crown colonies. Divided by war, unequal in political standing, by whom and by what means were they to be associated in one larger whole?[55] For most Englishmen and for not a few Afrikaners the imperial statesman whose name was most closely linked with the unification of South Africa was the Liberal, Sir Henry Champbell-Bannerman, who succeeded Balfour as prime minister in December 1905. Campbell-Bannerman had condemned the wartime concentration camps as 'methods of barbarism', and his courageous denunciation of them especially in the face of divided opinions in the party about future South African policy, was thought by Botha to have left the door open for Anglo–Boer reconciliation after the war. How precisely it came about has recently been the subject of critical reappraisal. On the generally accepted account Campbell-Bannerman had a talk with Smuts on 7

February 1906, on the basis of a memorandum Smuts had brought with him to London about the future of the former Boer Republics and it was Smuts' conviction to the end of his days that that talk had 'settled the future of South Africa'. On the following day, again by the traditionally received account, Campbell-Bannerman made a speech in Cabinet which is said to have persuaded his colleagues to agree to the scrapping of the constitution devised by the outgoing Unionist Colonial Secretary, Alfred Lyttelton and in its place to concede, without any intervening period of representative government such as Lyttelton had contemplated, responsible government to the defeated Dutch republics. This speech Lloyd George later told Lord Riddell was 'the most dramatic, the most important ten minutes' speech ever delivered in our time. In ten minutes he brushed aside all the checks and safeguards devised by Asquith, Winston and Loreburn;'[56] while to R. C. K. Ensor he described it as 'so unanswerable as to secure at once the unanimous assent of his hearers, many of whom had till then held a different opinion'. Just after Campbell-Bannerman's death, on 25 April 1908, the *Nation* commented 'without his intervention we doubt whether South Africa would have had self-government in a form which would have ensured the great practical aim of acceptance by the Dutch community. Thus at a stroke, he wiped out the worst leavings of the war . . .' The *Annual Register* 1908 drew attention to this judgment. In 1912, however, it was challenged by Asquith in a letter to J. A. Spender, claiming that the notion that Campbell-Bannerman won over the Cabinet was 'a ridiculous fiction. Between ourselves, he had little or nothing to do with the matter and never bothered his head about it. The Transvaal Constitution was worked out by myself, Loreburn, Elgin, Winston and Sir R. Solomon, with the help of [Sir John] Lawson Walton' (the Attorney-General).

The whole episode has been subjected to critical scrutiny, notably by Dr Hyam, who is at once sceptical of the overriding importance sometimes attributed to Smuts' conversation with Campbell-Bannerman, not least by Smuts himself in later years and of Campbell-Bannerman's rôle in Cabinet.[57] The first would seem well founded, the second to open but not to close enquiry. In respect of it old convictions may be unsettled, but no new certainties emerge. The weight of contemporary or near contemporary evidence in favour of the older, simpler version is too considerable to be lightly discounted. Asquith's remarks seemingly did not weigh over much with J. A. Spender to whom they were addressed. In his two volume biography of Campbell-Bannerman published in 1923, he gives Campbell-Bannerman all the credit for his 'act of faith', while nine years later in his biography of Asquith, also in two volumes and written in collaboration with Asquith's son, Cyril, Asquith's contribution is described in terms of the time and thought he had devoted to the drafting of the new Transvaal Constitution 'which in the end owed much to his efforts and his keen sense of the legal problems involved'. R. B. McCallum, nurtured in the Glaswegian stronghold of Scottish Liberalism, concurs in this distinction between the rôles of the two men, the one initiating, the other applying. In his history of the Liberal party, McCallum remarks that the matter of self-government 'was settled quickly and finally by Campbell-Bannerman and by him personally . . .' his 'claim to greatness' that 'he for once acted on the full logic of his principles'. Timing, too, was the essence of the matter and in this he was ahead of his contemporaries. In his biography of Asquith, McCallum agreed that 'Asquith took a considerable part in the greatest achievement of the Campbell-Bannerman Administration, the grant of responsible government to the defeated Boers of the Transvaal and Orange Free State. His skill in constitutional law was valuable in the framing of the ordinances.'[58] In other words, as was a feature of his premiership, Campbell-Bannerman gave the lead and then withdrew. Once the new policy had been set on course, the meticulous process of implementation he left to others. By drawing a distinction between policy-making and its implementation, while allowing for some exaggeration here and there, the two versions appear not quite so far apart as at first sight. What is fundamentally at issue is not the precise measure of individual responsibility, which in itself does not greatly matter, but the source and nature of the inspiration that went to the fashioning of a South African settlement, which was to have a major influence on subsequent Commonwealth thinking and development.

Responsible government was restored to the Transvaal on 6 December 1906, and to the Orange River colony, thereafter known once more as the Orange Free State, on 5 June, 1907, in both instances by Letters Patent, thereby avoiding the judgment of the House of Lords. It was as well for the application of Liberal policy that such a device could be employed, for the restoration of self-government to the Transvaal was described in the Commons by the Unionist leader A. J. Balfour as 'the most reckless experiment ever tried in the development of a great colonial policy'[59] and the large Unionist majority in the Lords had already shown themselves to be in no mood to defer in any matter to the opinion of the Liberal majority in the lower House. As for the decision to restore self-government itself, while certainly a bold political step, it was neither rash nor little considered, as opposition denunciations of it sought to suggest, nor for that matter so dramatic as Smuts' later comments upon his conversation with Campbell-Bannerman might lead one to suppose. Rather did it follow naturally from the strand of Liberal thinking, best represented by Campbell-Bannerman himself, about South Africa during and after the war.[60] The principle which guided Liberal policy was reconciliation with the Boers, made possible, despite all that had taken place, by a timely concession of political autonomy within the British Empire.

Neither the prime minister, nor, as the files abundantly testify, the Colonial Office, were unmindful of the implications of the decision taken in February 1906 to restore self-government forthwith to the former republics. It was not a leap-in-the-dark; it was a calculated risk, or, as Campbell-Bannerman's biographer wrote, 'an act of faith'.[61] More than forty years later General Smuts remembered it, and the man who was chiefly responsible for it, in an address delivered in the Senate House at Cambridge ' . . . I would specially mention', he said, 'one whose name should never be forgotten . . . Campbell-Bannerman, the statesman who wrote the word *Reconciliation* over . . . that African scene, and thus rendered an immortal service to the British Empire, aye, to the cause of man everywhere'.[62] Of course, even such an act of faith could not obliterate all the memories of war. Grass may grow quickly over a battlefield but it grows slowly over burnt homesteads and civilian concentration camps. And, even responsible government within the Empire could not compensate in most Afrikaner minds for loss of republican independence but at least it contributed, more than any other action conceivable in the circumstances could have done, to further Anglo–Boer reconciliation.

Liberal policy in 1906–7 did not bring about the union of South Africa but it made its advancement possible psychologically by helping to reconcile the Boers to existence within the Empire and technically by placing the four South African colonies on an equal footing in negotiation about future relations between them. But the nature of their relationship was something that after the South African war could be determined only in South Africa. The 'imperial factor' had to be and was firmly excluded. That was a condition of Afrikaner support for union. Accordingly, as earlier in Canada and Australia, the constitution was fashioned in debate and protracted conference by representatives of the four self-governing colonies. It was 'home-made'. This meant that the preconception and preoccupations of those who made it, and not those of the imperial government, determined its character. Those preoccupations were many and varied but through them all ran the consistent purpose of the Transvaal to create a strong, unitary state.

The wealth of the Transvaal constituted the occasion for war and was a condition of unification. Of necessity therefore the views of the Transvaal weighed heavily, even conclusively, in respect of the nature of a united South African state. The Transvaal government, with General Botha as its first prime minister, increasingly favoured strong and stable government. For this there were many reasons, some of them subsequently overmuch discounted. One such was the continuing antagonism of the great financial interests to the Boers and the deeply ingrained mistrust of the Boers for the financiers and mineowners, the Uitlanders of other days and more recently the instigators and beneficiaries of indentured Chinese immigrant labour on the Rand. In December 1906 General Smuts, expatiating once more on a subject which had loomed large in a memorandum he had brought with him to London and shown to British ministers in February that year, wrote to Merriman saying that the South African idea 'is waging a mortal war with organised money power which is corrupting politics and tampering with men's souls all over South Africa . . .' The existence of this power and its influence was a reason for favouring 'federation or rather (if possible) unification. Believe me, as long as we stand divided and separated in South Africa the money power will beat us in the Transvaal government and as a consequence over the rest of South Africa. I know the practical difficulties, which will be well-nigh insurmountable.'[63]

The phrasing verges on the melodramatic but despite some historians' doubts the sentiments were almost certainly authentic. Fear of financiers was supplemented by another and again possibly insufficiently regarded but more familiar factor. While Downing Street desired to discard its South African responsibilities, South Africans – English and Afrikaners in this at one – wished to discard Downing Street.

The one aim for us [Smuts told Merriman in 1906] is South African self-rule. But it sounds almost like a mockery at present – what with the malevolence of Conservative governments and the stupidity of Liberals. However we can but do our duty, knowing that the events of the last seven or eight years have stirred and set free forces in South Africa which are quite beyond the control of Downing Street or any other street or lane in London.

And in passionate climax, associating imperial with financial influences, he declared that he would rather suffer defeat in the cause of a united and free South Africa 'than triumph with the satanic hacks of a Milner or a Rhodes'. Clearly the more firmly united the South African colonies, the greater would be the measure of their effective independence from both. 'My own position,' wrote Smuts more temperately in August 1907 'is that federation or rather unification is a good and wise ideal; it is the only alternative to Downing Street which is a most baneful factor.'[64]

There remained – most important of all in terms of political as distinct from economic or administrative considerations – the place of non-Europeans in South Africa. The stronger the central government, the greater would be its control over native policy. Unified administration might result in the magnanimity that derives from assured authority, as many Liberals in England wished to believe, or, alternatively, in policies of repression which concentration of power would make practicable. What alone was certain was that while a federal government might preserve diversities, a unitary government predicated pressure towards uniformity and a concentration of European power and authority at the centre.

There was a press campaign against federation in which many have sensed the hand of Smuts. Certainly he was strongly opposed to a federal solution but then so were others, President M. T. Steyn of the Orange Free State among them. 'Surely,' the president wrote to Merriman on 30 January 1907, 'Australia ought to be an object lesson to us not to federate in haste', and he continued, 'Our duty I take it is to see we are not jockeyed into some or other ready-made federation scheme.' Merriman himself probed more deeply. The paraphernalia of four separate governments, judiciaries and administrations was, he pointed out to Goldwin Smith in a letter later that year, absurdly expensive. Yet some of the difficulties in the way of unification were very great – 'the local jealousies – the terrible native question which is always with us and to which we have added the Asiatic trouble'. How was the franchise to be determined in a unified state? The franchise at the Cape, without distinction of colour but with a high educational qualification, had 'on the whole . . . worked well'. 'Our natives have increased both in wealth and in habits of industry and civilisation. They have given little or no trouble . . . I must confess that viewed merely as a safety valve I regard the franchise as having served its purpose.' But none of the other colonies approached to this system. 'In the two Boer states they have refused the native civil rights – in Natal the whole system has been designed to keep him in a state of barbarism.' In any negotiations Merriman correctly surmised 'they will attempt to get us to abandon our franchise'. The best course, he thought, would be to adopt a franchise with a real educational test which would 'shut out all but the native who was fit to exercise the rights of a citizen, while not denying to any man the privileges of citizenship on the ground of accident of colour'. But he feared, again correctly, that this would be impossible and speculated about the alternative of retaining the Cape franchise, while allowing a differential franchise elsewhere. Was this possible? Were there precedents? The New Zealand practice was not altogether applicable. There was, it was true, separate representation for Maoris, but on the New Zealand basis that would mean in time the swamping of the white electorate in South Africa. 'There is this difference,' he concluded, '. . . in New Zealand the Maoris are the idle classes, the Europeans industrious. In the Cape the natives are the workers growing in riches as a result of their industry' and accordingly qualifying in increasing numbers for the franchise as time went on. There was, in sum, no solution in respect of the native question that was politically practicable and morally acceptable for the whole of a united South Africa. In that context questions of a unitary or a federal state were matters self-evidently only of degree.

The constitution of the Union of South Africa was shaped in successive conventions held at Durban, Cape Town and Bloemfontein in 1908–9.[65] The governments of the four colonies, Cape Colony, Natal, the Orange Free State and the Transvaal were represented as equals, but among equals the position of the Transvaal with its able and hard-working delegation and its expert advisers drawn from the ranks of Lord Milner's young men remained in all respects pre-eminent. That delegation, Smuts not least among them, presented the case for union as against federation with a logic, force and a persistence which their possible opponents altogether lacked.

The aim of the architects of union was the fusing of the two European races and thereby, to quote General Smuts, 'the remaking of South Africa . . . on a higher plane of political and national life'. The unitary form of government, subject to whatever safeguards were agreed, as advocated by the Transvaal delegation, was accepted partly because of obvious economic advantages and a general desire for efficient administration but chiefly because it was thought the more likely to weld white South Africa 'into one compact nationality inspired by one common pervading spirit', and, be it added, applying one consistent and coherent native policy. It meant – and despite some superficial concessions to the provinces was understood by the powerful Transvaal delegation to the convention to mean – strong centralised government with ultimate authority resting in the union Parliament. It meant also (as federation might not have done) that if the experiment of fusion failed then the majority white community would be well placed to control the government of the country should it so desire. The Canadian federal precedent which had ensured the safeguarding of French Canadian rights was considered but deemed inappropriate, partly because of very different financial, trading and transport problems and still more because the European peoples were geographically interspersed in South Africa as they were not in Canada. But it is also the case that the counterbalancing advantages of a federal system were insufficiently weighed because of the indolence and ineptitude of the political leaders in English-speaking Natal, the one province which had a clear interest in federation rather than union on almost every political and cultural ground. The case for federation went almost by default. 'I could always in the last resort', wrote Patrick Duncan, 'ask opponents in Natal whether under unification they thought their affairs would be more inefficiently managed than they are now and none of them could truthfully say that their worst apprehension went as far as that.'[66] In the sequel, union was in fact approved in Natal, alone of the four provinces, by popular referendum. Positively this illustrated more than anything else the impressive degree of confidence that prevailed in the principle of one white South African state at that time.

The Boers feared and the natives hoped that after the war the British government would insist on extending the application of Cape native policy to the northern provinces. In the event the fears of the Boers proved unfounded and the hopes of the natives were belied. There were two principal reasons for this. In the first place the thinking of the imperial government was dominated by what was called 'the Racial Question', by which was meant relations between the two European peoples in South Africa. And it was dominated for the very good reason that these white communities alone could at that time provide men locally, who could assume responsibility for the government of Southern Africa. Though not without its difficulties it was possible to think of the administration of the defeated republics with the co-operation of the defeated

Boers, but was it possible to think of their administration *against* the Boers? The second and more concrete point to be noted is that the Liberal governments were bound by the concession their Conservative predecessors had approved in respect of native policy by Article 8 of the Treaty of Vereeniging. That article read: 'The question of granting the franchise to natives will not be decided until after the introduction of self-government.' This was an explicit undertaking not to admit any native to the franchise in the Transvaal or the Orange River Colony while Britain had direct control over their domestic policies. Together with the other terms of peace, Article 8 was submitted to the high commissioner, the Colonial Office, the colonial secretary and the cabinet. In the Colonial Office, it was noted that 'it did not seem possible to debar the native, if duly qualified, from having the franchise under representative government' and suggested that the franchise should be granted before representative government was instituted but 'so limited as to secure the just predominance of the white race as in Cape Colony'. The official principally concerned, F. Graham, minuted, 'The native franchise is I think the only point worth hesitating about. As [the clause] stands the native will never have the franchise. No responsible government will give it to him.'[67] But neither the high commissioner, the colonial secretary nor the cabinet appear to have hesitated. Why should they? They had fought the war to ensure British supremacy, not to establish native rights. Later Milner conceded that acquiescence in Article 8 was a mistake. He added that he believed 'as strongly as ever that we got off the right lines when we threw over Mr Rhodes' principle of "equal rights for every civilized man" '.[68]

The Colonial Office files later abound in statements of what in these circumstances an imperial government could *not* do. It could not go back on Article 8 of the treaty. It could not interpret that Article narrowly, applying it only to the natives because, as a Committee of Enquiry under the chairmanship of Sir Joseph West-Ridgeway reported, the Boers had in good faith interpreted it as applying to all non-European inhabitants. The secretary of state, Lord Elgin, who thought it quite evident that 'the time must come when there will be danger of a collision between the white and coloured races unless the relations between them are fair and equitable',[69] anxiously considered what steps might be open to the imperial government. But when the steps 'open to us to secure the just interests of the natives' were reviewed one by one, the objections to each seemed well-nigh insurmountable. The secretary of state himself conceded that the terms of surrender 'absolutely preclude' representation of natives as in Cape Colony, and he felt obliged to infer that it also excluded representation of Coloured people. He weighed the possibility of making reservations in the grant of the constitution but noted that there would obviously be difficulty in framing any provision and that quite certainly any such provision would be objected to. The root of the problem was to reconcile the humanitarian aims of the Liberal government towards the non-European with their policy of generosity towards the defeated Boers in the form of restoring self-government to them. But there was in fact no way in which the imperial government could ensure improvement in the lot of the non-Europeans consistent both with the terms of Article 8 of the treaty and with their policy of self-government for the Europeans.

While nothing could be done before the restoration of self-government in respect of native rights, nothing could be done after because there was self-government. The debate in South Africa leading to union made it abundantly clear that either there was union with at most existing electoral laws in each colony, which meant an absolute political colour bar in the inland provinces and a nearly absolute political colour bar in Natal, or negotiations for union broke down. The Cape was no more prepared to sacrifice its liberal franchise than the Transvaal or the Orange Free State were prepared to extend it to their own territories. There were individuals, W. P. Schreiner notable among them, who foresaw many of the consequences of compromise and protested at acquiescence in illiberal northern practices. They enjoyed, however, only qualified support within the Cape and lacked any solid backing elsewhere. On a tour of the Transvaal after the convention had published its Report, Louis Botha had in fact great difficulty in preventing resolutions being passed for the removal of the Cape native franchise. 'All parties,' he wrote to Merriman on 17 March 1909,

> object most strongly to the provisions retaining in the Cape colony the native franchise for the Central Parliament . . . no other point has given me so much trouble as this and I must confess that it was all I could do to prevent mandates to amend this clause. I can assure you that a very great number of people in the Transvaal, English as well as Dutch, are quite prepared to wreck the union on this question.[70]

This was something not to be lightly discounted. Union without the Transvaal was at once unthinkable and impracticable. And so the solution was a compromise, with each province retaining its existing electoral laws. Self-evidently the issue was suspended, not concluded. Self-evidently too the balance of power would rest with the north. It was the Cape franchise which needed to be safeguarded and which was in fact entrenched in the constitution of the union – the South Africa Act 1909 – so that it might be amended only by a two-thirds majority of both Houses of the South African Parliament sitting together.

There was much debate before this electoral compromise was reached. It touched on matters of deep import for the future of South Africa and the Commonwealth; it illuminated some lasting questions inseparable from the political association of different races but the most enduring impression that emerges from later reading of it is the sense of bafflement. Smuts at all times was ready to give sophisticated expression to acquiescent agnosticism. Thus in 1906 he wrote to Merriman of the natives:

> I do not believe in politics for them. Perhaps at bottom I do not believe in politics at all as a means for the attainment of the highest ends; but certainly so far as the natives are concerned politics will to my mind only have an unsettling influence. I would therefore not give them the franchise . . . When I consider the political future of the natives in South Africa I must say that I look into shadows and darkness; and then I feel inclined to shift the intolerable burden of solving that sphinx problem to the ampler shoulders and stronger brains of the future. Sufficient unto the day . . .![71]

And two years later he returned to the same theme:

> On the question of the native franchise my mind is full of Cimmerian darkness and I incline very strongly to leaving that matter over for the Union Parliament. I also feel pretty certain that a native franchise imported into the constitution would make union impossible of acceptance by the people. Let us therefore adhere to the comfortable gospel of *laissez-faire*. To us union means more than the native question . . .[72]

So potentially explosive an issue could not even then be put to rest quite so easily as that, as Smuts himself had reason to know. In June 1908 J. A. Hobson, writing on behalf of The New Reform Club Political Committee (a radical group in London), enquired of him how he thought the coming unification of South Africa would affect the position of the natives. In his reply Smuts argued once again that the only sound policy at that stage was to avoid any attempt at a comprehensive solution. Public opinion on the subject of the natives was in a chaotic state and, that being so, any solution would be a poor compromise which would probably prejudice a fairer and more statesman-like settlement later. He also gave renewed warning of the graver danger that any constitution which conferred the franchise on natives would not be ratified. Then he proceeded:

> My view is that the different franchise laws of the several colonies ought to be left undisturbed . . . and that the question of a uniform franchise law be gone into only after the union has been brought about. You will then avoid the dangers I have referred to; and you will in the union Parliament, representing as it will all that is best in the whole of South Africa, have a far more powerful and efficient instrument for the solution of the question along broad and statesmanlike lines than you will have in the union convention . . . The political status of the natives is no doubt a very important matter, but vastly more important to me is the union of South Africa, which if not carried now will probably remain in abeyance until another deluge has swept over South Africa.

In that last sentence lay the crucial issue. Smuts had his order of priorities; at the head of it was union and that was understandable. But did he really believe, as he also wrote, that the right course for a British statesman concerned with the future of the natives was to 'trust the people of South Africa in this matter and commit the government of the whole of British South Africa [including the Basutoland, Bechuanaland and Swaziland protectorates] unreservedly to their charge' on the ground that it would best bring home to the South Africans 'their solemn duties in the matter'?[73]

Smuts sent to Merriman a copy of his reply to Hobson. On the practical and immediate issue both Hobson and Merriman were at one with Smuts. Hobson conceded that a uniform federal franchise appeared impracticable,[74] though pointing out with some emphasis that there was a pronounced objection on the part of the Liberals to any idea of handing over the protectorates to South Africa. Merriman commented, 'I entirely agree with you that it would be quite impossible to dream of any general native franchise at the present time. If it were adopted at the convention it would unquestionably lead to the rejection of the constitution in the majority of the states.'[75] The Cape would not abandon its non-European franchise in the interests of uniformity any more than the northern provinces would adopt it. The one sensible compromise was therefore agreement to continue existing and contrasted electoral practices. But looking to the future Merriman was not at one with Smuts. He was attracted by the idea of native territories governed as provinces with the natives allowed 'large privileges in local government' as in the Transkei. But the practical difficulties in the way of its general application appeared too formidable. So he was driven back reluctantly to the idea of a 'civilisation' franchise. The numbers of the natives 'constitute, and always will remain, our greatest menace'. There were four and a half million of them 'in different stages of progress but they are all progressing'.

To me personally [Merriman continued] the idea of a native franchise is repellent but I am convinced that it is a safety-valve and the best safety-valve, and that so far from its leading to any immediate danger it will be generations before the European political supremacy will be menaced, while it does undoubtedly not only safeguard the rights of the inferior race but also gives them a content which puts an end to the unrest that any unrepresented population always will have.

Behind these debates and compromise solutions lay the fact that the war, by bringing under one allegiance communities which differed so profoundly on race relations, had at once sharply accentuated an existing problem and brought it within the frontiers of an Empire soon to become a Commonwealth. And the problem thus accentuated was one to which men in office had no solution to offer. Even the most clear-sighted among them looked also 'into the shadows and darkness'. 'The great African group' of which Lord Crewe spoke with so much satisfaction (when piloting the South Africa Act through the House of Lords) as joining the great American and the great Pacific group and bringing the self-governing Empire into something like its final form,[76] brought with it unsolved, first into the circle of the dominions, and then of the Commonwealth, one of the most difficult and disruptive of all human issues. The dilemma of the imperial government was plain. They could not at one and the same time pursue a liberal and a humanitarian policy in South Africa and so perforce they consoled themselves with thoughts of the entrenchment of the colour-blind franchise at the Cape, continuing imperial responsibility for the high commission territories and the magnanimity that might come with union and with the assurance of strength. Milner had advised Asquith, prime minister when union was enacted, as long ago as November 1897:

> You have, therefore, this singular situation, that you might indeed unite Dutch and English by protecting the black man, but you would unite them against yourself and your policy of protection.
>
> There is the whole *crux* of the South African position . . . You say and say truly that self-government is the basis of our colonial policy and the keystone of colonial loyalty. That principle, fearlessly and unflinchingly applied, would make South Africa as loyal as Canada – but what would be the price? The abandonment of the black races, to whom you have promised protection . . .'[77]

Reluctantly that price in part was paid. What Ramsay MacDonald called the 'imperial standard' in dealing with native peoples was not maintained. This was no casual decision. It was taken to avoid the final alienation of the Boers, already embittered by their 'century of wrong'. It is widely assumed today that there was a practicable and preferable alternative policy open to the British government ensuring a measure of political rights for Africans. This may be so but it was not apparent to any British statesman with experience of government at the time. And the time was five years before the outbreak of the first world war.

4 The Pacific Colonies; Self-Government and Consolidation

> From the Cape to Australia – from political discord, the conflict
> of races ... and the perpetual interference of the imperial
> government, to a country where politics are but differences of
> opinion, where the hand of the imperial government is never
> felt, where the people are busy with their own affairs ... where
> everyone seems occupied, and everyone at least moderately
> contented – the change is great indeed.

So wrote James Anthony Froude on arriving at Adelaide from
Cape Town in 1885. And to what did he attribute so vast a
difference?

> One is a free colony, the other is a conquered country. One is a
> natural and healthy branch from the parent oak, left to grow as
> nature prompts it [the other] a branch ... withering from the
> point where it joins the trunk ... It is pleasant to turn from
> shadow to sunshine ... to a country ... where the closest ac-
> quaintance only brings out more distinctly how happy, how
> healthy English life can be in this far off dependency.[1]

The colourful contrasts may be somewhat discounted but assuredly
Froude struck the right chord in writing of 'a branch from a parent
oak' and English life in the far Pacific.

In the history of the Commonwealth there were two member
states that were exceptional, they were Australia and New Zealand.
They were, and are, exceptional in that they are British. Canada it
is true had a population predominantly British in extraction until
the second half of the twentieth century. But recognition in respect
of language and of provincial rights of the existence of another, a
French, culture was a condition of confederation. In South Africa
the majority of the population was non-European and of the
European minority, the majority was non-British. Of subsequent

111

members, the Irish Free State, with the six plantation counties of
Ulster excluded from it, lacked any substantial British settler
element, though for historical reasons it also had two official
languages; while Asian, African, West Indian and Mediterranean
additions were of other races, cultures or civilisations. So it was that
Australia and New Zealand, while constituting a fundamental
element and the strongest cohesive force in the limited European
Commonwealth which existed between 1917 when the designation
Commonwealth was first used in formal conference, and 1947
when India, Pakistan and Ceylon became dominions, lacked
counterpart or potential reinforcement. In the nature of things an
expanding Commonwealth would include no more such British
member states. The conditions for that did not and would never
exist despite imperialist illusions entertained from time to time
about close British settlement in climatically congenial areas in
Africa and also (James Bryce would have added) because of missed
opportunities of British sovereignty and settlement in southern
South America.[2]

The distinctive Australian–New Zealand contribution to the
Commonwealth is accordingly to be traced to the fact that they
were projections of England (or more precisely of Britain) overseas; they were, in the phraseology of Dilke exactly applied, parts of
Greater Britain. In Melbourne Froude found

> the Victorians and Victorian society . . . it was English life over
> again . . . All was the same – dress, manners, talk, appear-
> ance . . . I could not help asking myself what, after all, is the
> meaning of uniting the colonies more closely to ourselves. They
> are closely united; they are ourselves; and can separate only in
> the sense that parents and children separate, or brothers and
> sisters . . .[3]

If ever there was to be a *British* Commonwealth in the strict sense of
the term it would have consisted of Great Britain, Australia and
New Zealand. And it is further questionable if without the
existence of these two Pacific dominions there would ever have
been the diluted British Commonwealth of history.

The unique position of the Pacific colonies that became dominions largely predetermined their rôle in Commonwealth history. In difficult and vexing questions of racial and cultural
policies, Australia had nothing and New Zealand – despite the
unusually good relationship established between European majority and Maori minority – only a limited amount to offer by way of

experience that was fruitful in other and more complex Commonwealth contexts. Nor did either dominion, by reason of the origin
of the great majority of its population, possess that inner sensitivity
to the problems implicit in the reconciliation of indigenous,
national aspirations with Commonwealth membership; problems
with which Canada, South Africa and – with particular intensity –
the Irish Free State were so much preoccupied in an earlier and
India in a later phase of Commonwealth history. So it was that
Australia and New Zealand stood, paradoxically, at the very heart
of and at the same time somewhat apart from the main stream of
Commonwealth development, consciously British in their reaction
to non-British nationalist movements and notably conservative in
their response to those Commonwealth developments in the
inter-war years which are now seen to have been a condition of its
post-second world war expansion. But (and partly by reason of the
very fact that they were little troubled by problems of national or
cultural diversity) Australia and New Zealand were unusually well
placed to make contributions in different fields, most notably in
defence and security. For their peoples, whatever their differences
on lesser matters with Britain, there remained – at least until the
middle years of the twentieth century – one King, one Cause, one
Flag. The common origin of the great majority also made it easier
for them to enrich Commonwealth experience in other important
respects. The colonists, 'despite their pretensions to being *enfants
terribles*', had a respect for the traditional forms of English colonial
government but, so M. André Siegfried noted,[4] they advanced
beneath them to patterns of political or social democracy more
egalitarian in spirit and for the most part in practice than were to be
found elsewhere in the Empire. In New Zealand, 'the chosen land
of the most daring experiments', this was most in evidence in
matters of social policy, where the New Zealanders (so Siegfried
also observed early in the century), uninterested in the theory of
socialism 'have without doubt pushed the application of it further
than any other people'.[5] In Australia, more radical than New
Zealand in the temper of its citizens but less progressive in its social
legislation (partly because of the restrictive influence after 1901 of
its federal constitution) it was chiefly in the allied fields of law and
government that new precedents were established and radical,
popular practices applied.

From the time of its discovery by Captain Cook in 1770 and the
arrival of Governor Phillip in Botany Bay eighteen years later, one
problem had loomed large in Australian history – settlement. Who
was to populate the newly found continent – unexplored, un-

known, untenanted except for black aborigines who were few in number and backward in their customs, a continent without trace of earlier civilisation or previous migration, seeming to one visitor to bear not the slightest resemblance to the outside world: It was 'so primitive, so lacking in greenness, so silent, so old', with an 'appearance of exhaustion and weariness in the land itself . . .'[6] Was Britain alone to people this continent in the southern seas? The answer was in the affirmative. At one time that most notable of the pioneers of planned British settlement, Edward Gibbon Wakefield, contemplated emigration from 'those numerous overpopulated countries' by which the colonies 'are, as it were, surrounded', from the islands of the Pacific to the mainland of Asia and including 'the poorest class of Hindoos' and the Chinese 'by far the most industrious and skilful of Asiatics'.[7] But to that and all other such suggestions the response of the colonists was emphatic and consistent. Australia was to be kept white. The first Act passed by the Parliament of the Commonwealth of Australia in 1901 was to reaffirm on the new federal basis the sanctity of that white Australian policy. In so far, therefore, as the continent is popu-lated, it has been more than ninety per cent peopled by immigrants from the British Isles. This is to be attributed in some measure to planning on the British side but chiefly to the power of attraction of economic and social opportunity in temperate climatic conditions in new countries under the British flag – though in respect of the last it is worth recalling, without endorsing, Dilke's opinion that 'under separation we should, perhaps, find the colonies better emigration-fields for our surplus population than they are at present. Many of our emigrants who flock to the United States are attracted by the idea that they are going to become citizens of a new nation instead of dependents upon an old one.' With the separation of Australia from England a portion of these 'sentimentalists', he thought, might be diverted to that continent.[8]

The first British settlers were in no position to decide their own destination. They were some seven hundred convicts brought out by Governor Phillip in 1788 as the result of a government decision that Australia should take the place of the independent American colonies as a convict settlement to which criminals might be transported. This continuation in another continent of the policy of penal colonisation did not pass unchallenged. The philosophical Radicals, with Jeremy Bentham as their spokesman, condemned it as vicious. But it lasted well into the nineteenth century. The number of transported convicts, reckoned to be just under two thousand in 1825, rose fairly consistently thereafter to over four thousand in 1833. Against this the number of free immigrants was only a matter of hundreds until the late 1820s when the total rose to some two thousand a year.[9] Radical opinion strongly pressed for organised migration of free settlers to Australia on a scale sufficient to outnumber the convicts and submerge the character of the earlier settlement.[10] From Newgate prison Wakefield produced his blue-print,[11] his chief concern being to ensure orderly and balanced settlement. Colonial development, he thought, depended upon the maintenance of a right relation between capital and labour, since the one was dependent upon the other. In order to ensure such a balance he recommended first that unoccupied land in the colonies should be sold and the funds thus obtained be used to finance immigration on the scale required and second that the sale of waste land should be controlled in such a way as to ensure a reasonable balance between people and territory. 'As a wise man eats just as much as will keep him in the best health, but no more: so a wise government would grant just enough land to enable the people to exert their utmost capacity for doubling themselves, but no more.'[12] He urged that the government should fix a price for waste land high enough to ensure that land already occupied should be reasonably exploited and valued before new land was settled. The application of this vicinity-maximising or dispersion-preventing principle would, so Wakefield thought, bring about that degree of concentration in settlement at which he aimed. It was also (if incidentally) a principle favouring middle-class rather than working-class occupation of new land since capital was a condition of the acquisition of it.

Earlier experience was not encouraging in respect of planned emigration; attempts to organise it after the Napoleonic wars had been unusually disappointing in their results. Thus in 1823, at a time when the government was actively engaged in promoting emigration overseas, fifteen thousand British people went to British territories under government-sponsored schemes, while unorganised private emigration accounted for some sixteen thousand. None the less, the settlement of South Australia, founded in 1834, between the established colonies of New South Wales and Van Diemen's Land, provided after some vicissitudes substantial practical vindication for Wakefield's ideas. Nor was it his only contribution to British settlement in the Pacific. With Molesworth, Wakefield was also responsible in 1839 for the formation of the New Zealand Company, the initial enterprise of which was claimed (though questionably) to have been decisive in stirring a hesitating and uncertain government to forestall the

116   *Foundation Members and Nature of their Association*

French and to proclaim the islands a British colony a year later.[13]
By the later 1830s total British emigration to Australasia had
climbed to some fifteen thousand a year with a temporary peak of
nearly thirty-three thousand in 1841.[14] If not assured, their British
future was at least beginning to take shape.

In New Zealand the impression of Wakefield upon the pattern of
colonisation was even more pronounced than in South Australia.
He had deplored the fact that these Pacific territories should have
been so long regarded 'as fit only for the residence of convicts,
labourers, mechanics and desperate or needy men'. The Greek
colonies, he emphasised, contained a mixture of all classes of
society; he claimed that it was for that reason that they had risen to
wealth and eminence much earlier than they would otherwise have
done and their example ought therefore to be followed. In
accordance with such preconceptions, a cross-section of British
Victorian society lacking only in its extremes of wealth and poverty
was transplanted to New Zealand. Settlement there – solid,
bourgeois and respectable[15] – faithfully reflected the aspirations of
its promoters. The purposes behind the planning were given
succinct expression in one sentence of a report of the directors of
the New Zealand Company, 1847, which read:

> The aim of this company is not confined to mere emigration
> but is . . . to transplant English society with its various gradations
> in due proportions, carrying out our laws, customs, associations,
> habits, manners, feeling – everything of England, in short, but
> the soil.[16]

One consequence implicit in this composition of New Zealand
society was the strongest possible attachment on the part of the
settlers to their mother country. Another was a measure of cultural
and intellectual dependence upon Britain, which proved a source
of recurrent frustration to New Zealand's intelligentsia in later
times.

The accidents of history and of geology contributed much in the
case of New Zealand and more in the case of Australia to
determining the character and pace of settlement. In both instances, until the mid-twentieth century, up to 97 per cent of these
settlements remained British. That was the fundamental factor.
But there were others, one of which has already been noted.

> Australia had a bad start [wrote the Liberal, F. W. Eggleston]. It
> started as a gaol, and those who started it appeared to plan it for

that purpose and for nothing else. Though I do not think that this 'birth-mark' left any criminal taint in the community, the deficiencies of the original plan caused extraordinary difficulties which lasted for generations.

Professor Shaw agreed that socially the convict settlements did Australia no great harm while economically they greatly helped Australian development. Transportation had provided a labour force which, if less efficient than free workers, was far better than no workers at all.[17] Then in the middle years of the century the exodus from Ireland after the famine brought many, mostly embittered, emigrants to Australia to reinforce the settlers both convict and free and to swell the existing Irish population, estimated in 1837 (if Catholics and Irish be near equated) at close on twenty-two thousand. A Young Irelander of the 1840s, Charles Gavan Duffy, became prime minister of Victoria and was knighted. Succeeding generations had a spokesman in Archbishop Mannix, who expressed in public utterances over a long period of years as well as in private practices – he posted his letters with stamps bearing the monarch's head upside-down – something of the transplanted, transmuted, but by no means wholly extinguished nationalism of his country of origin. More important in terms of settlement however were the motley crowd of hardy adventurers brought to the continent by news of discoveries of gold, first in the Bathurst district and elsewhere in New South Wales and subsequently in Victoria, Queensland, Western Australia and the South Island of New Zealand.

The excitement of the first discoveries of mineral wealth in Australia was as intense as it was later to be at Kimberley or on the Rand. Some of them were made by chance, others by intuitive reasoning. Notable among the latter, and giving in fullest measure the dramatic quality which in some degree belonged to them all, was Hargraves's strike in the Bathurst district. Hargraves, an Australian who migrated to California, disclaimed all pretensions to scientific knowledge. But he became convinced, by comparing in his own mind what he saw before him in California with what he had seen in Australia eighteen years earlier, that there was gold in Australia. In the light of that conviction he returned to Sydney and journeyed on horseback to the remembered site. Memory had served him well and the resemblance of the formation was beyond doubt. He dug a panful of earth, and sure enough there was gold in it. In his excitement he exclaimed to his guide, 'This is a memorable day in the history of New South Wales. I shall be a baronet, you will be knighted, and my old horse will be stuffed, put into a glass-case, and sent to the British Museum.'[18] The first alone was true; and it was enough. In succeeding years there were to be even more memorable days in the history of Victoria.

It is quite impossible for me [wrote Lieutenant-Governor Latrobe to Earl Grey at the Colonial Office][19] to describe to your lordship the effect which these discoveries have had upon the whole community, and the influence which their consequences exercise at this time upon the position and prospects of everyone, high and low. The discoveries early in the year in the Bathurst district of New South Wales unsettled the public mind of the labouring classes of all the Australian colonies ... The discoveries within our bounds [Victorian] ... exercise a far wider influence upon our excitable population ... Within the last three weeks the towns of Melbourne and Geelong and their large suburbs have been in appearance almost emptied of many classes of their male inhabitants ... cottages are deserted, houses to let, business is at a stand-still and even schools are closed. In some of the suburbs not a man is left ...

From other countries and all continents men came to Australia to join in the search for gold. The pattern of its society, its thinking, the pace of economic development – all were profoundly affected. Nor was New Zealand left out. While no such rich or widely publicised discoveries were made there, gold was found in Otago in 1861, turning Dunedin almost overnight from a quiet country town into a rough and – for the older inhabitants – frightening mining centre. But it also brought new population to stimulate economic development and to confirm European numerical preponderance over the Maoris.[20]

The fever of the gold rushes passed but the social and economic consequences of them remained. As it became apparent that as much – possibly more – money might be made out of gold miners than out of gold mines, the camps of pioneering days gave way to mining settlements, with their stores, services and sense of community and these, in turn, to townships. The wealth of the gold fields percolated through the townships to the cities and served as a magnet drawing new population from across the seas. The 'image' – if the terminology of mid-twentieth century political scientists may be retrospectively applied to the Pacific colonies of the mid-nineteenth – of young, adventurous, even if improvident communities where hand-in-hand went hardship and opportunity, destitution and riches spectacularly won, an image which owed so much at the outset to the drama of the gold rushes, continued thereafter to draw to the far south young men who felt the flavour of life in England was long since spent.

The overriding importance of increasing population, despite the accretions from the gold rushes, continued to be a constant preoccupation of the British settlements in the Pacific, throughout the colonial and the succeeding dominion phase in their history. In the later Victorian age there were confident prognostications from Seeley, Dilke and others about the expansion of the British people overseas until the population of Greater Britain would equal or surpass that of the mother country herself. There were sanguine forecasts in Australia also but there prognostication however confident was more apt to be balanced by a present sense of realities. And not the least significant among those realities was the existing pattern of widely scattered seaboard settlements round the coast of a continent, and of a tremendous hinterland which except for isolated mining or other centres remained largely uninhabited and partly unexplored. 'Don't let us be mistaken,' warned Sir Henry Parkes in 1890 in presenting his arguments for the federation of Australia, ' . . . population is the one great basis for the growth of nations either here or anywhere else . . .'[21] And in relation to size and resources adequate population in Australia was woefully lacking.

Questions of population also occupied the minds of settlers in New Zealand though not for quite the same reasons. Australia was a continent; New Zealand an island, or rather islands – even if in Auckland and Wellington men preferred to speak of the mainland with an island to the south. But while the islands were thinly populated in relation to resources there was not so much a problem of empty spaces to be filled as a concern on the part of the settlers that a native population (one, moreover, among the most advanced and adaptable of all the indigenous peoples in the Empire) should be matched and ultimately outdistanced in numbers. New Zealand, like South Africa but unlike Australia, had a native question. If it was, by comparison with that of southern Africa, modest in its dimensions, this by no means necessarily implied it was susceptible of an easy, straightforward solution. In New Zealand there also loomed large familiar questions of land and franchise policies in which Colonial Office views of an 'imperial standard' by no means always coincided with settler interests or settler opinion.

Neither the Australian nor the New Zealand colonists were the pioneers in the advance from representative to responsible colonial government. That trail was blazed in North America. But, conditioned by not dissimilar circumstances in terms of environment and political heritage, it is not surprising that they were stirred by emotions and aspirations similar to those entertained by their Canadian contemporaries. In 1852 Lord Salisbury heard a din of indignation against Downing Street from 'bishop to pot-boy', from the Cape to New Zealand. Each colony had its own individual causes of complaint but there were also the common sources of friction which Lord Durham had diagnosed, chief among them being the alienation of an executive, appointed by a governor, from a representative assembly to which it was not responsible. Where there was no indigenous people with rights or interests to be safeguarded and where there was a sufficient settler population to sustain the responsibilities of self-government, there were also thought to be no continuing imperial interests or considerations of policy sufficient to warrant withholding the concession of self-government or incurring the odium which would almost inevitably result from so doing. Individual doubts or reservations certainly remained, but generally speaking British statesmen, in the words of Professor Ward, had come to treat 'responsible government as a normal institution of British politics, to which colonies with large British populations, political maturity and stability were entitled'.[22] Accordingly government on the Canadian model was granted to the Australian colonies from the middle years of the century onwards as they became sufficiently populated to sustain it. It was also granted to New Zealand, but there – because of the existence of a substantial indigenous population with interests to be safeguarded – it could not be conceded without reservations. It was with reluctance that the British government had decided to annex New Zealand in 1839 and a determining factor had been concern to protect the rights of the Maoris from settlers who had come hitherto chiefly from Australia but whose numbers were about to be increased by migration organised by the New Zealand Company. A policy of protection implied limitation in respect of powers of settler self-government.

In 1846 representative institutions were conceded to New Zealand on the basis not only of a General Assembly with an elected House but also of provincial councils, each with an elected House of Representatives. The governor, Sir George Grey, felt misgivings at the prospect of control by some twelve thousand colonists over 'the well-armed, proud and independent' Maoris,[23] especially in the provincial assemblies, and as a result the constitution was not brought into force. In 1852, however, pressure by the new

Canterbury settlers led by an Anglo–Irishman, John Robert Godley – who protested that he would rather be governed 'by a Nero on the spot than by a board of angels in London' on the ground that if the worst came to the worst Nero's head could be cut off whereas the board would remain beyond reach – hastened the enactment of a New Zealand Constitution Act. The Act established a General Assembly, consisting of two Houses, together with six provincial councils (which survived until 1876) for dealing with provincial affairs. This was government on a grand scale! But in respect of representation a key question remained. Who was to be entitled to vote? The Maoris at that time still outnumbered the settlers. They had been guaranteed 'all the rights and privileges of British subjects' in the 1840 Treaty of Waitangi. Was exclusion from the vote consistent with such assurances? In one sense the question was at that time theoretical rather than practical. The majority of the Maoris, living on their own land, apart from the new settlers, were not yet adapted to European political practices. But the issue of principle remained. It was met by a franchise based on a low property qualification, with the Maoris disfranchised in practice by reason of their system of land tenure. Their system was communal and individual Maoris consequently failed to qualify for the vote. But the question could not rest there.

When the first New Zealand Parliament met on 24 May 1854 (Queen Victoria's birthday) in Auckland, the first capital – some of the Otago members had taken two months to travel there – members declined to conduct business until a ministry responsible to Parliament was appointed.[24] The principal ulterior purpose behind this demand was to establish settler control over the disposal of Crown Lands. Parliament was first prorogued and then dissolved, a further election taking place in 1855; it having by this time become apparent that there was no reasonable alternative, a responsible ministry was appointed the following year. But the extent of its responsibility in one all-important particular remained in dispute. The governor, Colonel Thomas Gore Browne (who succeeded Grey in the same year), had pronounced views on the responsibilities of his office and without the specific authority in his own or his predecessors' Instructions, took steps to reserve control of native affairs to the Crown, which meant in practice largely to the governor. He did so in the belief that 'the interests of the two races were antagonistic', and that such a division of responsibility was a matter of principle because it would be wrong in such circumstances to subject one race to the other.[25] In practice this diarchical arrangement proved unworkable. The settlers were

intent upon securing free sale of land, which meant individualis-
ation of land-holding in the Maori communal areas. Despite the
opposition of the governor and of the imperial government they
managed to force the issue. They also underestimated the Maoris
and wars followed. The Maoris were defeated but the settlers
learned by painful experience the merits of compromise.

In respect of representation, the long-term outcome of the
Maori wars was the special allocation of four seats to the Maoris on a
basis of adult suffrage, with a view to the ultimate standardisation
and merging of electorates. Like so many devices intended to serve
a temporary purpose, this special representation for Maoris has
continued down to the present day. If anomalous in principle, it
has proved workable in practice. It has meant in turn over-
representation and under-representation in relation to Maori
population though not, in the second case, in relation to Maori
registered voters.[26] From the time of the first European settlement
until 1900 the Maori population steadily declined but since then it
has risen consistently and in recent years at a rate faster than the
European. While it would be over-sanguine, especially in view of
increasing Maori urbanisation, to think of the problems of race
relations in New Zealand as belonging only to the past, none the less
through a chequered history and a reliance upon pragmatic
solutions in social as well as political life, a spirit of inter-racial
community has developed which is generally in accord with the
later professed principles of the Commonwealth.

There are two further aspects of New Zealand development
which have a place in the context of Commonwealth history. The
first is of Australasian, the second of more widespread interest.
From the early years of settlement Australian and New Zealand
colonists thought in terms of exclusive British predominance in the
Pacific. England, commented André Siegfried, 'remains in the eyes
of Australasians the pre-eminent nation, the chosen worker of any
civilising mission. The colonials, an integral part of the superior
race, work by its side.' A sure instinct had warned them from the
very first that it was necessary for them to remain as far as possible,
'alone and without troublesome neighbours in the South Pacific'. In
this way the programme 'Australasia for the Australasians' developed into 'Oceania for the Anglo–Saxons'.[27] M. Siegfried wrote
with something less than enthusiasm of the colonial jingoism that
might be called Australasian imperialism – understandably so
since the French, after all, were by no means the least of the
European powers the colonists wished to exclude. But he was right
in the importance he attached to it. The Colonial Office also had

good reason to feel its force and good cause to seek to restrain its impetuosities.

In the last three decades of the nineteenth century New Zealand's imperial, or imperialist, aspirations in the Pacific received their strongest expression and have had, in Professor Angus Ross, their historian. Even before New Zealand became a British colony, the New Zealand Company had thought of New Zealand as 'the Britain of the south' with an imperial destiny of its own. With steady consistency of purpose, successive New Zealand prime ministers sought first to secure the annexation and government of the Pacific Islands or, failing that, to ensure that control over them did not pass into the hands of foreign imperial powers. On 17 October 1873 Sir Julius Vogel, the prime minister of New Zealand, prepared a memorandum for the Colonial Office which conveys in graphic phrases something of the outlook of New Zealanders and the purposes which they had in mind. The memorandum urged that 'a policy or line of conduct should be decided on, not alone in connection with one or two clusters of islands, but applicable to all Polynesia', with a view to Britain taking up 'the work of reducing to civilisation the fertile islands of the Pacific'. New Zealand would gladly cooperate in the task:

> Ministers venture to urge that Great Britain . . . may with justice be proud of having reproduced herself in the 'Great Britain of the south' as New Zealand has aptly been called . . . but there is a lesson which New Zealand teaches, and that is that local efforts to maintain peaceful relations with an uncivilised race are far more successful than those directed by a distant power. It may be worth consideration whether, if Polynesia is not to be abandoned to foreign nations, it would not be well to entrust to New Zealand, which possesses so much experience in dealing with the government of a mixed race, the task of aiding in extending the British sway to the islands of the Pacific . . . the Parliament of New Zealand would cordially entertain proposals which had for their object to give to the colony the opportunity of assisting Great Britain in the great national work of extending the British dominion throughout the unappropriated islands of the South Pacific.[28]

The British government, however, was unreceptive. They had other interests and other priorities, chief among them being relations with the European powers. In the critical years between 1880 and 1886 Gladstone was much more concerned to reach some tolerable understanding with Germany on colonial questions than to satisfy the New Zealand ambitions – strongly backed though these were throughout the period by the Australian colonies. Vogel was written off in the Colonial Office as 'an imperial busybody', while Germany and France by agreement extended their colonial empires to the Pacific. In practice as well as in theory foreign policy remained in the last resort the preserve of the imperial power. New Zealanders and Australians might lament lost opportunities of Anglo–Saxon hegemony in the Pacific but having failed to persuade London to act in accordance with their aspirations they were without remedy – except for the no doubt wry satisfaction, afforded in 1919 to the prime minister of New Zealand, Mr Massey, of telling the House of Representatives in Wellington how right New Zealand leaders had been in urging that Samoa should have been annexed either by Britain or New Zealand and not allowed to pass into German hands.[29]

Of more lasting consequence than her imperial aspirations were New Zealand's social reforms. The Liberal Party, dominant in New Zealand politics in the late nineteenth and early twentieth century, had affinities with the new Birmingham School, inasmuch as the chief trends in its thinking were imperial development and expansion on the one hand and domestic social reform on the other. Manhood suffrage on a property or residential qualification, introduced in 1889, was followed in 1893 by votes for women, conceded for the first time in British history. This in its turn was followed, during the Liberal Party's long tenure of office (which lasted from 1891 to 1912), by pioneering legislation in education which created a national system of primary schooling, free, compulsory and secular for all children under thirteen. In 1894 was enacted legislation on industrial conciliation and arbitration, described as being at once the most novel of the labour measures and one of the most decisive in moulding New Zealand society.[30] Between 1896 and 1901 there was introduced a whole code of labour legislation, including the regulation of working hours, factory inspection and non-contributory pensions.

To what causes are these pioneering social reforms to be attributed? Chief among them would seem to have been the patterns and ethics of New Zealand society. Unlike Australia, New Zealand was populated – save only at the extremes of wealth and poverty – by 'a virtual slice' of nineteenth-century English society, by people who had gone out 'not in despair but in hope'.[31] The government was in a particular sense the government chosen by and representative of the people. It was too close and familiar to inspire the mistrust that comes with remoteness and there were accordingly few psychological reservations on the part of the people about the extension of its powers – on the contrary, it was felt to be the duty of the state to promote the happiness of the people and to better their lot. The most effective way in which it could do so was by social legislation; government was considered to 'be benign'.[32] There was no deep cleavage of view about the theoretical limits of its responsibilities; there was rather a constant clamour for state action. The New Zealanders were not a race of theoreticians; their approach to such matters was direct and practical. They thought in terms of their own welfare and, in more exalted moments, of a mission to humanity and of their destiny 'to show the old world the paths of social progress'. 'A people can advertise itself, just as a merchant or a manufacturer can,' noted M. Siegfried. And he added that the New Zealanders, well aware of this fact, had not chosen the worst means 'for, since the passing of such measures as those for compulsory arbitration and woman suffrage, everybody has heard of the little antipodean colony of whose very existence people were once scarcely aware.'

There were men, two in particular, as well as measures to be remembered in New Zealand's reformist years. The first was Richard Seddon, 'King Dick', prime minister from 1893 to 1906. With his 'burly frame and a chest like Vulcan's', his 'cheery laugh' and his 'crushing hand-grip' (as James Bryce found it) went an approach correspondingly robust and practical. Of humble origins, his friends said he never read a socialist book, his enemies that he never read a book. This however was not true. In the House of Representatives he relied on Erskine May's *Parliamentary Procedure* and he was also once observed by a colleague reading a history of pirates in the Spanish Main. While James Bryce thought him wanting in learning and eloquence he acknowledged that he had force and drive. It was well observed of him, commented Bryce, that he 'never could estimate the precise value of comparatives and superlatives and seemed to the last to imagine that strong language was the only language befitting a strong man'. Yet Bryce also remarked upon his adroitness as a parliamentary leader and his closeness to the people. 'His audiences, especially in the provinces,' noted Pember Reeves, of Seddon's semi-regal progresses through his dominions, 'welcomed both the visits and the oratory. They liked to hear their own views, feelings and wishes . . . given back to them in language not too far removed from their own. They liked the comforting official statistics, the patriotic platitudes, the inevitable reference to "God's own country" . . .'[33]

William Pember Reeves, minister of education, justice and labour 1891 to 1896 (when he went to London as New Zealand's Agent-General), and Seddon's principal lieutenant, provided a counterpart. Reeves, well remembered as the author of *The Long White Cloud*, a most readable general history of New Zealand, supplied the intellectual force behind its social legislation in this great period of reform. Siegfried described Reeves's socialism as experimental and practical, noted his rooted distrust of financiers and capitalists and admired him as one possessing a power of logical analysis peculiarly associated with Frenchmen.[34] Not altogether surprisingly perhaps Reeves ended his days far from New Zealand, becoming closely associated with the Fabian Society and third director of the London School of Economics and Political Science.[35] Yet the reforms he had helped to shape remained and they fixed upon New Zealand the image of an egalitarian society desiring to become still more egalitarian and one which in so doing gave Empire and Commonwealth a pattern of social legislation from which all – including Britain herself – could learn; and which many, including countries in South Asia in later years, sought at least in part to adapt to their own, and often very different, circumstances.

The development of a distinct political identity in New Zealand has about it a certain air of paradox. It might be supposed that New Zealand's dreams of Anglo–Saxon hegemony in the Pacific, combined with the common British origins of New Zealand and Australian settlers, would bring British colonists throughout the Pacific into one political community. But on the shorter term at any rate it was not to be. New Zealand cherished the idea of Empire, but for New Zealanders Empire meant most of all close and continuing association not with neighbouring Australian colonies but with the mother country. Many New Zealanders became ardent advocates of imperial federation. But it was federation on that larger and not on a limited Pacific scale to which they aspired. For them it was an all-embracing imperial system or nothing.

The case for Australasian federation, buttressed as it was by not unimpressive arguments of political, economic and even strategic advantage, did not go by default. On the contrary it was considered and deliberately rejected by New Zealanders. The arguments against it were conveniently summarised by Captain W. R. Russell, a New Zealand delegate at the Australasian Federation Conference in Melbourne in 1890. He argued first that New Zealanders living under different climatic conditions, colonised in an entirely different manner, having had 'a very much rougher time than the colonies of Australia', were likely to develop a very complete individuality – a distinct national type. They had no wish to be submerged in a greater Australasia where their population of seven hundred thousand would be heavily outnumbered. Nor was he much impressed by the strategic argument. A federal army might involve New Zealanders in expenses they were not prepared to meet while its value in the event of a sudden assault upon the islands was questionable: the issue might well be decided before news of the attack ever reached Australia. There were also likely to be differences of interest and of opinion on trading policy. Would New Zealand be wise, would she be prepared, to join irrevocably in a customs union which might bring about more protection than already existed? There was also the question of native administration. The New Zealand delegate argued that it was bound to be one of the most important questions in New Zealand politics for many years to come. Were responsibility for that question to be handed over to a federal Parliament – 'to an elective body, mostly Australians, that cares nothing and knows nothing about native administration, and the members of which have dealt with native races in a much more summary manner than we have ventured to deal with ours in New Zealand' – it might well provoke renewed and disastrous conflict between settlers and Maoris in the islands.[36]

The outcome of the debate was that New Zealand was left free to join in the contemplated federation, but in fact it did not opt to do so. Nor would Sir Charles Dilke have been surprised. Englishmen, he learned on his Pacific travels, were 'given over to a singular delusion as to the connection of New Zealand and Australia'. They were apt to think the comprehensive designation Australasia appropriate and meaningful. But Dilke was made aware only of the separateness and the indifference of the one to the other.

> The only reference to New Zealand [he recalled] except in the foreign news that I ever found in an Australian paper, was a congratulatory paragraph on the great amount of the New Zealand debt; the only allusion to Australia that I detected in the Wellington *Independent* was in a glance at the future of the colony, in which the editor predicted the advent of a time when New Zealand would be a naval nation and her fleet engaged in bombarding Melbourne or levying contributions upon Sidney.[37]

While federation did not come to New Zealand at all, it came only after long delay and protracted discussion to the Australian colonies. For this a number of explanations have been offered. The main centres of population were geographically widely dispersed along the seaboard, the settlers themselves were of varying social backgrounds, most of them had become accustomed to domestic self-government over a comparatively long period of time – in New South Wales and Tasmania since 1855, in South Australia since 1856, in Victoria and Queensland since 1859 – and they were apt to feel that what had been so comparatively long enjoyed should not be lightly abandoned. Vested interests had been entrenched with the passage of time and there were fears, as in the case of New Zealand, on the part of the less densely populated states, that their interests should be subordinated or even altogether overlooked in a federation inevitably dominated by New South Wales and Victoria. For all these reasons, debates about the possibility of federation, which was pursued intermittently from the middle of the century and of which Dilke heard much in the 1880s, were apt to concentrate upon its negative implications in respect of the status and authority of the individual colonies. Mr (later Sir Edmund) Barton, a delegate from New South Wales to the Federal Convention at Adelaide in 1897, even then felt obliged to remind his audience that the purpose of federation was not to diminish but

> to enlarge the powers of self-government of the people of Australia ... That is a proposition which, from the many discussions that have taken place in public in various parts of the colonies, appears to have been lost sight of. The idea of surrender seems to have occupied a large place in the minds of the people. Federation really adds to the powers of self-government, a fact which seems to have been put aside and left out of consideration.[38]

While explanation is required as to why progress towards federation was so slow – given in particular the homogeneity of the colonial populations – it is also necessary to consider why in the last decade of the century the idea of 'a nation for a continent and a continent for a nation' suddenly gathered momentum. The most evident environmental change had come with the intrusion of European powers other than Britain into the Pacific in the 1880s. It was a change much resented by the colonists but one in which Britain acquiesced, as evidenced most notably in the case of New Guinea (where unauthorised annexation by the Queensland government was repudiated by the colonial secretary in order to allow of a mature consideration which in turn – and incidentally – gave Germany time to organise an expedition and in 1884 to proclaim

north-eastern New Guinea a German colony). With the arrival of
newer European imperialisms, dreams of undisputed Anglo–
Saxon hegemony in the south-west Pacific dissolved. The Australian colonies, hitherto free from all experience or even serious risk
of war, now had a challenge (however remote it might appear) to
their continuing security. It was time for them to consolidate their
strength and resources.

Sir Henry Parkes, who had championed the cause of federation
over many years, deployed arguments of this kind forcefully at the
Australian Conference in Melbourne in 1890. He said that he had
no doubt whatever in his mind that if there had been a central
government in Australia in 1883 New Guinea would have been
annexed to Australia. This was almost certainly untrue. Alfred
Deakin, as prime minister of the Commonwealth of Australia, was
unable (much to his annoyance) to exercise any effective influence
over British negotiations with France in 1904–6 leading to the
Anglo–French condominium over the New Hebrides. But that did
not necessarily lessen the impact of Parkes's contention. He also
played more generally upon Australian anxieties in saying: 'Those
great armed powers of Europe which are shut in from the sea are
not only wanting more earth for their multitudes to live upon, but
are wanting the earth which fronts the ocean in any part of the
world . . .' Again, however questionable as a matter of political fact,
this was an interpretation of European expansionist aims which led
on naturally to the conclusion that Australia 'ought to be mistress of
the southern seas'.[39] Such, in Parkes's view, was indeed Australia's
destiny. But that destiny was one of the two great objects 'which can
only be properly attained, properly promoted, by a federal
government'. The other was the increase of national and individual
wealth. Parkes produced figures purporting to show that the
average private wealth per inhabitant in Australasia exceeded and
in many cases far exceeded that in Austria, Germany, France, the
United Kingdom and even the United States. 'There is not one so
wealthy as we . . .' That wealth had been used to establish systems of
education, to construct means of communication and to make 'such
progress as has excited the admiration of the best of other
countries'. Further advance and development was conditional
upon arrangements, management and regulations that a single
national authority alone could make. The grandest purpose of all,
however, was the making of a united people who would appear
before the world as one and form a federal dominion for ever part
'of one beneficent Empire'.[40] Throughout the language was
sanguine, even grandiose and to many Australians must have had a

flavour of irony in the economic crisis that followed. But in a new country these were the days for expansive reflections and while historians are apt – not unreasonably – to discount the emotional, as against strategic, economic or political factors, in this case it may be that Sir Henry Parkes was wiser than they. Oratory, noted Alfred Deakin who employed it with great effect, was not likely to make 'hard-boiled inter-colonial politicians fall weeping on each other's shoulders amid universal protestations of indissoluble federal brotherhood'. No doubt – but without the use of oratory would the federal idea have passed from its parliamentary to its successful popular phase?[41]

The final stages of the federation movement in Australia may be briefly recorded. A conference of all the colonies was held in 1883 at the instigation of Sir Henry Parkes and a Federal Council, experimental in character and advisory in function, was then established. It enjoyed, however, neither popularity nor unanimous state support since, apart from New Zealand, New South Wales from the first refused to be represented at its deliberations and South Australia later withdrew from them. There followed, among important landmarks, the Melbourne Conference on Australasian federation in 1890 and in the succeeding year a further conference at Sydney at which the draft of a Commonwealth Bill was produced. The purposes of the draft-bill were publicised through the organisation of the Federation Leagues and by 1895 it was agreed, with the approval of the several colonial governments and Parliaments, to hold a convention in Adelaide in 1897 to prepare a further and final draft Bill. The convention was duly held in March of that year; it went to work, so Joseph Chamberlain later informed the House of Commons, 'in that business-like spirit which we flatter ourselves distinguishes British proceedings throughout the world'.[42] The convention produced a draft which after submission to the respective colonial Parliaments and redrafting in the light of their suggested amendments finally emerged after further discussion in Melbourne and Sydney as the Commonwealth of Australia Bill.

Federation in Australia was not, however, to be the outcome (as it had been in Canada) of inter-governmental debate alone. It was to carry also the sanction of the people. From the outset it had been accepted among the representatives of the several colonial governments that ratification by popular referendum was a necessary precondition of the final adoption of any measure upon which they might agree. And in fact there was not one but two referenda, the proposed measure not securing on the first occasion the prescribed

minimal majority of eighty thousand in New South Wales. In the
second referendum, in which the electorates of New South Wales,
Victoria, South Australia, Queensland and Tasmania took part –
but not Western Australia which of its own choice stood apart –
there was a vote of 377,000 for the Bill and 141,500 against.
Accordingly it was submitted to Westminster not only with colonial
parliamentary but also with colonial popular sanction for legislative
enactment.

There was, it has been remarked,[43] no Damascus Road miracle
about Australia's conversion to federation and this is certainly true.
One reason was the toughness of the bargaining and the ma-
noeuvring for position among the states' representatives, so
illuminatingly and often entertainingly described in Alfred
Deakin's *The Federal Story*, and in his biographer's analysis of
Deakin's rôle, especially in Victorian politics, where he was 'the very
symbol of the federal cause'.[44] But while the advance was slow it
also carried with it an impressive air of a growing conviction on the
part of governments, parliaments and peoples alike. There was
faith that federation was the right way, the ideal course.

A federal constitution [Deakin had declaimed in 1898] is the last
and final product of political intellect and constructive ingenuity;
it represents the highest development of self-government
among peoples scattered over a large area . . . I venture to submit
that among all the federal constitutions of the world you will look
in vain for one as broad in its popular base, as liberal in its
working principles, as generous in its aim as this measure.

There were many Australians who were convinced these things
were so.

The procedures by which federalism was adopted in Australia
showed some significant contrasts with those employed in bringing
the Canadian confederation into existence. Such differences were
by no means fortuitous. The cultural homogeneity of the Australian population, coupled with its social composition, favoured a
predominantly radical approach to questions of politics which
found expression in this instance in the insistence that, unlike
Canada, there should be approval by the people for the new
federation and its constitution. It was even reflected in some
measure in the title 'Commonwealth' with its republican overtones,
as against a dominion with its imperial associations. It also
accounted at least in part for the less conservative character of the
Australian constitution in which once again reliance was placed – as

it had not been in Canada – upon the people for the final resolution of contentious issues. But there were also, of course, other influences.

Canada was the neighbour of a great and (as it seemed in the 1860s) potentially aggressive power; Australia, despite the recently established French and German colonies, remained still virtually isolated in the southern seas. Where the fathers of Canadian confederation had been deeply influenced by American experience, which had impressed them with the dangers of divided authority that derived from strongly entrenched states' rights, the Australians entertained no such misgivings, in fact were altogether otherwise predisposed; the Canadian confederation, with its bias towards the centre, being generally regarded as an example not to be followed. 'I am quite sure', remarked a South Australian delegate at the Adelaide Convention, 'that no one who has studied the question of a federal form of government will contend that the essence of federalism in the strict sense of the term is to be found in Canada.' But a federation in the strictest sense of the term was what the majority of Australians looked for because that would bring into being, not a Commonwealth with subordinate states, but a Commonwealth and states which would be equal and coordinate in their powers. Not Canada but the United States must be, as Deakin observed, their source of inspiration. The constitution of the Commonwealth of Australia accordingly gave to the federal parliament only powers over matters listed and defined in the constitution. Residual powers were left not with the centre, as in Canada, but with the states. 'I hold it', said Richard O'Connor at the convention at Adelaide in 1897, 'to be a basic principle of this federation that we should take no powers from the states which they could better exercise themselves, and that we should place no power in the federation which is not absolutely necessary for carrying out its purposes.' This was in essence the principle that was applied. And, as Joseph Chamberlain explained to the House of Commons when introducing the Commonwealth of Australia Bill on 14 May 1900, the result was that whereas in Canada the underlying purpose of the constitution was 'substantially to amalgamate the provinces into one dominion, the constitution of Australia created a federation for distinctly definite and limited objects of a number of independent states, and state rights have throughout been jealously preserved'.[45]

The constitution of the Commonwealth of Australia is embodied in the Commonwealth of Australia Act passed by the British Parliament in 1900 and having effect from 1 January 1901. The bill was drafted, amended and, as has been noted, finally approved both by governments and people in Australia before its final submission for legislative enactment in London. There was no discussion preliminary to or in the course of drafting such as had taken place between the Canadian leaders and the colonial secretary before the enactment of the British North American Act 1867. This did not however mean that Joseph Chamberlain acquiesced in the view that his rôle as colonial secretary was limited to piloting a measure agreed and approved by Australians through the House of Commons. On the contrary, he asserted that while 'the bill has been prepared without reference to us' it should none the less receive in the imperial Parliament 'the fullest consideration and even the fullest discussion'.[46] If need be Chamberlain was prepared and felt entitled to propose and urge any amendments he thought desirable on grounds of general imperial interest; and in fact in respect of appeals to the judicial committee of the Privy Council he did so, even if only with very qualified success. But he also reminded the House of the realities of the situation. There was a limit beyond which the imperial government could not prudently go.

We have got [said Chamberlain] to a point in our relations with our self-governing colonies in which I think we recognise, once for all, that these relations depend entirely upon their free will and absolute consent. The links between us and them at the present time are very slender. Almost a touch might snap them. But, slender as they are, and slight as they are, although we wish, although I hope, that they will become stronger, still if they are felt irksome by any one of our great colonies, we shall not attempt to force them to wear them.[47]

It was a significant and statesmanlike admission. It meant that by the turn of the century the British government recognised, even in respect of matters of admitted imperial importance such as appeals to the judicial committee of the Privy Council, that it could and should proceed to secure what it deemed to be imperial interests only by discussion and through exchanges of view.

The preamble to the Commonwealth of Australia Constitution Act[48] recorded that the people of New South Wales, Victoria, South Australia, Queensland and Tasmania had 'agreed to unite in one indissoluble Federal Commonwealth under the Crown of the United Kingdom of Great Britain and Ireland' and under the constitution established by the Act. The first eight Articles of the Act dealt with matters of formal importance – the citation of the Act, the succession to the Throne, the binding character of Acts made by the Parliament of the Commonwealth, the meaning of the term 'Commonwealth' and of the term 'the States' and the admission of Western Australia as an original state on the result of a referendum held before the Act came into force. The constitution of the Commonwealth of Australia was set out in section 9. While the Act itself could be amended only by the imperial Parliament, the constitution as embodied in section 9 prescribed the means whereby it might itself be amended by the Australian Parliament and people. This distinction between constitution and the Act in which it was embodied, together with the provisions for the indigenous amendment of the constitution, represented a notable departure from Canadian precedent. It had, moreover, its counterpart in a corresponding difference in respect of judicial interpretation. Under the British North America Act, it will be recalled, final judicial interpretation of the Act was vested in the judicial committee of the Privy Council. The Australians, however, desired the interpretation of their constitution to be vested in the Australian high court. To this there were objections from the imperial government which gave rise to protracted argument. Chamberlain was insistent upon the importance of preserving intact the ultimate authority of the judicial committee of the Privy Council, the Australians little disposed to make the concession this would have required of them. A compromise was proposed which was much to the satisfaction of the Australian delegates in London, the chief among them being Deakin, who told Dilke when its terms were first communicated to him: 'This is all we want and if we get this we shall secure a great victory.'[49] The compromise which was suggested and adopted did not exclude appeals to the judicial committee in principle but vested ultimate authority, in respect of the allowance of them, in the high court of Australia. Section 74 of the constitution, as finally agreed and embodying the compromise laid it down that:

> no appeal shall be permitted to the Queen in Council from a decision of the high court upon any question, howsoever arising, as to the limits *inter se* of the constitutional powers of the Commonwealth and those of any state or states, or as to the limits *inter se* of the constitutional powers of any two or more states, unless the high court shall certify that the question is one which ought to be determined by Her Majesty in Council.

The high court has in fact used the power of decision conferred upon it by section 74, as the Australians intended and Chamberlain feared. A certificate giving leave to appeal to the judicial committee has been granted in one case only and legislation has been passed by the Commonwealth Parliament to ensure that appeals from the supreme courts of the states in respect of *inter se* questions should lie to the high court only.[50] These were matters of more than strictly legal significance. They reflected something of the outlook of the architects of Australian federation. They cherished Empire as much as Chamberlain but their notions of Empire did not coincide with his. Already they were thinking in terms of equality under the Crown. Australians, remarked Deakin, would be proud to fight and if need be to die for Queen and Country, but he had never heard of anyone prepared to die for the judicial committee of the Privy Council. Chamberlain's notions of its significance as a link of Empire he discounted as high-flown and exaggerated. More positively the Australians were clear that they wished federal-state relations to be interpreted by an indigenous court familiar with Australian law and practice. While therefore the right of the judical committee to hear appeals from the Australian high court was preserved in principle, the interpretation of Commonwealth-states rights was effectively vested in practice in the high court which alone could grant leave to appeal to the judicial committee. This was a case in which Australians were able to profit from Canadian experience by not following Canadian example.

There were other interesting and in some cases ingenious innovations in the Australian constitution. As in Canada, Parliament consisted of a governor-general as representative of the Crown and two Houses, a Senate and a House of Representatives. But while forms coincided, neither attitudes nor composition nor the balance of power were by any means identical. In respect of actual status, the designation of governor-general was somewhat misleading, there being no official hierarchical relationship between him and the governors of the several states. On the contrary, the governors continue to be appointed by the Crown and to serve as symbols of the separate and coequal identity of the states with the Commonwealth, precedence however being yielded to the governor-general at dignified functions.[51] More important, there was a pronounced coolness on the part of Australians towards the office of governor-general. To Alfred Deakin the title appeared 'to be little better than a glittering and gaudy toy', while to John Cockburn, another Founding Father, the governor-general's highest function was 'to be a dummy'.[52] Not only was Australian language about the office altogether less respectful than Canadian but there was also a corresponding Australian desire to limit in practice the discretionary authority of the holder. Professor Crisp commented in 1955 that the history of the governor-generalship in the first fifty-four years of the Australian federation was a history 'of gradual but constant encroachment upon the initially very restricted personal initiative and discretion of its incumbents'. And he added that in becoming 'ever more innocuous and politically unobtrusive' the governor-generalship had provided 'an ever more satisfactory keystone to the constitutional arch'.[53] But in 1975 the Governor-General, Sir John Kerr, brought the office out from the shadows into the full glare of public and press controversy by dismissing the Prime Minister, Mr Gough Whitlam, from office, the occasion being the Prime Minister's refusal either to compromise or to advise a dissolution when the Senate refused to pass the Government's appropriation bills.[54]

The governor-general, convinced after seeing the party leaders, Gough Whitlam and Malcolm Fraser on 6 November 1975, the 'decisive day' when the Senate denied supply for the third time, that in his own words they were 'on the point of collision',[55] armed himself with an opinion from the Chief Justice of the High Court, Sir Garfield Barwick, who advised first, that the Senate had power to refuse supply, second that a Prime Minister who could not ensure supply must either advise a General Election or resign and third, should the Prime Minister in such circumstances refuse to do either, the Governor-General had the constitutional authority to withdraw his commission as Prime Minister. The Governor-General then proceeded in, according to Mr Whitlam, his newly soundproofed study – Mr Whitlam was convinced that the key to the entire operation was secrecy and surprise[56] – to ask Mr Whitlam directly in person on 11 November whether he was prepared to advise a dissolution and, on receiving the answer, 'No', told him 'I have decided to terminate your commission. I have a letter for you giving my reasons.'[57] The Governor-General forthwith invited the leader of the Opposition, Mr Malcolm Fraser, to form a government. The new Prime Minister secured the passing of the Supply Bill through the Senate and advised a double dissolution (see pp. 137–8) on the same day and just before the House of Representatives passed a vote of no confidence in his administration. The Governor-General's political judgment was fully vindicated in the ensuing December election, but even with acceptance of the Chief Justice's ruling – the request for this by the Governor-General was itself held to be of questionable propriety – the Governor-General's action stretched the conventional exercise of his prerogative powers to an extent little in keeping with traditional Australian or indeed other views of the rôle of the office, the crucial feature in the whole dramatic episode being the Governor-General's manipulation of a dissolution against the advice of a Prime Minister who retained a majority in the Lower House.

The composition of the two Houses of the Australian Federal Parliament and the relationship between them underlined most strikingly the difference in purpose of the Australian and the Canadian Founding Fathers. The Australian Senate consisted originally of six, and subsequently of ten, senators from each state. They are elected for six years by the people of the states voting on the same franchise qualification as for the Federal Lower House, the House of Representatives, but with each state voting not in separate constituencies as for the Lower House but as one electorate. So far as possible the members of the Lower House were to be double those of the Senate, the relation between them being in certain circumstances of practical importance. The purpose of these arrangements was to ensure that the Senate should serve as the guardian of states' rights and in particular as the protector of the less populous states which, it will be noted, had equal representation with those of greater numerical resources. On paper this was a Senate very different from its nominated Canadian counterpart, with a specific function to fulfil and popular sanction behind it. In practice however the contrast has not been so pronounced. The large constituencies for Senate elections coupled with the tightness of Australian party organisation (particularly on the left) and the rigours of Australian federal politics generally have combined to ensure party predominance in the Upper as in the Lower House.

The democratic outlook of the Australian constitution-makers, again by contrast with the Canadian, as well as their ingenuity was well illustrated in the devices adopted for resolving differences between the two Houses of the Federal Parliament and for amendment of the constitution. Under section 57 of the constitution the rejection by the Senate of a measure passed by the House of Representatives on two occasions with an interval of three months between them in the same or the next session of Parliament entitled the government to advise a double dissolution, that is to say a dissolution both of the House of Representatives and Senate, and if after the subsequent election the Senate should again and for a third time reject the same measure, there was to be a joint sitting of both Houses at which the will of the majority would prevail. Such a double dissolution has in fact taken place in 1914, 1951, 1974 and, as has been noted, in 1975. In three cases the government was returned with control of both Houses so that no joint sittings were required, but in 1974, with continued deadlock after the May elections, the relevant provision of the constitution (section 57) took effect for the first time in the history of the Commonwealth, a joint sitting being held on 6 August 1974 at which all of the six bills in dispute were passed.

In the critically important field of constitutional amendment there was likewise reliance upon appeals to the people. Under section 128, a proposed amendment to the constitution had to be passed by an absolute majority in each House of the Federal Parliament and then submitted to the electors. If there was a difference between the two Houses, an amendment passed by an absolute majority on two occasions by one House and twice rejected by the other might also be submitted to the people in a referendum. In the referendum, approval of the proposed amendment required a double majority, that is to say a majority of the electors in the Commonwealth as a whole and also a majority in a majority of states. If the amendment affected a particular state then additionally there had to be a majority in the state (or states) concerned. These majorities were not readily obtained. Of the thirty-six proposals for amendment of the constitution submitted to referenda in the first eighty years of federation, only eight were carried.[58] This was the more significant in that many of the amendments proposed, for example by the Labour government immediately following the end of the second world war, were designed to extend federal powers in order to help reconstruction and ensure uniformity and improvement in social services as a whole. Even in times of high political emotion the conservatism of the electors remained pronounced. One example may suffice. In 1951, during the period of the Korean war, in which Australian forces were engaged, the Menzies government dissolved the Communist Party and seized its property. Their action was challenged in the courts and on appeal, the high court (which had been stigmatised in slogans painted on the walls above the Yarra the night before judgment was delivered as a 'capitalist stronghold' and was hailed the evening after in hastily amended letters as the 'guardian of the people's rights') declared the legislation *ultra vires*. The government responded by proposing a constitutional amendment to validate their action. It secured the necessary approval of both Houses and was duly submitted to the people but was narrowly defeated in the country as a whole and also failed to secure the support of a majority in a majority of states.

In so far as there has been enlargement of federal powers it has been mainly by judicial interpretation. For the rest the strong bias towards states' rights evident in the constitution as enacted remains, with only such matters as are expressly listed in the schedule to the constitution as vested in federal authority falling within its competence and everything not expressly so attributed remaining with the states.

> If any country and its government were to be selected [wrote James Bryce] as showing the course which a self-governing people pursues free from all external influences and little trammelled by intellectual influences descending from the past, Australia would be that country. It is the newest of all the democracies. It is that which has travelled farthest and fastest along the road which leads to the unlimited rule of the multitude.

Bryce, who could hardly imagine a representative system of government in and through which the masses could more swiftly and completely exert their sovereignty, viewed the prospect with some misgivings. He reminded his Australian readers of the maxim that nations must not presume too far upon their hereditary virtue and he thought it might be said of the Australian system of government what Macaulay said 'not quite correctly, of the United States government. It is "all sail and no ballast".'[59] But Bryce (like other and later commentators) underestimated the ballast of a people's conservatism behind the sometimes brash expression of radical sentiments.

5 'The Business May Seem Prosaic'; Co-operation by Conference, 1887–1911

'Prodigious greatness' – such were the terms in which Sir John Seeley wrote of England in the widely read and highly influential published version of his Cambridge lectures of the spring of 1881 on *The Expansion of England* .[1] 'We seem,' he reflected, in one of the most quoted (if more questionable) of his sentences, 'as it were, to have conquered and peopled half the world in a fit of absence of mind.'[2] It was the peopling, not the conquest, that appeared to him of first importance. The 'English Exodus' had been 'the greatest English event of the eighteenth and nineteenth centuries'.[3] It had brought into being a Greater Britain comprising mother country and colonies of settlement. The growth of that Greater Britain was 'an event of enormous magnitude'.[4] Yet associated with Greater Britain were colonies not of settlement but of conquest, India chief among them, not united to Britain by blood – the strongest of ties – and in that and most other respects on quite a different footing. They were by no means necessarily a source of strength – not even the greatest among them. 'It may be fairly questioned', observed Seeley, 'whether the possession of India does or ever can increase our power or our security, while there is no doubt that it vastly increases our dangers and responsibilities.'[5]

While Seeley in his pioneering but by no means restrictively academic study of the imperial dimension in British history, marvelled at the greatness of the British Empire he was also somewhat fearful. His fears were not of declining dominion – on the contrary he rightly sensed that it would be yet further extended – but of corrupting influences. 'Bigness', he warned, 'is not necessarily greatness; if by remaining in the second rank of magnitude we can hold the first rank morally and intellectually, let us sacrifice mere material magnitude.'[6] Others, he recognised, were more confidently expansionist and he suspected they were less wise. It offended him to hear 'our Empire described in the

140

language of Oriental bombast';[7] and for the 'bombastic' school of imperialists 'lost in wonder and ecstasy at its immense dimensions',[8] advocating the maintenance of Empire as a point of honour or sentiment, preoccupied with notions of further expansion regardless of its purpose, Seeley had contempt mingled with some concern. The Empire, which took over the rule of unassimilable races, he admonished them, was weakening its health, perhaps weakening it fatally. Had not Empires in the past declined into nothing more than 'a mere mechanical union of alien nationalities'?[9] Indeed, once a state advanced beyond the limits of nationality its power became precarious and artificial and that, Seeley believed, was the condition of most empires and 'the condition for example of our own Empire in India'. The subcontinent rested heavily upon his mind. 'India is really an Empire and an Oriental Empire'; withdrawal would be 'the most inexcusable of all conceivable crimes' but none the less retention carried its own risks and weighty responsibilities. Might not the possession of India also prove corrupting, 'drag us down, or infect us at home with Oriental notions or methods of government?'[10] Seeley, without dismissing the possibility, discounted it. India was not attached to Britain as the Roman Empire had been to Rome and the foundations of English liberty might accordingly remain secure. Moreover, while the connection with India especially gave cause for some sobering reflections, Seeley entertained few doubts on this or other grounds about the destiny of the British Empire. History, he felt, when studied and rightly interpreted, could be seen to have marked out for Britain a place in the first rank of states with Russia and the United States, and in a higher rank than the states of the European continent.[11] The important practical question was, how was this place to be attained and retained? It was a question that had begun to preoccupy the minds of many of his contemporaries.

Neither Britain's resources nor her manpower were concentrated as were those of her continental rivals of the future. Might not this alone exclude the prospect of equal greatness? Seeley thought not. Why? His assurance in this regard derived neither from the extent of the Empire nor even from contemporary indications of reviving imperial sentiment. Disraeli, that harbinger of a new imperialism, in his speech at the Crystal Palace nine years earlier, had poured scorn on the opinions of Liberal 'statesmen of the highest character, writers of the most distinguished ability' who had 'proved to all of us that we have lost money by our colonies' and had shown 'with precise, with mathematical demonstration, that there never was a jewel in the Crown of England that was so truly costly as the possession of India', had gone on to appeal directly to considerations of power, prestige and pride of nationality.[12] With these later day Disraelian imperialist sentiments Seeley sympathised only in part for, as we have seen, he was not among the growing number who were carried away by the romantic notions of grandeur, which the queen's assumption of the title of Empress of India – 'theatrical bombast and folly' Gladstone termed it[13] – supremely symbolised. 'When we enquire into the greater Britain of the future', Seeley insisted firmly, 'we ought to think much more of our colonial than of our Indian Empire'. It ought to be thought of more because it was not only a part but the condition of the greatness of the future. The population of the colonies, Seeley predicted confidently and more sensibly than many of his contemporaries, would greatly expand. 'In not much more than half a century', he wrote,[14] 'the Englishmen beyond the sea – supposing the Empire to hold together – will be equal in number to the Englishmen at home, and the total will be much more than a hundred millions'. But in essence his argument rested not upon uncertain prognostication of numbers, but upon the actual existence of British settler states in North America, in the Pacific, in southern Africa and, Seeley added, in conformity with contemporary opinion, in the West Indies. What was required, in his view, was to build upon the foundation which they, and they alone, provided and to organise a United States of Britain to take its place in the future, coequal in power, status and extent with the United States of America and with Russia. The contemplated means were federal and the goal an imperial federation.

Sir John Seeley was thinking of the future in the light of the past. Others with more direct responsibility for the formulation of political aims inclined, though not always for the same reason, towards a similar conclusion. They noted that the balance of power in Europe had been decisively changed by the German victories of 1870–1, that in consequence of them, the German Empire had emerged as the most formidable military power in the world and furthermore, that a new, more active and more dangerous era in great power rivalries had opened. In this situation there was self-evident need to look more closely at Britain's resources in relation to her world wide obligations and to consider afresh her ability to discharge them on the basis of existing imperial organisation – or lack of it.

The many wars in which Britain had been engaged since 1815 had, with the exception of the Crimean, all been 'small wars' and most of them the 'small wars' of Empire. The waging of them was costly and the advantages gained usually debatable at a time when it was becoming a constant concern of Whig-Liberal administrations (in the main) to limit and if possible to diminish military expenditure. This concern was understandable. In 1846–7 the total cost of the army and navy accounted for roughly 73 per cent of the national expenditure (excluding debt services) and one third of the total cost of the army was spent upon colonial garrisons. Partly because of traditional mistrust of a standing army at home and partly because of contemporary thinking on colonial defence 'as if the defence of each separate part of the Empire was a problem entirely self-contained',[15] many of these garrisons were apt to be more fully manned than would otherwise have been required. With colonial self-government a new concept was introduced, well-expressed in the phrase 'self-government begets self-defence'. This was a favourite theme of Gladstone, whose argument spelled out was that self-government was a condition of self-reliance and self-reliance in its turn a condition of self-defence, neither of which could grow so long as colonists were taught that 'come what would, they would be defended by a power thousands of miles away'.[16] In 1862 the House of Commons, after considering the report of a parliamentary committee known from the name of its chairman, Arthur Mills, as the Mills Committee, enunciated the principles that should determine the allocation of defence responsibility between Great Britain and her colonies in a resolution which read:

> That this House (while fully recognising the claims of all portions of the British Empire to imperial aid in their protection against perils arising from the consequences of imperial policy) is of the opinion that colonies exercising the rights of self-government ought to undertake the main responsibility of providing for their own internal order and security and ought to assist in their own external defence.

The moral was driven home for the colonists by the subsequent withdrawal of British garrisons from Canada, the Australian colonies, New Zealand and (partially and temporarily as it proved) from southern Africa. But restatement of principles was not accompanied by a parallel redefinition, for practical purposes, of future imperial-colonial responsibilities for defence expenditure or contributions and in his Crystal Palace speech Disraeli drew attention to this omission. Self-government should have been conceded in the first instance, he argued, as part of a great policy of imperial consolidation. It ought to have been accompanied by an imperial tariff and 'by a military code which should have precisely defined the means and the responsibilities by which the colonies should be defended, and by which, if necessary, this country should call for aid from the colonies themselves'.[17] But instead the principal – indeed to many the all-sufficient – justification for 'the recall of the legions' had been the economies thereby effected and the appeasement of anti-imperialists.[18]

The assumption made by the critics of imperial expenditure on colonial defence (shared, it would seem, by the great majority of their fellow countrymen) was that the colonies, incapable of defending themselves, could be thought of only in terms of financial or military obligation, rarely, if ever, of contribution. As Dilke put it in 1868, in a passage remarkable for its insight into the pattern of the future even if it was mistaken in its forecast:

> It is not likely, however, nowadays, that our colonists would for any long stretch of time engage to aid us in our purely European wars. Australia would scarcely feel herself deeply interested in the guarantee of Luxembourg, nor Canada in the affairs of Servia. The fact that we in Britain paid our share—or rather nearly the whole cost—of the Maori wars would be no argument to an Australian but only an additional proof to him of our extraordinary folly. We have been educated into a habit of paying with complacency other people's bills – not so the Australian settler.[19]

Yet in 1878 Disraeli gave dramatic cause for reconsideration, if not in respect of colonial at least in respect of possible imperial reinforcement of British resources in a European theatre, by moving Indian troops into the Mediterranean to strengthen the garrison at Malta at a time when Anglo–Russian tensions over the terms of the Treaty of San Stefano neared breaking point – and by so doing incidentally inspiring a parody of what Sir Henry Lucy described as the 'popular music-hall doggerel' of the day:[20]

> We don't want to fight;
> But, by jingo, if we do,
> We'll stay at home and sing our songs
> And send the mild Hindoo.

Already the Russian war scare had led, with prompting from the colonial secretary, Lord Carnarvon, to the appointment of an interdepartmental defence committee. As a result of its reports and recommendations a Royal Commission under the chairmanship of Lord Carnarvon (whose interest in defence continued unabated despite his resignation from the government on its policy towards Russia) was set up in the following year to enquire into 'the defence of British possessions and commerce abroad'. The appointment of colonial representatives was considered but not effected. Some famous colonial personalities, however, testified before it, including Sir Henry Parkes from New South Wales and Sir John A. Macdonald from Canada, who believed that no common system of defence could be established and that it was better to trust to a loyal and patriotic response under the stimulus of crisis than to grants of men or money in times of peace. Gladstone's return to office in 1880, after impassioned Midlothian denunciations of jingoism and of the financial profligacy of Disraeli's administration in the pursuit of 'false phantoms of glory',[21] gave cause for doubt about the Commission's continued existence. But the need for it was accepted by the new government, albeit reluctantly, and it was enabled to complete its work. The outcome was the first systematic survey of British imperial defence in the nineteenth century and one that was made not in the old pecuniary but in the new power context. Recommendations for future organisation were set out in three Reports, none of which was published in full. The emphasis was upon the sea communications of Empire, the conditions of their security and the contributions the colonies might make, chiefly by way of harbour facilities and coaling stations. The Commission allowed that the cost of the navy must for the time being fall upon imperial funds but noted that the capacity of the colonies to share in imperial defence would continually increase and the relative apportionment of burdens, as between the mother country and her colonies, would accordingly require to be adjusted in time. Of broader significance was the fact that new alignments in world power had shifted British defence interests from problems of the local security of particular colonies or outposts to those of imperial defence and strategy conceived as a whole, with each individual colony or territory having a rôle to play and a contribution to make.[22]

Changes in the patterns and practices of international trade were no less significant than the shifts in the balance of world power. So long as England's industrial supremacy remained, all she wanted was access to the markets of the world. Free trade and peace were her self-interested, but none-the-less enlightened, objectives. The Manchester School had believed that in time others would follow along the same liberal, progressive road but after 1870 most European states, with Germany in the lead, far from continuing the advance towards the free trade goal, reversed course and from behind protective tariffs began to compete with Britain in world markets. Germany became fully protectionist in 1879, Russia increased her tariff in 1881 and 1882, France and Austria–Hungary in 1882 and Italy in 1888. When France and Germany entered the colonial field in Africa and Asia they surrounded their new possessions with tariff walls; evidently they believed there was a connection between sovereignty and economics, between colonies and trade. Did not this suggest that some reconsideration of accepted economic notions in Britain might also be due or even overdue? The depression of the 1880s and evidence of Britain's declining share of world trade strengthened the case for critical reappraisal, not least of the rôle of the Empire overseas in the British trading system. One characteristically English reaction was the foundation of the Fair Trade League in 1881 favouring imperial preferences and – more important – tariff retaliation against foreign countries (always apt to be suspected of not trading 'fair'), with a view to reducing imports of food from protectionist foreign states and increasing supplies from the colonies on a long term, developing basis.[23] Nothing, however, came – or perhaps could have come – of these proposals, which were before their time and in conception near-impracticable.

Superimposed upon military and commercial factors were the less tangible considerations of the inter-relation between Empire and national power and prestige. Was Empire the foundation of British greatness? Gladstone thought not, spacious though he recognised that Empire to be.

There is no precedent [he declared in the opening speech of his Midlothian campaign, on 25 November 1879] in human history for a formation like the British Empire. A small island at one extremity of the globe peoples the whole earth with its colonies. Not satisfied with that, it goes among the ancient races of Asia and subjects two hundred and forty millions of men to its rule. Along with all this it disseminates over the world a commerce such as no imagination ever conceived in former times and such as no poet ever painted. And all this had to do with the strength that lies within the narrow limits of these shores. Not a strength that I disparage; on the contrary, I wish to dissipate if I can the idle dreams of those who are always telling you that the strength of England depends, sometimes they say upon its prestige, sometimes they say upon extending its Empire, or upon what it possesses beyond these shores. Rely upon it the strength of Great Britain and Ireland is within the United Kingdom.[24]

But in England this view was increasingly challenged while on the continent many writers, principally (though not only) German, failed, so A. J. P. Taylor has written, 'to grasp the truth about the British Empire – that it had come into being as the result of British commercial enterprise and industrial success; and they asserted the reverse, that the prosperity and wealth of Great Britain were due to the existence of her Empire.'[25] Yet while their arguments remained questionable they possessed superficial force and they were heavily underscored with popular emotional overtones. Even Bismarck, who late in life told the Reichstag that he had never been a 'colonial man', found it advantageous to let colonialist currents fill his diplomatic sails. Was Britain alone, the possessor of the greatest of European Empires, to stand aside aloof and detached, to discount its Empire's potential and to allow her colonies and possessions, unorganised and little regarded, to drift away into independence as casual sentiment suggested or circumstances decided on the complacent assumption that greatness resided not in Empire but in its own small island state? The answer – in the last quarter of the century as distinct from its middle period – was an increasingly emphatic and often a strident negative. The 'pomological theory' of colonies[26] was discarded and homely analogies from the orchard were superseded by harsher parallels from Darwinian concepts of the survival of the fittest. No longer ripeness but greatness was all!

The Imperial Federation League which was founded in 1884 reflected the new thinking. It numbered some distinguished figures including Joseph Chamberlain and W. E. Forster among its converts but it was important historically not because its aims were fulfilled but because the gradual realisation that they were impossible of fulfilment exposed the fundamental misapprehension about the aspirations and interests of the self-governing colonies – as entertained or interpreted by the colonists themselves – which had brought the League into existence and in so doing helped to focus the minds of British statesmen, albeit in many cases reluctantly, upon more limited but realisable ends. The misapprehension (which Seeley, himself associated with the league for several years, shared) derived from a belief that the British people at home and in the overseas colonies would, or should, form not several states but one state or even nation. In an address to the Philosophical Institution of Edinburgh on 5 November 1875, W. E.

Forster suggested, as conditions of the imperial federal union of the future, that all the self-governing communities of the Empire should agree in paying allegiance to one monarch, in preserving a common nationality, and 'not only in maintaining a mutual alliance in all relations with foreign powers but in apportioning among themselves the obligations imposed by such alliance'. Forster understood that the comprehensive character of his last condition was likely to provoke colonial objections but he argued that the very essence of a continuance of the imperial connection was 'a common patriotism; the feeling throughout all the different communities that, notwithstanding the seas that roll between them, they are yet one nation; and that all their inhabitants are fellow-countrymen'.[27] But therein, concisely stated, lay the fundamental federal misconception. Englishmen overseas though somewhat divided in mind were for the most part preoccupied not with building up a common nationality or a single state but with the development of the distinct and separate political identities of their own territories, on the basis not of one but of several states or nations. In so far as they were moved by deliberate intention, that intention was antagonistic to the aims of the federalists. This was something that federalists, carried along with the rising tide of imperial sentiment, were slow to perceive and reluctant to acknowledge. Their propaganda did, however, serve a constructive purpose but not the purpose it was intended to serve; not for the first time did the championing of an impossible cause concentrate attention upon what was possible. In itself this was no mean achievement but it is important that it should be recognised for what it was. The idea of federation, once actively publicised and promoted, acted as a catalyst stirring into action over the years the forces that were predestined to provide the alternative to it.

The chief purpose of the Imperial Federation League was to ensure effective reorganisation of Empire under continuing control of London. If the early federationists forgot or ignored India that was because, as an Indian writer has observed, 'she was quiet and securely in hand'.[28] It was the colonies of settlement – enjoying responsible self-government and advancing towards a state of autonomy that might lead by easy stages to sovereign independence – which gave point to the slogan 'federate or disintegrate' and on which federationists' attention was accordingly focused. It had been alleged by the same Indian writer that their concept of a federal Empire to be confined in practice to colonies of European settlement was for this reason 'frankly racial'. In as much as the purpose of federation was – in the words of James Anthony

Froude – to 'reunite the scattered fragments of the same nation', this was true. But would it not be truer to say that it was this immediate purpose of the federationists – namely, to retain these 'scattered fragments' within an Empire to which they seemed by no means securely attached – which gave to their propaganda its racial tone rather than the existence of a sense of racial exclusiveness which inspired their aim? The balance is not easy to strike; but there is no doubt that federationists for the most part were profoundly influenced by a particular example – the reunification of the majority of the German people in one state – which certainly had its cultural and racial overtones.

The advocates of imperial federation were apt to think more spaciously than those actually holding responsibility for the conduct of imperial affairs. At the first Colonial Conference, held in London in 1887, the year of Queen Victoria's Golden Jubilee celebrations, the prime minister, Lord Salisbury, was at some pains to make clear that imperial federation with its 'grand aspirations' was a matter 'for the future rather than for the present'. The Empire, which 'yields to none – it is, perhaps, superior to all – in its greatness' had about it one peculiarity which distinguished it from other empires – 'a want of continuity; it is separated into parts by large stretches of ocean; and what we are here for today is to see how far we must acquiesce in the conditions which that separation causes, how far we can obliterate them by agreement and by organisation'. The geographical factor meant that the British Empire could not emulate the German Empire in conducting all its imperial affairs from one centre and Lord Salisbury was sceptical as to whether it would ever be possible for it to do so. There were however other prospects before it. He hoped that they might 'present to the world the spectacle of a vast Empire, founded not upon force and upon subjection, but upon hearty sympathy, and a resolute cooperation in attaining those high objects of human endeavour which are open to an Empire like this'. But such cooperation was conditional upon agreement among themselves and could rest only upon continued self-reliance and self-determination in respect of domestic policies. So much indeed was already implicit in the imperial-colonial relationship and in turn it predicated the nature of the Conference's conclusions. 'The decisions of this Conference', Lord Salisbury remarked, 'may not be, for the moment, of vital importance; the business may seem prosaic, and may not issue in any great results at the moment. But we are all sensible that this meeting is the beginning of a state of things which is to have great results in the future.'[29]

Some ninety years have passed since Lord Salisbury spoke of the deliberations of the first Colonial Conference in these deflationary terms. On two points – superficially unrelated but in fact closely associated – he may be seen from this vantage point in time to have shown considerable foresight. The Colonial Conference of 1887 did mark the beginning of a state of things which had great results, not despite but largely because of the prosaic nature of its business. A long succession of imperialists was to express disappointment at the pedestrian character of the proceedings, the limited aims, the meagre results first of colonial then of imperial conferences, and in more recent times of Commonwealth Prime Ministers' Meetings. Yet had those imperial or Commonwealth gatherings concentrated their attention, as imperialists wished, on grand designs and spacious purposes then it may be remarked with some assurance that there would have been no later Commonwealth of Nations.

The prime minister had reason for supposing that the proceedings of the first Colonial Conference would be prosaic. There was debate on the arrangements for the naval defence of the Australian colonies; discussion on postal and telegraphic communications in general and a resolution in favour of a trans-Pacific cable in particular. Other questions that were considered related to the Pacific islands, to the adoption by the colonies of parallel legislation to that proposed in the United Kingdom regarding merchandise, marks and patents. There was a report from Canada on the Canadian Pacific Railway as a new Empire route important alike in its naval, military and political implications. All these were matters of moment to men concerned with practical affairs; they were hardly of a kind to excite the emotions of the multitude or to satisfy the aspirations of the new imperialists. But the latter were not left altogether comfortless.

A conference, even if it had been a rather casual gathering composed of public men from the colonies who happened to be in London for the Jubilee celebrations and one to which colonial premiers were not as such specially invited – though three in fact attended – had, after all, been held. Nor did it pass unremarked that while Lord Salisbury discounted possibilities of imperial federation he spoke in more qualified terms of other lessons that might be drawn from German experience. First he reminded members of the Conference that there had been a *Zollverein*, or customs union, and also a *Kriegsverein*, or a union for military purposes, before the German Empire came into existence. Then he argued that so far as the British Empire was concerned, the former, the *Zollverein*, though not to be dismissed as impractical by reason of the Empire's geographical dispersal had for the time being to be put 'in the distant and shadowy portion of our task' while the latter, the *Kriegsverein*, or union for purposes of mutual defence, which Lord Salisbury assured them was 'the real and most important business upon which you will be engaged', was to be regarded as a question for immediate and explicit consideration. It was also a matter of common interest. It was not only Britain but the colonies too who might be threatened by the changing patterns of world power and by the enormous increase in the means of communication. 'The English colonies', Lord Salisbury observed in thinly veiled admonition, 'comprise some of the fairest and most desirable portions of the earth's surface. The desire for foreign and colonial possessions is increasing among the nations of Europe.' Not only a sense of obligation to the mother country but considerations of self-interest should prompt colonial governments and peoples to assist Great Britain in discharging the obligations of imperial defence. The colonies for their part were not unresponsive though neither could they be called uncritically acquiescent. From Cape Colony, J. H. Hofmeyr proposed a 2 per cent *ad valorem* tax on all imports, the revenue deriving from it to be expended on imperial naval defence. This was at once unacceptable and deemed impracticable, though in principle it approximated to British ideas of colonial contributions to the upkeep of the Royal Navy. The terms of agreement about Australasian naval defence, concluded at the 1887 Colonial Conference after two years of negotiations, introduced a more realistic note. The Australian colonies and New Zealand were to pay a contribution of £126,000 per annum towards the support of an auxiliary squadron of ships which would reinforce the ships of the Royal Navy in Australasian waters, and which it was specifically agreed should not be reduced in number. Under Australian pressure the Admiralty reluctantly conceded that the ships should not be employed outside Australasian waters without the consent of Australasian governments.[30] The principle of contribution though not of unrestricted contribution was thus introduced.

In 1894 a further conference met in Ottawa at the invitation of the Canadian government. In Canada but not in Britain it has been regarded as being in the strict sense a Colonial Conference. Its proceedings (which did not include defence) were again prosaic. The record of them fills some four hundred pages[31] and there was a new departure in the passing of resolutions. Questions that were discussed included once again the Pacific cable project, and proposals for a fast line of steamships across the Pacific, particularly between Australia and New Zealand; ranging more widely were resolutions in favour of imperial legislation to enable the colonies to enter into agreements of commercial reciprocity with one another and recommending, in principle, imperial trade preferences between Great Britain and the colonies. It was however further resolved that the colonies should proceed to make arrangements between themselves about trading preferences until such time as Britain, free trade discarded, was able to participate in them. Herein was foreshadowed one of the great imperial debates of succeeding years.

The Colonial Conference of 1897 which met in London at the time of Queen Victoria's Diamond Jubilee celebrations was unquestionably in the true line of succession. It was called by Joseph Chamberlain and attended in addition by the prime minister of Canada and the premiers of New South Wales, Victoria, New Zealand, Queensland, Cape Colony, South Australia, Newfoundland, Tasmania, Western Australia and Natal, all of whom were received as honoured guests at celebrations which, in their ordered magnificence and in the variety of the people's participation in them, marked the heady apogee of Empire.[32] At the Conference Chamberlain expressed his opinion that there was a real necessity for some better machinery of consultation between the self-governing colonies and the mother country. He remarked:

> ... it has sometimes struck me – I offer it now merely as a personal suggestion – that it might be feasible to create a great council of the Empire to which the colonies would send representative plenipotentiaries – not mere delegates who were unable to speak in their name without further reference to their respective governments but persons who by their position in the colonies, by their representative character and by their close touch with colonial feeling, would be able, upon all subjects submitted to them, to give really effective and valuable advice. If such a council were to be created it would at once assume an immense importance and it is perfectly evident that it might develop into something still greater. It might slowly grow to that federal council to which we must always look forward as our ultimate ideal.[33]

The principal colonial representatives were however either critical or reserved and the Conference contented itself with a resolution (carried with two dissentients, one of them being Richard Seddon) stating that the existing political relations between the United

Kingdom and the self-governing colonies were 'generally satisfactory'. But notwithstanding this resolution, there was a feeling that some preparatory step should be taken in the direction of giving the colonies a voice in the control and direction of imperial interests[34] – but only within the accepted framework of colonial self-government. Chamberlain's proposals transgressed this proviso. He was of course right in thinking that any council the members of which could commit their countries to certain imperial policies without reference to their own governments would assume immense importance; where he was mistaken was in supposing that the majority of the self-governing colonies would be prepared to impair in this way the responsibility of individual governments to individual parliaments.

The colonial secretary pressed the colonial premiers more urgently in respect of defence. He reminded them of the military review they had seen as part of the Jubilee celebrations and he told them that later in the week they would see at Spithead 'an astounding representation' of naval strength, by which alone a colonial Empire could be bound together. 'You are aware', he said to them, 'that that representation – great, magnificent, unparalleled as it will be – is nevertheless only a part of the naval forces in the Empire spread in every part of the globe.' This 'gigantic navy' and the military forces of the United Kingdom were maintained at heavy cost. But they were not maintained exclusively for the benefit of the United Kingdom or the defence of home interests. They were maintained still more as a necessity of Empire, for the maintenance and protection of imperial trade and of imperial interests all over the world. Every war, great or small, in which the United Kingdom had been engaged during Queen Victoria's reign had, so Chamberlain alleged, 'at the bottom a colonial interest, the interest that is to say either of a colony or of a great dependency like India. That is absolutely true, and is likely to be true to the end of the chapter.' If it was the case that Chamberlain was attributing the root cause of the greatest of these wars, the Crimean, to the Indian interest, he was indulging in his gift for overstatement. At any rate the colonial premiers listened, but they responded only in modest measure. Cape Colony offered an unconditional contribution to the Royal Navy but the Australian colonies contented themselves with the renewal of their earlier contribution, which was still restricted to the protection of Australasian interests in Australasian waters. As for Canada, explained Sir Wilfrid Laurier, the question of a contribution, now that it had become a practical one, would no doubt be considered but, he proceeded, in reply to Australian criticism of Canadian inaction, the Canadian position was different from the Australian in that Canada was an inaccessible country.[35]

There was however a more noteworthy reponse in circumstances which Chamberlain cannot have altogether relished. At the outbreak of the South African war, the colonial secretary saw little reason to doubt War Office forecasts of an early, victorious conclusion to hostilities. How sanguine they were may be judged by the prospect held out to the young Winston Churchill by the British commander-in-chief, Sir Redvers Buller, on the troopship that carried them both to South Africa in the late autumn of 1899, who opined that they should be in time for one final engagement before Pretoria.[36] But there was no 'promenade to Pretoria'. As the war dragged on, contingents came from the Australian and New Zealand colonies and also from Canada where participation in an imperial war (although placed on a voluntary basis) still remained a source of much controversy between English and French-speaking Canadians. The colonial contributions were significant. Instead of English defence of colonial interests there was colonial reinforcement of England in a war in which the colonies had little or no interest. For nineteenth-century thinking about the colonies of settlement as defence liabilities, there was thereby ushered in a new phase in which they were earning the right to be thought of as military assets. Yet British feelings about colonial assistance in South Africa were inevitably mixed. It was heartening that this help should have been forthcoming; it was disturbing that it should have been required. Rudyard Kipling (whose reputation was never quite the same again after the war) sought to drive home the moral in *The Islanders*, written in 1902 in passionate advocacy of conscription which alone, he believed, could give to Britain the measure of military self-sufficiency she required and which South African experience had shown to be lacking.

> And ye vaunted your fathomless power and ye flaunted
>   your iron pride,
> Ere ye fawned on the younger nations for the men who
>   could shoot and ride!
> Then ye returned to your trinkets; then ye contented
>   your souls
> With the flannelled fools at the wicket or the muddied
>   oafs in the goals.

The Colonial conference of 1902 was the third conference to meet at a time of Royal celebrations, in this case the coronation of

King Edward VII. The sobering experiences of the South African war rested heavily upon it. Gone was the exuberant imperialism of earlier years. 'I feel', said Chamberlain, 'that . . . it would be a fatal mistake to transform the spontaneous enthusiasm which has been so readily shown throughout the Empire into anything in the nature of an obligation which might be at this time unwillingly assumed . . .' Accordingly, a new emphasis upon the weight of British responsibilities was counterbalanced by a greater British sensitivity as to the nature of the colonial connection and enhanced appreciation of its value. 'We do require your assistance,' Chamberlain told the Conference, 'in the administration of the vast Empire which is yours as well as ours. The weary Titan staggers under the too vast orb of its fate. We have borne the burden for many years. We think it is time that our children should assist us to support it . . .'[37] Here were echoes not of great powers ever becoming greater but of Matthew Arnold and his weary Titan –

> Staggering on to her goal;
> Bearing on shoulders immense,
> Atlanteän, the load,
> Wellnigh not to be borne,
> Of the too vast orb of her fate.[38]

And there followed an appeal – more insistent than in 1897 – for organised colonial contributions for defence. As international dangers had multiplied so had expenditure on armaments increased. They involved a cost per head of the United Kingdom of twenty-nine shillings and threepence per annum on naval and military defence whereas in Canada the comparable expenditure was only two shillings per head; in New South Wales three shillings and fivepence; in Victoria three shillings and threepence; in New Zealand three shillings and fourpence and in the Cape and Natal somewhere between two and three shillings per head of the white population. 'Now, no one,' said Chamberlain, 'I think, will pretend that that is a fair distribution of the burdens of Empire. No one will believe that the United Kingdom can, for all time, make this inordinate sacrifice.'[39] The Admiralty rubbed in the lesson with a memorandum showing a breakdown of the figures in respect of naval expenditure. They told even more strikingly the same statistical story. Per head of the population in the United Kingdom such expenditure amounted to fifteen shillings and one penny, in New South Wales to eightpence-halfpenny, in Victoria to nearly one shilling, in New Zealand to sixpence-halfpenny, in the Cape of

Good Hope to one shilling and a penny-farthing and in Natal four shillings and fivepence-threefarthings per head of the white population, and in Canada nil.[40] Was such a disparity warranted? When the colonies 'were young and poor', the colonial secretary conceded, they had clearly been incapable of providing large sums for their defence, but now that they were rich and powerful, growing every day 'by leaps and bounds', with their material prosperity promising to rival that of the United Kingdom itself, it was inconsistent with their position and their dignity that they should leave the mother country to bear the whole or almost the whole of the expense. Nor was it wise. 'Justification of union,' argued Chamberlain, 'is that a bundle is stronger than the sticks which compose it, but if the whole strain is to be thrown on one stick, there is very little advantage in any attempt to put them into a bundle.'[41]

A constructive proposal for spreading the strain – and incidentally a display of the colonial initiative for which Chamberlain had hoped – came from Richard Seddon, the prime minister of New Zealand. It was not novel but it was not on that ground the less welcome. It contemplated the creation of a joint colonial and imperial reserve force. The colonial secretary underlined the need for such a reserve at the conference table. He acknowledged with appreciation the assistance of colonial forces in South Africa. But what, he felt obliged to ask, had it amounted to? In the case of Canada one thousand men out of a population of five million. What the situation had demanded was something like ten thousand to twenty thousand men, already trained and in being as a reserve force, in each of the colonies according to its population and resources. But the provision and organisation of such forces were matters for the self-governing colonies themselves to decide. Regrettably it had been made plain to him that, other than New Zealand, in the existing conditions of public opinion in the colonies it would not be practicable to bring any such scheme into effect. 'That being the fact,' concluded Chamberlain severely, 'I am bound to say that in my opinion public opinion in these colonies must be very backward. I think it will have to progress, and that it cannot in the natural course of things but progress, especially as the dangers which lie all round you are better appreciated.'

On the naval side the colonies were only a little more forthcoming. The Admiralty underlined in a memorandum which they prepared for the Conference, the importance of command of the sea, supporting their argument with a wealth of historical illustration ranging from Salamis and Actium to Lepanto, Chesapeake

Bay, the Peninsular war, the expedition to the Crimea and the South African war, the last three being used as examples of great military enterprises which could have been carried out only by a power supreme at sea. To maintain such supremacy the Admiralty asked for colonial contributions to naval strength, not in the form of local navies but of subsidies to the Royal Navy. The reason for this was their conversion to the newer orthodoxy of Admiral Mahan which demanded concentration of naval power at the decisive point and, as a necessary consequence, centralised control. The first lord, Lord Selborne, drew the particular attention of the colonial prime ministers to the elimination from the Admiralty memorandum of any allusion to the word 'defence', on the ground that the term suggested an outdated and heretical approach to contemporary strategic requirements. The colonial response was varied. Cape Colony and Natal offered unconditional contributions of fifty thousand and thirty-five thousand pounds respectively. For New Zealand, Seddon vigorously repudiated the notion of a separate navy and disliked the idea of a fixed contribution but finally agreed to a payment of forty thousand pounds a year, later increased to one hundred thousand pounds a year. Laurier excused Canadians from all contribution on the ground of heavy expenditure on domestic development and especially on transcontinental railroads – a point on which he had some exchanges with Chamberlain – while for Australia Sir Edmund Barton, after placing on record the existence of strong popular support for a local navy in the Commonwealth,[42] agreed upon an increase in the Australian contribution to the Royal Navy from one hundred and twenty-six thousand pounds a year – the figure determined under the Naval Agreement negotiated in 1887 – to two hundred thousand pounds a year, which was one hundred thousand pounds a year less than the Admiralty had asked for, the short fall being justified, as with Canada, on the ground of heavy expenditure at home on railways. Even so, Barton's action came in for heavy criticism in the federal Parliament. This was chiefly because successful Admiralty insistence upon the need for undivided responsibility so as to allow for concentration of forces should need arise, meant that Admiralty control of the ships in the Australian squadron was not limited, as heretofore, by the need for consultation with the Australian government about their employment outside Australian territorial waters. Even though not ready to undertake the responsibility of a separate navy, most Australians were not prepared to discard earlier notions of the value of local defence. Despite vigorous criticism, however, in Parliament and the press the subsidy was approved and continued to be paid, though with steadily diminishing conviction of its appropriateness, until the Naval Agreement of 1909.

   The nature of British-colonial differences on defence respon-sibilities in 1902 was variable. and at times elusive. They had a socio-economic content in Australia and most notably in Canada, where as Laurier emphasised there was a small population develop-ing a huge territory – the precise opposite of the position in the United Kingdom – and fixed military contributions were likely in consequence to impose a quite disproportionate burden. But the root source from which such differences stemmed was clear. It was not economic or strategic but political; the colonies were instinc-tively averse to any development which might impose a limit to the growth of their autonomy and an imperial military force might do precisely this. The colonies had decided the extent and the nature of their contribution to the South African war and they wished to decide the extent and nature of their contributions to future and possibly greater wars. This was true of all except New Zealand but of none was it more true than of Canada. Canada's business, said Sir Wilfrid Laurier in 1900, was Canada's business. 'I claim for Canada this, that in future, Canada shall be at liberty to act or not act, to interfere or not interfere, to do just as she pleases, and that she shall reserve to herself the right to judge whether or not there is cause for her to act.'[43] Did that mean no cooperation on imperial issues? Clearly not; the South African war even if recruitment had been on a voluntary basis had shown as much. But it had also shown that Canadian cooperation and the nature of it would be condi-tional upon the approval of and determined by the Canadian government.

   The insistence of colonial governments and especially that of Canada upon their powers of decision was at least in part defensive. Before he left for the 1902 Colonial Conference, Sir Wilfrid Laurier remarked that there was 'a school in England and in Canada, ... which wants to bring Canada into the vortex of militarism which is now the curse and the blight of Europe.'[44] What might be the effects in Canada if it were even partially successful in securing identification of Canadian with British imperial interests? Chamberlain himself was warned in a letter from Canada that should Laurier agree to a Canadian financial contribution for imperial defence, there would be a cry of 'Tribute' from Quebec and, added the correspondent, 'We do not want a French Ireland in Canada between us and the sea.'[45] It had already become apparent before 1902 that the future rôle of the colonies in imperial defence would have to be thought of, not on traditional lines, but in conformity with their status and aspirations as self-governing political entities. In 1902 colonial concepts were formulated chiefly by negative responses to imperial propositions. In respect of military forces they were final. But no parallel categoric responses were, or could be, made in respect of naval forces. The new strategic orthodoxy, coupled with self-evident dominion dependence upon the Royal Navy, saw to that. So it was that in the naval sphere the 1902 Colonial Conference marked less an ending than the opening of a new phase in imperial-colonial relations.

While the initiative in respect of the political and defence organisation of the Empire was taken by the United Kingdom, in respect of trade it lay with the colonies. For this there was good reason. The colonies enjoyed a freedom of manoeuvre which the mother country did not possess. Their approach was pragmatic, that of the United Kingdom rigid. They were free trade or protectionist as suited their particular needs at a particular moment; Great Britain remained, despite some misgivings, a country doctrinally committed to free trade. As a necessary consequence proposals for tariff reform came not from London but from the colonies. While the elder Hofmeyr's 1887 proposal for an imperial customs tariff with the revenue from it to be devoted to the general defence of the Empire came to nothing, a new departure was made between 1894 and 1897, with the Canadian government deciding to give British goods tariff preferences, which amounted at first to 25 per cent and were subsequently increased to 33⅓ per cent. They were preferences voluntarily accorded by Canada on British taxable goods imported into the dominion. The Canadian initiative was followed by other colonial governments. But it was not requited. Might the British government not be persuaded to do so?

At successive Colonial Conferences the British government had been categoric in its assertions that it desired to increase the volume of Empire trade, which amounted to about one-third of Great Britain's total trade. But, in the first instance at least, it was not in terms of imperial preference that British statesmen were thinking. Their thoughts ran on a more ambitious scale and in a different direction. What was uppermost in their minds, and most notably in the thoughts of the secretary of state for the colonies, was a customs union, or *Zollverein*, on the German model. Free trade within the Empire was a first object. That, were it feasible, would bring substantial benefits in its train. It would, so Chamberlain told the

Colonial Conference in 1902, 'enormously increase our inter-imperial trade . . . it would hasten the development of our colonies . . . it would fill up the spare places in your lands with an active, intelligent and industrious, and above all a British population . . . it would make the mother country entirely independent of foreign food and raw material.'[46] But there was no acceptance of the argument or its implications in the colonies. Why? Professor Hancock has summarised the reasons in two brief sentences. For them Chamberlain's *Zollverein* was impossible because 'it meant tariff assimilation with Great Britain and a surrender of tariff personality. Tariff personality was an essential element in self-government.'[47] Even with the concessions that Chamberlain was prepared to make, an imperial customs union meant centralised direction; that meant loss of fiscal autonomy and might well mean more besides. Association within a free trade area with one of the most industrially advanced societies in the world would imperil the future of growing colonial industries. The advantages in terms of an assured market for raw materials and primary products were accordingly likely to be offset, or more than offset, by diminished prospects of industrial development. And thinking in politico-economic terms, as did colonial leaders almost without exception, that meant in turn a readiness to postpone or even abandon hopes of building up a balanced economy within their own frontiers. The sacrifice was not to be contemplated and they held (and again almost without exception) – to quote Professor Hancock once more – 'to the national system of political economy'.[48]

For the British government, for Chamberlain personally, imperial preference – the cause for which he sacrificed the later part of his political career – was a second-best. But for the colonies with Canada in the lead, it was their first choice. They too wished to increase imperial trade and imperial preference might well enable them to do so in a manner consistent with their national economic aspirations. Preferences were at once compatible with policies of protection at home and with special trading relations with the Empire overseas. In fact as it appeared to colonial statesmen preferences presented only one major problem: a free trading Britain could not participate in an imperial preferential system. The practical choice before the colonies, therefore, was preferences without requital from Britain or no preferences. For the most part the colonies chose the first course. Increasingly, however, they applied pressure, at times beyond the limits of what was conventional, upon successive British governments. Their persuasive efforts yielded no fruit for more than thirty years but this was not because the issue went by default in British domestic policies.

During the South African war the chancellor of the Exchequer, Sir Michael Hicks Beach, imposed duty of a shilling a quarter on imported corn as a temporary war-time fiscal measure. It was proposed that this duty should be retained after the war but that the colonies should then be allowed to import free. Before he left on a tour of South Africa, Chamberlain understood that agreement had been reached on such a basis by all the members of the cabinet except C. T. Ritchie, Hicks Beach's successor at the Exchequer. While the colonial secretary was away however the cabinet, much influenced by Ritchie, an out and out free trader, decided that the duty should be altogether repealed. With that decision there disappeared the last chance of introducing some qualified form of preference without major assault upon the citadel of free trade.[49]

On his return Chamberlain resigned from the cabinet in order to be free to campaign for imperial preference and the more senior and ardent free traders resigned to oppose it, leaving Arthur James Balfour, as prime minister, to try out the possibility of avoiding a final party split on fiscal issues with the insubstantial but characteristically ingenious suggestion that tariffs be imposed, but only as retaliatory measures against unfair foreign competition. The idea served a purpose – that of prolonging Balfour's period of office – but it satisfied neither the out and out free traders nor the imperial trade reformers.[50] And in the statistical confusion of the nation-wide debate upon the fiscal issue that followed one thing emerged clear beyond dispute. The English working man was not prepared to risk the chance, and free traders assured him it was a certainty, of dearer food in the supposed interests of imperial unity and greatness.

In the broader setting of imperial organisation, colonial backing for imperial preference as against Empire free trade showed that, as in defence and politics, the colonies were in fact resolved to establish and confirm their several and separate identities and not to allow them to be submerged in a greater imperial whole. The protagonists of imperial integration were thus confronted by the champions of nascent dominion nationalism – Chamberlain by Laurier, the spokesman of Canada's 'everlasting no'; as one shrewd observer, Richard Jebb, noted,[51] by the time of the Colonial Conference of 1902 the forces of patriotic nationalism were triumphing over the forces of imperial loyalty. Jebb did not think that the unity of the Empire would be thereby impaired; rather that in the future it would of necessity rest upon the foundation of colonial nationalism. Chamberlain, it is clear, was by no means so certain. 'His ideal is an independent Canada and he is certainly not an imperialist in our sense,' Chamberlain remarked of Laurier on 25 August 1902, in a letter to his son, Austen.[52] It was true; and it was the imperialism of Laurier that was destined to survive.

In succeeding years changes in name serve to illustrate the developing character of imperial relations. In 1902 the desirability of altering the name 'Colonial Conference' to 'Imperial Council' was referred to governments for consideration. In 1905 the colonial secretary, Alfred Lyttelton, formally suggested in a dispatch to colonial governors that the title 'Colonial Conference' which 'imperfectly expresses the facts' should be discarded and replaced by 'Imperial Council'. The Canadian government objected strongly. They pointed out that the change in name would be interpreted 'as marking a step distinctly in advance of the position hitherto attained in the discussion of the relations between the mother country and the colonies', the term 'Council', with its implication of a formal assemblage possessing an advisory and deliberative character, suggesting to them, in conjunction with the word 'Imperial', a permanent institution which might eventually encroach upon dominion autonomy; 'Conference', a neutral term, implied no more than an unconventional gathering for informal discussions.[53] In the light of these objections (and as the Canadian government itself proposed) the adjective was retained, the noun discarded, and after 1907 the Colonial Conference was re-named not 'Imperial Council' but 'Imperial Conference'.

It was the changing nature and purpose of the Conferences that were responsible for the change in their designation. Gone was the indeterminate character of the 1887 gathering and in its place was a Conference with a defined composition and an established status. In 1907 the designation 'dominion' supplanted the older title of colony in the Conference record for the first time and it was dominion governments which were to be represented at future Conferences. It was decided also that the re-named Imperial Conference should meet every four years and that at its meetings 'questions of common interest may be discussed and considered as between His Majesty's government and His governments of the self-governing dominions beyond the seas. The prime minister of the United Kingdom will be *ex officio* president, and the prime ministers of the self-governing dominions *ex officio* members of the Conference.'[54] The colonial secretary was also to be an *ex officio* member. There was debate about the making of arrangements for the Conference. Was it right that its work should be organised by the Colonial Office? Was it in accord with the principles of dominion autonomy? Was it likely to ensure due and proper attention to the affairs of the dominions? Alfred Deakin, now in his second term as Prime Minister of Australia, thought not. He came prepared for controversy, an entry in his diary after his first visit reading, so his biographer tells us: 'Informal meeting at C.O. – Battle with Elgin [secretary of state] and C.O. begins'.[55] 'Affable Alfred's' affability, indeed, never extended to the Colonial Office. In 1887 he had complained of its 'natural *vis inertiae*' and in 1907 he followed this up with an allegation that it was not fitted to conduct relations with self-governing dominions nor to organise Colonial Conferences. Although he said he would have preferred, if he could thereby have accomplished his object, to handle the subject without 'brushing the dust off a butterfly's wings', he did in fact launch a major frontal assault upon the department.

The Colonial Office, so Deakin argued, was no more than a department of the British government, and one moreover associated with past days of colonial subordination. The manners of its officials, he alleged, were apt to be casual, while dominion representations were met with an understanding neither of the real causes from which they sprang nor of precise dominion intentions. 'Our responsible and representative governments are dealt with as you deal with a well-meaning governor or well-intentioned nominee council.' He complained about 'an attitude of mind'. The Colonial Office had about it

a certain impenetrability; a certain remoteness, perhaps geographically justified; a certain weariness of people much pressed with affairs, and greatly overburdened, whose natural desire is to say 'Kindly postpone this; do not press that; do not trouble us; what does it matter? we have enough to do already; you are a self-governing community, why not manage to carry on without worrying us?'

It may be added by way of complementing the picture, and as Deakin no doubt in part sensed, that Colonial Office officials (in the words of an understanding interpreter of their views) found white colonial leaders 'at best touchy, brash and incompetent', Deakin being notorious for 'misrepresentations' and for 'twisting the lion's tail for the amusement of his people'.[56]

Deakin's conviction that the Colonial Office was ill-fitted to deal with dominion affairs led him to conclude that a new department was required which would be genuinely representative of all the governments attending the Imperial Conference and serve as a Conference secretariat. It would be in the strict sense an imperial body. But other dominion leaders, notably Laurier (whatever their private reflections about the Colonial Office), had not the least wish to see it replaced for these purposes by a new and nominally imperial body with uncertain powers and uncertain responsibilities. Their reasons were not far to seek.

In an earlier discussion, General Botha had remarked that the root objection to the adoption of the word 'Council' was that it might make an infraction upon the rights of responsible government in the various self-governing colonies. 'On this point', he said, 'I am conservative.'[57] But might not an imperial or Conference secretariat carry the same threat? In logic the case for the secretariat was strong. Why should responsibility for arranging and organising the business of Imperial Conferences be vested in the hands of officials in a government department responsible to one government alone? Was not the logical alternative a body with shared responsibility to all governments, British and dominion? But on the other hand, in practice might not such diffused responsibility in fact lead, possibly by slow stages, to the emergence of a quasi-autonomous administrative authority? The secretary of state, Lord Elgin, feared this might be so. He said it would be very difficult, for that reason, for His Majesty's government to agree to the establishment of a body with independent status. 'In the self-governing colonies, as with us,' he continued, 'I need scarcely remind the members of the Conference [that] the basis of all British government is the responsibility of ministers to their Parliaments: not only, as here, our responsibility to the British Parliament, but your responsibility to your Parliaments.' That responsibility could not and should not be impaired. Sir Wilfrid Laurier was even more disturbed. The notion of a Council had been happily disposed of but there now appeared the possibility of a surviving secretariat. Laurier enquired about its functions. Would members of the secretariat give independent advice? What reports would they make? What would they do during the four or five years between conferences, all on their own? He had no doubt of the answers. Of necessity such a body would always be inclined to act independently. He was convinced that it should not be brought into being and he was altogether of the view of Lord Elgin that, on the principle of responsible government, no one should give advice of any kind except a man who was directly responsible through Parliament to the people.[58]

Such misgivings were not universally entertained. The New Zealanders did not share them. On the contrary, neither for the first nor for the last time they had put down at the head of their proposals resolutions about an Imperial Council and secretariat for discussion at the Conference. If they did not endorse what Deakin said, they sympathised with his general aims. The most British and the most distant of the dominions was, neither then nor later, fearful of measures of centralisation such as might ensure more speedy and effective attention to imperial needs.

The upshot of debate was in one respect strange and in another significant. The Colonial Office felt obliged to bring into nominal existence not an imperial but a conference secretariat, and one was duly created, theoretically separate from, but in respect of personnel wholly a part of the Colonial Office itself. This secretariat had no distinct existence and served no purpose – not even that of appeasing Deakin; a phantom suspended in a void, in due course it vanished almost as though it had never been. The reorganisation of the Colonial Office as from 1 December 1907 into three departments, the first of which – the dominions department – was to be responsible for relations with the overseas dominions was, however, another matter. While to outward appearance the change was not great – and to dominion reformers correspondingly disappointing – administratively it marked the beginning of a new phase. One day the dominions department, under another name, was to absorb the parent Colonial Office.[59] When that day came it marked the completion in terms of administrative responsibilities – as 1907 marked the first administrative recognition in London – of the transformation of Empire into Commonwealth. It was recognition accorded under Australian pressure and however short it fell of Deakin's original purpose it was his achievement. 'An eloquent, or at least a fluent, smart sort of fellow', wrote John Morley disparagingly of him, and added, echoing the views of the Colonial Office – 'Laurier is excellent, but Deakin is intolerable.' One reason for it was Deakin's aggressiveness, another, however, was his persistence in pursuit of his aims. He was not in fact a man easily to be deflected from his purpose or cajoled by compliments. If there was something a little ironic in Sir Wilfrid Laurier's graceful acquiescence, against earlier inclination, in the conferment of a knighthood at the Jubilee Conference in 1897, there was something altogether characteristic in Alfred Deakin's consistent declining of honours, even to the point of twice refusing an honorary degree from the University of Oxford. 'Perhaps you will excuse my saying', wrote the vice-chancellor in studied rebuke on the first occasion, 'that we have only once before had this degree refused.'[60]

The pattern of emerging Commonwealth was also to be traced in Conference deliberations on trade and defence. In 1907 the debate on preferences was renewed and once more was protracted. Pressures upon the United Kingdom government to modify traditional trading policies were so considerable, especially from Deakin (who spoke far more than anyone else at the Conference and who by reason of some of his public utterances was accused of intervening in British politics), that General Botha thought it worth while to remark that Britain also was a self-governing state. But essentially the position remained unchanged and the Conference of 1907 had no option but to reaffirm the resolution of 1902, which had stated that the conference favoured reciprocal preferences 'with the exception of His Majesty's government, who was unable to give its assent, so far as the United Kingdom was concerned, to a reaffirmation of the Resolutions in so far as they imply that it is necessary or expedient to alter the fiscal system of the United Kingdom'.[61] Whatever else might be the case, it was apparent by 1907 that the developing relationship between Great Britain and the dominions would not in the near future be strengthened by an imperial preferential trading system.

In defence, as distinct from trade, there were indications of new thinking and of closer British-dominion accord. The Committee of Imperial Defence, first formed in 1902 as a consequence of the national searchings of heart over the South African war and formally created by a Treasury minute dated 4 May 1904, played an important part in bringing it about. The committee, an advisory body to be summoned by the prime minister, normally included the heads of the service departments and of the Treasury, the Foreign, Colonial and India Offices, in a membership which was not precisely defined. It had a permanent secretariat, but since the committee was itself only a consultative body the secretariat was without specified administrative or executive functions.[62] It was however not only vested with the responsibility of preserving a record of proceedings and decisions but with collecting and co-ordinating for the use of the committee 'information bearing on the wide problems of imperial defence and to prepare any memoranda or other documents which may be required . . .' The services of both committee and secretariat were at the disposal of the national organisations within the Empire for the working out of their defence policies but it was for dominion governments to decide how much use to make of them. There was no obligation.

The committee, though concerned with the defence of the Empire, was neither in composition nor constitution an imperial but only a United Kingdom body and was rightly named (as L. S. Amery noted) a Committee of Imperial Defence, not an Imperial Committee of Defence.[63] In 1903 Sir Frederick Borden, the Canadian minister of militia, attended both sessions of the committee while in London for other reasons. Formal agreement was recorded at the 1907 Colonial Conference both to the effect that the dominions might refer to the committee any local questions in regard to which expert assistance was thought desirable and that a representative of a dominion might be summoned to attend as a member of the committee during the discussion of questions raised at its request. But as Lord Hankey (first appointed as naval assistant secretary to the Committee of Imperial Defence in 1907) later recalled, no immediate opportunity occurred for translating this resolution into effect. The dominions referred no question to the committee and nominated no representative to attend.

At the 1907 Colonial Conference the secretary of state for war, R. B. Haldane, restated the principles of imperial cooperation in defence in terms that took due account of dominion susceptibilities. On the level of practical cooperation he spoke of plans for the interchange of General Staff officers between Britain and the dominions and of a corresponding broadening of the basis of the recently created General Staff – 'a purely advisory organisation of which command is not a function' – so as to provide for the association and liaison of dominion forces with it. 'The beginning,' he proceeded cautiously, 'of course, would have to be very modest.' But most important would be agreement upon aims broadly conceived. ' . . . we know that this thing must be founded simply upon the attaining of a common purpose, the fulfilment of a common end. It cannot be by the imposing of restrictions or by rigid plans which might not suit the idiosyncrasies of particular countries.'[64] This was an approach well calculated to win dominion acceptance.

The Conference had before it a series of papers on the possibility of assimilating war organisations throughout the Empire, on patterns and provision of equipment and stores for colonial forces, and – always allowing for the particular circumstances of individual colonies – on the need for agreement upon measures that would make common action effective if and when it was desired. In the paper prepared by the General Staff and submitted by the prime minister, it was accepted as a first and fundamental principle that the maintenance of the Empire rested primarily upon supremacy at sea. The second principle which (it was stated) should govern the military organisation of the Empire was that each portion of it should as far as possible maintain sufficient troops for its own self-defence. And the third principle was 'the great one' of mutual support in time of emergency. Changes in the pattern of warfare were underlined and the new dangers and the new responsibilities which they brought with them outlined.

> Since the last Conference, the paper argued, there had been a great conflict between two nations powerful on land and sea and that conflict, [the Russo–Japanese war] . . . had taught us lessons, tactical and strategic, ashore and afloat. [But] . . . the one great lesson which stands out clear and well-defined, admitting neither argument nor disclaimer, is that the nation of which the naval and military authorities are in a position to make their preparations for emergency on a definite plan and with a full knowledge of the strength and organisation of the forces which they will be able to put in the field at the critical moment, starts with an incalculable advantage over an opponent who does not enjoy the same position. War is in the present day becoming more and more an exact science.[65]

The mother country, it was affirmed, was seeking to live up to these principles. It was for the dominions to consider them and to contribute what they might to imperial resources.

But it is not to be supposed that imperial defence problems could be disposed of merely by drawing lessons from the experiences of others or the enunciation of mutually satisfying principles. There were the often vexing questions of their application. In 1907 there was unanimous support for the establishment of a General Staff for the Empire, working on a basis of co-operation and having as its principal tasks the surveying of the defence of the Empire as a whole, and for the bringing about of the uniformity in weapons and training that would make possible effective cooperation in a great war. But at the same time the dominions declined to enter into advance military commitments, as a necessary part of their resolve to retain in their own hands decision as to the nature and extent of their participation in a war; nor were they strongly pressed to do so, partly because it was recognised to be inadvisable but equally because the British government (and not least the Colonial Office) entertained an indifferent, even at times a contemptuous view of possible dominion military contributions in a war waged by the professional armies of Europe.

In respect of naval policies the position was rather different and the outcome of the 1907 Conference correspondingly less clear-cut. In the Memorandum already referred to which Lord Selborne, as first lord of the Admiralty, had submitted to the 1902 Conference, the doctrine of naval concentration had received classic statement:

The sea [the memorandum read] is all one, and the British Navy therefore must be all one; and its solitary task in war must be to seek out the ships of the enemy, wherever they are to be found, and destroy them. At whatever spot, in whatever sea, these ships are found and destroyed, there the whole Empire will be simultaneously defended in its territory, its trade and its interests. If, on the contrary, the idea should unfortunately prevail that the problem is one of local defence, and that each part of the Empire can be content to have its allotment of ships for the purpose of the separate protection of an individual spot, the only possible result would be that an enemy who had discarded this heresy and combined his fleets will attack in detail and destroy those separated British squadrons which, united, could have defied defeat.[66]

A strategic doctrine asserting unequivocally the need for unified control of naval forces was bound at all times to possess some unpalatable political implications for the dominions. In naval as in military matters dominion governments (with the one exception of New Zealand) felt a strong and continuing interest in the development of local defence, with local dominion navies providing an essential element in it. Was there not here then a conflict between a strategic and the national principle? And if the navy were to be under unified control, did not that mean determination of policy by a single authority? And would not that single authority inevitably be the imperial authority? Was any purpose then to be served by the development of autonomous dominion navies? In the event of Anglo–German naval war, what happened in the North Sea was likely to be conclusive. If the Royal Navy were defeated in a major engagement there, what resistance could dominion navies in distant waters offer to a victorious German High Seas fleet? If, therefore, the Admiralty principle were applied in practice and the logic of the strategic situation accepted, would it not mean that the appropriate dominion contributions – in whatever form they were made – would be for the strengthening or maintenance of the Royal Navy? Successive British governments, as has been noted, certainly inclined to this view. Strategically it may well have been the correct view. On the other hand, it inevitably meant a delay or even the indefinite postponement of the creation or expansion of separate dominion navies. Could some compromise be reached here? This was not merely a matter of imperial-dominion relations; it was a matter of vigorous domestic dominion controversies and of dominion self-esteem. The peoples of the dominions could derive but little emotional satisfaction from contributing to the building of a dreadnought or a battleship they might never see. They desired to have their own ships under their own control, cruising in their own waters and based on their own ports. 'They want,' as the first lord of the Admiralty, Winston Churchill observed with insight and understanding, 'to have something they can see, and touch, and take pride in, with feelings of ownership and control. Those feelings, although unrecognised by military truth, are natural. They are real facts which will govern events.'[67]

In 1909 the British government were brought face to face with the realities of German naval competition. It was not merely that Germany was building 'all big-gun' ships at a faster rate than Britain – four to two in 1908 and with a further four to follow – but that German construction was more rapid. It seemed, despite continued superiority in total numbers, that British naval supremacy was being rapidly eroded. Both cabinet and people were alarmed. There was a cry for acceleration in the building – 'We want eight, And we won't wait' in the words of a music hall refrain. The apprehension spread to the dominions. There was evident need for consultation which was met by a supplementary Imperial (Defence) Conference in 1909.[68] The temper of the Conference held against so threatening a background was realistic; so too was the approach of the Admiralty. They showed a readiness to yield some ground in the face of dominion objections – most forcibly stated over the years by the Australians – to the subsidy principle and themselves advanced alternative proposals on the basis of the coming into existence of supporting but separate dominion navies. The memorandum they submitted first restated the contention that 'the greatest output of strength for a given expenditure is obtained by the maintenance of a single navy with the concomitant unity of training and unity of command' and that 'the maximum of power would be gained if all parts of the Empire contributed, according to their needs and resources, to the maintenance of the British Navy', but this proposition was followed by a second which, recognising the desire of some dominions to create their own local navies, argued that on this premise the aim should be the formation of a distinct fleet unit capable of being used in its component parts in time of war. This second proposal contemplated dominion responsibility for the maintenance of a certain naval strength, each in its own sphere of interest 'thus relieving the imperial fleet of direct responsibility in distant seas'. Were the principle to be adopted, then there would in the future be a United Kingdom fleet unit in the East Indies and China (with the aid of the New Zealand contribution), an Australian squadron in the South Pacific, and a Canadian squadron in the eastern Pacific, each squadron being capable of action individually not only in defence of coasts but also of trade routes, and the three in conjunction forming a far eastern fleet.

Neither Admiralty proposition was acceptable to Canada. They rejected the idea of subsidy, and as Laurier later explained to the Canadian House of Commons, Canada's double seaboard rendered the provision of one fleet unit for the time being impracticable. He proposed in the Navy Bill he introduced in 1910 that Canada should make a start with cruisers and destroyers, part of which were to be stationed on the Atlantic seaboard and part on the Pacific, the double seaboard being vital to the Canadian position. There was however some closer approximation of Admiralty and Australian views. It was given formal expression in a Naval Agreement by which the British government undertook to keep in the Indian and Pacific Oceans double the force of the Australian fleet unit. For Australia this seemed to promise reinsurance in respect of regional security and also a direct incentive to increase her naval strength. But in fact the agreement was never fully implemented, the British government seeing small reason for overmuch preoccupation with Pacific security in view of the Anglo–Japanese alliance and the Anglo–Russian Convention, 1907. Nonetheless the 1909 Conference led on to the creation of the Royal Australian Navy.[69]

At the next, and full, Imperial Conference in 1911, preoccupation with the threat of impending war in Europe was responsible for a dramatic departure from precedent in the Conference Proceedings. At specially convened sessions of the Committee of Imperial Defence, reinforced in its membership by the prime ministers of the dominions, Sir Edward Grey, the secretary of state for Foreign Affairs, gave an exposition of British foreign policy as seen against the circumstances and realities of the struggle for power in Europe. At the conclusion of the Conference Asquith remarked that this was an event in itself in that it was the first time that the dominions had been admitted into the innermost parts of the imperial household. 'What in the old classical phrase were called *arcana Imperii* have been laid bare to you without any kind of reservation or qualification.'[70] This was however not quite the case. Sir Edward Grey was choosing his words carefully when he said that 'we are not committed by any entanglement that ties our hands. Our hands are free, and I have nothing to disclose to our being bound to any alliances which is not known to all at the present time.' The Anglo–French and Anglo–Russian staff talks were not alliances or commitments of this kind and Lloyd George recalled that the fact of these talks having taken place was not disclosed to dominion prime ministers any more than it had been to most members of the British cabinet.[71] But in making this qualification, Lloyd George also remarked upon the range and candour in other respects of the foreign secretary's review. It was not of course presented merely to satisfy a natural dominion interest. Dominion governments were far removed from Europe; they might underestimate the dangers that threatened to engulf the continent and Britain herself; they might the better appreciate the gravity of the German naval challenge to British sea power if the facts and their implications were authoritatively expounded to them and might finally be moved to contribute more to collective imperial resources. All the evidence suggests that the impression in fact made upon the dominion prime ministers by the foreign secretary's disclosures was marked. General Botha, breakfasting with Lloyd George a few days later, told him he was going back to South Africa apprehensive of war with Germany and that should it come he would invade German south-west Africa at the head of forty thousand men.

On the naval side the agreement of 1909 was followed in 1911 by a further Anglo-dominion understanding to the effect that, while the armed forces of Canada and Australia would be exclusively under the control of their respective governments, training and discipline in their navies would be generally uniform with the training and discipline of the Royal Navy. Furthermore there would be inter-changeability of officers and men. It would be for each dominion to place its naval service at the disposal of the imperial government in time of war and in that event the dominion ships would form an integral part of the British fleet and would remain under the control of the British Admiralty during the continuance of the war.[72] The Canadian government furthermore enquired in what form temporary and immediate aid might best be given by Canada, receiving the reply that 'such aid should include the provision of a certain number of the largest and strongest ships of war which science could build or money supply'. Robert Borden (who succeeded Sir Wilfrid Laurier as prime minister on the defeat of the Liberals in the elections of September 1911) introduced a Navy Bill on 5 December 1912 to authorise a Canadian contribution of some thirty-five million dollars for the construction of three battleships for the Royal Navy.[73] The Bill passed the Commons but was rejected by the Senate with its continuing Liberal majority, and as a result Canadian naval strength at the outset of war amounted to no more than two cruisers which were at once transferred to Admiralty control. New Zealand however contributed one battleship and offered another should need arise. In so doing it earned high commendation from the first lord of the Admiralty.

In giving a splendid ship to strengthen the British Navy at this decisive point [Churchill told the House of Commons in March 1914] . . . according to the best principles of naval strategy, the dominion of New Zealand have provided in the most effective way alike for their own and for the common security. No greater insight into political and strategical points has ever been shown by a community hitherto unversed in military matters.[74]

Before the Imperial Conference of 1911 assembled, Asquith had a paper specially prepared by the Committee of Imperial Defence setting out the various ways in which greater and more effective dominion participation in imperial defence might be secured. In it the principal aim of the United Kingdom was stated to be the creation of administrative machinery which would ensure that at the moment of the outbreak of war the measures decided upon would be taken without delay. The position of the dominions, however, introduced an element of uncertainty. While it was possible for the Committee of Imperial Defence to discuss the construction of machinery for enforcing measures agreed to in the United Kingdom, in India and in the Crown colonies, the cooperation of the dominions could be obtained only by consultation. It was thought most likely to be forthcoming if permanent, in place of occasional, representation of the dominions on the Committee of Imperial Defence could be secured. But there was here a difficulty later to become familiar. Permanent dominion representatives were likely to lose touch with their home governments and peoples; members of dominion cabinets, on the other hand, while in a position of responsibility, were unlikely to be able to attend meetings with the desired regularity. The answer, it was therefore thought, might best be found in the constitution of a dominion defence committee in each dominion, keeping in the closest touch through its secretariat with the Committee of Imperial Defence in London. From the discussion of these proposals at the Imperial Conference certain conclusions emerged: that one or more representatives appointed by the respective governments of the dominions should be invited to attend meetings of the Committee of Imperial Defence when questions of naval and military defence affecting the oversea dominions were under consideration, and secondly an acceptance in principle of the idea of establishing defence committees in each dominion, subject to separate dominion decision in practice. The resolutions were not published because of reservations about publication entertained by some dominion representatives, notably Sir Wilfrid Laurier who had had dialectical exchanges with Reginald McKenna, First Lord of the Admiralty, over what happened to Canadian warships if Britain was at war and Canada at peace, in the course of which he enunciated the doctrine Mackenzie King was later to make familiar that only the Canadian parliament could bring Canada into war. But in the later opinion of Lord Hankey, if any single episode can be selected as bearing more than any other on the stupendous effort of cooperation which the dominions made in the Great War it was those quiet discussions in the friendly atmosphere of Disraeli's old room at 2 Whitehall Gardens (the offices of the CID which led to these understandings about cooperation through co-ordination of war plans.[75]

It was not to be supposed however that even on the eve of the first world war the dominion prime ministers were chiefly preoccupied with high matters of defence or still less of foreign policy. In respect of the latter at least they were present to understand but not to determine. Responsibility for foreign policy, Asquith told the 1911 Imperial Conference, could never be shared. This was an overstatement which perhaps concealed his own doubts; but at that time at least it was not shared. Apart from defence, it was about detailed questions of imperial cooperation in its political, social or economic aspects that dominion prime ministers and governments – as private papers and official records make clear – were chiefly preoccupied. For the most part then, the proceedings of the Conferences of 1907 and 1911 continued to be prosaic. The matters to be considered were selected on the principle laid down by Elgin in a dispatch of 4 January 1907 and reaffirmed by Lewis Harcourt, as secretary of state, on 20 January 1911, that preference should be given to subjects proposed by the dominions and that subjects should have precedence according to the number of dominions proposing them, regard being had to the intrinsic importance of the subjects and the possibility of arriving at a definite result by discussion. The topics that qualified were important and varied but for the most part unexciting. They included the position of British Indians in the dominions, natural-isation, enforcement of arbitration awards, uniformity of laws, weights and measures, merchant shipping and navigation laws, currency and coinage, income tax and death duties, treaties and commercial relations, wireless telegraphy, land settlement – this was in 1907 with a paper for consideration submitted by Rider Haggard – emigration, an all-red mail route and penny post.[76] Some of these matters were easily settled or disposed of, others required detailed and technical enquiry. But one way or the other it was important for people in the dominions or in Britain that so far as possible they should be considered and that action should be taken on them.

More enlivening debate in 1911, as in 1907, was prompted by a variety of proposals of Australian or New Zealand origin for the formal strengthening of the ties of Empire by administrative reorganisation or federal reconstitution. Harcourt considered in advance with Asquith what concessions might be made and the outcome of their deliberations was submitted in a paper to their cabinet colleagues. With regard to renewed pressure for the reform of the Colonial Office, prime minister and colonial secret-ary came to the conclusion that the least that could be conceded was 'a bifurcation of the Office below the secretary of state' (i.e. the creation of two permanent under-secretaries – one for dominions and one for Crown colonies) and 'the addition to the secretariat of the Imperial Conference of a standing committee which will include the high commissioners or other representatives of the dominions'. The arguments in favour of departmental bifurcation were thought to be 'of a purely sentimental nature' but not for that reason to be disregarded.

Ministers of the younger 'Dominions' [the paper proceeded] appear to feel some degradation in any association with the Crown colonies, some of which were almost autonomous before the discovery of Australia or the civilisation of South Africa. The demand for dissociation from the other possessions of the Crown is in the nature rather of social precedence than administrative efficiency.

The secretary of state conjectured that the dominion prime ministers would reject the offer of 'bifurcation' if they understood the arguments against it. In domestic terms it would create undesirable administrative dualism and result in the conduct of affairs by permanent officials who would not have knowledge both of dominions and Crown colonies. From the dominion point of view the loss would be equally considerable.

> It appears almost certain [wrote the colonial secretary in a passage of imperial prognostication strange for a Liberal states-man] that in a future not very remote the dominions in temperate zones will desire to acquire for themselves 'hothouses' for consumable luxuries and other purposes. It may not be unreasonable to contemplate the ultimate absorption of the West Indies by Canada; of the Pacific Islands by Australia and New Zealand; of Rhodesia and the native protectorates (even of Nyasaland) by South Africa. But if the complete bifurcation of the Colonial Office is to be effected at once, these dominions will be divorced far more completely than at present from any knowledge of, or interest in, or indirect influence over, their neighbouring Crown colonies than they would be under a homogeneous Colonial Office with a single permanent under-secretary, possessing the daily knowledge of and control over the administration of both branches.'

The Paper further gave (and in these cases, surely deservedly) short shrift to proposals that the prime minister should take over control of the dominions, leaving the Colonial Office to deal only with Crown colonies, and to the suggestion that if bifurcation took place the secretary of state should in future be styled secretary of state for 'the dominions, Crown colonies and protectorates' – a 'cumbrous and rather ludicrous title'.[77] In the event Harcourt was not pressed to adopt it, not even sufficiently strongly to give effect to the changes he himself was prepared to make. In 1911 there was no confrontation on such matters and the Colonial Office emerged from the Conference without suffering even bifurcation!

There were other suggestions not alluded to in the secretary of state's Paper. The Australian government proposed that the judicial functions exercised by the Judicial Committee of the Privy Council in respect of the dominions should be vested in an Imperial Appeal Court, so as to ensure effective representation from overseas. The New Zealand government suggested that, in the interests of the governments of the United Kingdom and of the

oversea dominions alike, there should be an interchange of
selected officers of the respective Civil Services with a view to a
widening of knowledge of questions affecting Britain and the
dominions. Neither proposal was accepted in the form in which it
was submitted chiefly because of the practical difficulties involved.[78]

Altogether more far-reaching was the resolution submitted by
the prime minister of New Zealand, Sir Joseph Ward. Seemingly
unmindful of the significance of the exchanges of 1905 about
Council or Conference, he proposed in 1911 the creation of an
Imperial Council of State. This proposal was alluded to in the
secretary of state's cabinet Paper. Harcourt was confident it would
not commend itself to the Conference. 'I know,' he wrote, 'that it
will be opposed by General Botha and it is certain to secure the
vehement hostility of Sir Wilfrid Laurier . . .' He was right. By way
of the longest and possibly the most confusing speech ever
recorded at such a gathering Ward submitted his resolution. The
following exchanges sufficiently indicate the reaction of his conference colleagues to it:

Sir Joseph Ward: . . . My opinion is that there ought to be
established an Imperial Council or an Imperial Parliament of
Defence, in the interests . . .
Sir Wilfrid Laurier: There is a difference between a council and a
parliament. What do you propose, a parliament or a council? I
want a proper definition of what you mean, because you have
proposed neither so far.
Sir Joseph Ward: I prefer to call it a Parliament of Defence.
Sir Wilfrid Laurier: Very well.
The President (Mr Asquith): That is a very different proposition
to the one in your Resolution. Your Resolution is 'An Imperial
Council of State' – nothing about defence – 'advisory to the
Imperial Government'. It is limited, as I understand the Resol-
ution, to giving advice.
Sir Wilfrid Laurier: When it is started it is to be a parliament; who
is going to elect that parliament?
. . . . . .
Sir Joseph Ward: I would point out that the resolution is 'with
representatives from all the self-governing parts of the Empire.
Sir Wilfrid Laurier: But you say 'Council'. Is it a council, or is it a
parliament?
It is important that we should know exactly what is the proposal.
Sir Joseph Ward: I prefer to call it a parliament.

Sir Wilfrid Laurier: Very good, then; now we understand what you mean.

Sir Joseph Ward: I prefer to call it a parliament, although I admit there is a good deal in the name.

Sir Wilfrid Laurier: There is everything in the name.[79]

Sir Joseph Ward's proposals, conciliar or parliamentary apparently derived from his reading of two Round Table memoranda, one by Lionel Curtis and one by Amery which, against the wishes of the Group in London, were passed by Curtis (then in New Zealand on peripatetic mission to the dominions, promoting the cause of organic union of the Empire) to the Governor who showed them to the Prime Minister, with results that were deemed disastrous by the Group (who in order to impose some future constraint upon Curtis furthered his appointment as Beit Lecturer in Colonial History at Oxford) and in Milner's later comment 'calculated to dishearten imperialists everywhere'.[80] The extent to which this was so was the measure of imperialist-Round Table illusions about dominant dominion sentiment. However skilfully propounded proposals of the kind adumbrated by Ward had no chance of adoption and no one put the reasons more clearly than General Botha, an inflexible champion of imperial decentralisation.

> If any real authority [he argued] is to be vested in such an imperial council, I feel convinced that the self-governing powers of the various parts of the Empire must necessarily be encroached upon, and that would be a proposition which I am certain no Parliament in any part of the Empire will entertain for one moment.
>
> If no real authority is to be given to such a council, I fear very much that it would only become a meddlesome body which will continually endeavour to interfere with the domestic concerns of the various parts of the Empire, and cause nothing but unpleasantness and friction.[81]

No parliament in any part of the Empire was likely when it came to the point to entertain the thought of conciliar derogation from its authority – in that General Botha had put his finger on what to parliamentarians was the essential issue; and so long as parliamentarians decided the forms and methods of cooperation within the Commonwealth there would not be a council or any other central authority such as might impair the responsibility of their own cabinets to their own parliaments.

More significant than the defeat of particular and ill-digested
proposals for centralisation was the newer force of dominion
nationalism gathering strength and insistent upon continuing
decentralisation of imperial authority. Laurier and Botha were its
spokesmen. 'Laurier and I have renewed our friendship,' Botha
told Smuts in a letter of 15 June 1911. 'He and I agree about
everything.' And he proceeded: 'The Conference work is going
quite well. We have destroyed root and branch the proposal for an
Imperial Council of State or Parliament, and we have succeeded in
keeping the Conference as a round table affair.'[82] The balance of
power within the self-governing Empire had perceptibly shifted
with the addition of a united South Africa to the number of the
dominions.

It would however be a misconception to conclude a review of
dominion/British relations on the eve of the first world war in
terms of negation. The first and most important fact about them
was that they existed and subsisted on the basis of cooperation in
peace and also (in Hankey's opinion, which was almost certainly
correct despite some Anglo–Canadian exchanges in 1911), in the
event of any major war after the Conference in 1907 on the
principle 'United we stand: divided we fall'.[83] The second was that
over a wide range of subjects they were conducted on terms of
equality. 'In the early Victorian era,' Asquith reminded the
Conference in 1911, 'there were two rough-and-ready solutions for
what was regarded with some impatience, by the British statesmen
of that day as the "colonial problem". The one was centralisation . . . The other was disintegration.' But after seventy years'
experience, he continued, neither view commanded the slightest
support at home or overseas.

> We were saved from their adoption – some people would say by
> the favour of Providence – or (to adopt a more flattering
> hypothesis) by the political instinct of our race. And just in
> proportion as centralisation was seen to be increasingly absurd,
> so has disintegration been felt to be increasingly impossible.
> Whether in this United Kingdom, or in any one of the great
> communities which you represent, we each of us are, and we each
> of us intend to remain, master in our own household. (Hear,
> hear.) This is, here at home and throughout the dominions, the
> life-blood of our policy. It is the *articulus stantis aut cadentis
> Imperii.*

This was warmly received by dominion prime ministers – even if not all of them may have shared Asquith's liking for classical quotation.[84]

On 1 August 1912 there was a discussion at the Committee of Imperial Defence which may serve at once by way of epilogue and pointer to the future. The new prime minister of Canada, R. L. Borden, accompanied by four of his ministers, was present and showed himself as interested in foreign policy as in defence, the discussion ranging, according to Hankey, 'around the whole of "British foreign policy and the international situation" '.[85] Borden reminded British ministers that south of the Canadian border people had a direct and immediate voice in the government of their country, including all matters of foreign policy, while north of it foreign policy remained reserved to a distant imperial power. Borden allowed that the contrast had not as yet impressed itself strongly upon the imagination of the Canadian people but he had no doubt that it would begin to do so in the very early future as the country advanced in wealth, population and resources and more especially 'as it advances in its conception of what a national spirit demands'. His colleague, C. J. Doherty, put the point concretely. As the Canadian government was willing that the dominion should take a larger share in contributing in one form or another to imperial defence, then some means should be found by which it could be given a voice in the direction of the foreign policy of the Empire. The difficulties were well known. What was required was examination of them as evidence that there was not only a recognition of the principle that the dominions ought to have a voice in foreign policy, but further, an intention that they should be given one.[86] Within a year of Asquith's dictum about responsibility for foreign policy as something that could never be shared, representatives of the senior dominion were discussing the sharing of it.[87]

PART TWO

The British Commonwealth
of Nations, 1914–21

'Then if we are to continue as nations and to grow as nations and govern ourselves as nations the great question arises: How are we to keep this Empire together?'

'The British Empire is . . . the most hopeful experiment in human organisation which the world has yet seen. It is not so much that it combines men of many races, tongues, traditions and creeds in one system of government. Other Empires have done that,.but the British Empire differs from all in one essential respect. It is based not on force but on goodwill and a common understanding. Liberty is its binding principle.'

'We cannot consent to any abandonment, however informal, of the principle of allegiance to the King, upon which the whole fabric of the Empire and every constitution within it are based. It is fatal to that principle that your delegates to the Conference should be there as the representatives of an independent and sovereign state. While you insist on claiming that, conference between us is impossible.'

6 The Catalyst of War

If Joseph Chamberlain, in Curzon's already quoted phrase, was 'colony-mad', that was not an affliction widespread among British politicians of his generation. For the most part, in colonial affairs they heeded Talleyrand's advice – 'pas trop de zèle' – instinctively and without effort. Another but a misleading impression, it is true, is apt to be conveyed by overmuch reading of Seeley, Froude and Dilke or even of Goldwin Smith and Hobson and still more of composite volumes such as *The Empire and the Century*[1] with its contributions from no less than fifty hands and prefaced with a poem of Rudyard Kipling's reminding readers of *The Heritage*:

> Our fathers in a wondrous age,
>   Ere yet the Earth was small,
> Ensured to us an heritage,
>   And doubted not at all
> That we, the children of their heart,
>   Which then did beat so high,
> In later time should play like part
>   For our posterity.
>
> A thousand years they steadfast built,
>   To 'vantage us and ours,
> The Walls that were a world's despair,
>   The sea-constraining Towers:

The British public had its moments of Kiplingesque exaltation: British politicians however experienced them comparatively rarely. But in neither instance was it aroused by or extended to the dominions. They were (with the partial exception of South Africa) too ordinary, too British, too sensible to be romanticised. Even the set speeches with which Colonial and Imperial Conferences opened and closed rarely took wing, though in their own way they may be as inimical to balanced understanding as eulogistic appreciations of the prospects and purposes of Empire. Students of the

Commonwealth are indeed well advised on general grounds to eschew them as staple reading diet. They are, moreover, unusually unreliable in one respect, namely as a guide to British preoccupations. From 1907 a British prime minister presided over such Conferences by virtue of his office. This was designed to enhance their status and it was successful in doing so. But in so far as it may suggest that dominion affairs were becoming a major interest of British prime ministers or cabinets, it is misleading. Apart from great occasions, it was not prime ministers but colonial secretaries who were responsible *inter alia* for relations with the dominions. What manner of men were they? That is the important personal question. The calibre of Joseph Chamberlain was as evident to critics as to friends but who were the men who followed him at the Colonial Office? Were they men of political stature, close to the heart of the British electorate and to the springs of power? The answer is a qualified but revealing negative.

From September 1903 to December 1905 Alfred Lyttelton was colonial secretary. The Colonial Office was the only cabinet post he ever held. He was not a dominating figure. 'In the world of shadows,' he wrote to Milner, 'I was called your political chief. But in the world of realities you must know that I always thought of you as mine . . .'[2] It is true that others succumbed no less to the power of Milner's personality but in the case of Lyttelton the record of his period at the Colonial Office reinforces the impression of a secretary of state with authentic interest in colonial development but a secondary force politically and otherwise. Lyttelton's successor was the ninth Earl of Elgin. He had been viceroy of India but his had not been a momentous viceroyalty. During the tenure of Lansdowne and Elgin – 'these two acquiescent, unimaginative men' – the viceroyalty, in the opinion of Dr Gopal, 'reached its lowest ebb' in the nineteenth century and he notes especially of Elgin that he had no firm views and was happy to leave the power of decision to Whitehall.[3] Elgin's period at the Colonial Office is clouded by recollections of its close. Asquith, on succeeding Campbell-Bannerman in April 1908, decided to dispense with Elgin's services. He neglected, however, to tell Elgin. News of his impending dismissal appeared in *The Daily Chronicle*, but Elgin's first intimation was a letter from the new prime minister, which remarked on the need for advancing younger men, but made no acknowledgment of Lord Elgin's past services and, by way of adding insult to injury, concluded with the query: 'What about a marquessate?'[4] The incident fairly reflected Asquith's lack of tact and Elgin's lack of political weight. Departmentally, it has been persuasively argued, Elgin was an altogether more considerable figure than has hitherto been supposed.[5] His comments on the Colonial Office files certainly show a man of experience and sound judgment, with a firm grasp of the essentials of British-dominion relations. They also suggest a man of conservative temper conscientiously trying to remember that he was a member of a Liberal administration.

Elgin was succeeded at the Colonial Office by Lord Crewe, who was much esteemed for his skill in the easing of party differences and in inter-party negotiation. Unlike his predecessor, he had, in consequence a distinct and recognised political rôle. But this was counterbalanced, in respect of his tenure of the Colonial Office, by the lack of any marked interest in imperial affairs, Crewe being concerned most of all that they should run smoothly. He was followed in 1910 by Lewis Harcourt, later Viscount Harcourt, who held office till the first wartime coalition, 1915. As a young man, and under the soubriquet of 'Loulou', he had acquired, through his father, Sir William Harcourt, the most intimate knowledge of the intrigues and dissensions that finally destroyed Lord Rosebery's shortlived administration.[6] Departmenal evidence suggests that in respect of routine administration Lewis Harcourt may have been underestimated as colonial secretary. On the other hand the cabinet paper he prepared for the 1911 Imperial Conference, and already alluded to, contemplating as not unreasonable the ultimate absorption of the West Indies by Canada, and of Rhodesia, the Protectorates and even Nyasaland by South Africa, would seem to indicate a lack of realistic appreciation of the problems and patterns of the future. Certainly in relation to the towering personalities of Asquith's prewar administration, Lewis Harcourt was an altogether minor force.

In sum, Chamberlain's successors at the Colonial Office down to the outbreak of the first world war were conscientious and in many respects enlightened men, none of whom, with the possible exception of Crewe, exercised a major influence in cabinet or in the country. Nor were any of them, including Crewe, of a calibre to have probed the major issues of colonial policy in depth. They responded to dominion pressures, usually with understanding and often with wisdom, albeit of a negative kind, but the initiative in the development and progressive redefinitions of British dominion relations rested increasingly (as was perhaps inevitable) overseas.

The record invites the further question: Why were colonial secretaries after Joseph Chamberlain, as indeed before him, for the most part men of secondary political significance? The answer

would seem to be twofold. Generally speaking, younger men of
political capacity and ambition did not seek the office. In this, it is
true, as in so many other matters Winston Churchill was an
exception. In 1908 he asked Asquith for it, setting out his
qualifications in a letter which hardly could be said to have erred on
the side of modesty and suggesting that the government would
have much to gain 'from a spirited yet not improvident administration of an imperial department'.[7] Asquith appointed him
instead to the Board of Trade. The second part of the answer is not
unrelated to the first. Men of ambition did not generally opt for the
Colonial Office because the affairs with which it dealt, including
final responsibility for the administration of Crown colonies as well
as for relations with the dominions, were not deemed to be of first
importance either to the British electorate or in themselves. The
former was hardly open to dispute; the latter more questionable. It
was alleged, not only overseas, that the British public and parliament, by their comparative neglect and want of interest in the
growth of the self-governing dominions, showed a lack of political
perspective. One illustration may suffice. Sir Henry Parkes' proposals for the federation of Australia were laid before the premiers
of the other Australian colonies at the same time as the kaiser paid a
dramatic visit to the Turkish sultan. In the British press the first
passed virtually unnoticed while the second attracted much attention. The *Pall Mall Gazette* complained on 4 November 1889 of the
fact that the two chief organs of

> a government which professes above all things to be imperialist
> should devote columns of criticism this morning to the chances
> and changes in eastern Europe, but have not a word to say of the
> new departure taken at the Antipodes. Decidedly, Europe is too
> much with us . . . The future of eastern Europe is no concern of
> ours; but the future of Australia is of enormous concern in every
> way both in itself – as a greater England – and for its bearing on
> the Empire as a whole.

Yet statesmen, journals and the public showed themselves far more
interested in the German emperor's phrases and the sultan's smiles
than 'in watching the development of a policy which, conceived in
the fertile brain of Sir Henry Parkes, may be destined to mould the
future of the whole British Empire'.[8] The implications of these
comments were just in so far as they suggested that readers of
British newspapers were as much predisposed to the playing-up of
the importance of moves in European politics as they were to the

discounting of the possible significance of imperial developments. One reason was clear – relations between Britain and the dominions were good and good relations were not – and are not – news. Another was the attitudes of governments and their advisers. 'What is curious,' wrote John Morley from the India Office to the viceroy, Lord Minto, at the time of the Colonial Conference 1907, 'is that India – the most astonishing part of the Empire – is never mentioned, and people are very much obliged to you and me for keeping it under an extinguisher.'[9] The less the information or news, the less was likely to be the trouble!

Colonial leaders, apt to assume that their sense of priorities ought to be shared in London, were resentful when they found this was not so even in the Colonial Office itself. Deakin's assault upon the Office in 1907 was given edge by his conviction that its staff had got their priorities – in this case imperial priorities – wrong. And away from the Office, colonial interests were lightly regarded and colonial representatives were thought of in many influential circles as men to be humoured and entertained but not to be taken over-seriously. John Morley, in his correspondence with the viceroy made no secret of his anxiety for the day when Britain's colonial guests would have come and gone.

At this moment [he wrote on 12 April to Minto, who had served as governor-general of Canada from 1898 to 1904] people are going to be bored out of their lives (the boredom is already felt) by our colonial kinsfolk, of whom you know something. Your Canadians are excellent, but some of the others are uncommonly rough diamonds. The feasting is to be on a terrific scale, and we shall listen to any amount of swagger on one side and insincere platitude on the other. Yet the Empire is a wonderful thing for all that.

By 26 April Morley feared: 'The Colonial Conference is becoming the greatest bore that was ever known.' And by 24 May he was telling the viceroy – who had reminded him that 'these rising nations are the young life-blood of the Empire', like 'all young things full of conceit and full of confidence, but . . . young and strong' – that while he was not out of sympathy with them, the fact remained that 'our young colonial kinsfolk are apt to be frightful bores, and if you had been condemned to eat twenty meals day after day in their company, and to hear Deakin yarn away by the hour, I believe you would have been as heartily glad to see their backs as I am.'[10] In his perceptive biography of Asquith, Roy

Jenkins,[11] did not even allude to the Imperial Conference of 1911. The list of papers circulated to the cabinet in the years before the first world war and the prime minister's daily accounts to the king of cabinet proceedings both serve to show how rarely the cabinet's attention was occupied with dominion (including South African) affairs or problems.[12] Nor is it suggested or to be supposed that the cabinet sense of priorities was in this respect misconceived. Domestic politics and the possible approach of a European war dominated cabinet thinking. At the Colonial Conference in 1897 Chamberlain had sought to persuade colonial premiers to think in terms of larger colonial contributions to imperial defence with the argument that every war in which Britain had been engaged since the queen's accession had had 'at the bottom' a colonial interest and by the inference that this would continue to be so.[13] By the close of the first decade of the new century no such contention could be advanced at such a gathering with even a semblance of conviction. As European tensions intensified, great power colonial rivalries eased. With the signature of the Anglo–Russian Entente in 1907 it became probable, and with the Bosnian crisis of 1908–9 it became certain, that any major war would be fought by the great powers of Europe in Europe and with a European *casus belli*. Was it not then at once right and inevitable that Britain's external preoccupations should be overwhelmingly European at this time and, as a necessary consequence, that imperial, including dominion, affairs should be relegated to the background, except in so far as the Empire had a rôle to play in a European war?

While it is important not to overestimate the place of the dominions in British thinking and still less in the determining of British attitudes or the shaping of British policies before the first world war, it is also important not to discount or disregard it. The dominions – even collectively – were not a great but they were a growing factor, influencing certain aspects of British policy. It was true (to recall Asquith's candid comment) that responsibility for foreign policy was not shared before 1914. Equally however the dominions were not without opportunities for making their views known and thereby exerting pressure from within. In the later nineteenth century questions of foreign or defence policy directly affecting the interests of colonial governments were accepted in practice as being matters for some degree of consultation between the colonial government or governments concerned and the imperial government. Indeed in one instance the practice provoked the indignation of Bismarck. The year was 1884 and the occasion German enquiries about the protection of German traders at Angra Pequeña; enquiries which were soon to be formulated as claims for the occupation of what was later known as German south-west Africa. Procrastinating tactics were adopted by the Foreign Office, and the foreign secretary, Lord Granville, explained an inordinate delay in replying to German enquiries by asserting that in such a matter the British government could not act 'except in agreement with the government of the colony, which has an independent Ministry and Parliament'. On this Bismarck commented: 'That is untrue, and does not concern us; if it were true, we should have to maintain a legation with these British colonial governments.' When the German ambassador conveyed the chancellor's mounting dissatisfaction to the foreign secretary, Granville explained once again that this had happened 'owing to the independent position of our colonies, which we cannot get over with the best will in the world'.[14] Cape representations about possible German occupation of south-west Africa had their parallel, over an extended period of time, in the more strident though no more effective pressure of Australian and New Zealand colonies for the exclusion of foreigners and the establishment of Anglo–Saxon hegemony in the Pacific. In all cases colonial views were subordinated in the last resort to the demands of European diplomacy, but the expression of them was not denied nor did they pass unconsidered. In fact Bismarck, in his allusion to legations to be accredited to colonial governments, may be thought to have hit upon an underlying truth. As representative government was a step on the road to responsible government, so expression of opinion on matters of foreign policy – albeit only those of limited local interest – was likewise a first and often (as the Australians found) a frustrating step on the road to participation in the determination of such issues and ultimately to full and separate control of foreign policy.

There was good reason for this. In constitutional terms control of foreign and defence policies was reserved to the imperial government. But in terms of political realities the situation had changed from one in which the colonies relied upon British protection to one in which dominion assistance was still a small but an increasingly significant factor in Britain's plans for imperial defence. By 1914 the dominions were not suppliants seeking favours; they were states with military and naval contributions to offer. Those contributions remained conditional in form, even if it could be (as it was) assumed that, in Lord Hankey's cautious words, 'it was unlikely that any dominion would not offer to co-operate'[15] in the event of war. Indeed it was only on such an assumption that the agreement reached in 1911 – by which on the outbreak of war dominion fleets were to be placed by dominion governments under the control of the imperial government, and to form 'part of the imperial fleet and to remain under the control of the Admiralty . . . and be liable to be sent anywhere during the continuance of the war' – had meaning. It was an assumption, too, which underlay the discussions in the same year about the nature of military cooperation which had taken place; the planning to make it effective through dominion association with the Committee of Imperial Defence; the creation of dominion defence committees and the preparation in all the dominions of war Defence Schemes in the form of 'War Books' on the British model. None of these things was sufficiently advanced – Hankey felt one more Imperial Conference was required to bring them past the experimental stage[16] – but there had been progress in planning for coordination in war efforts that in 1907, and still more in 1902, would have seemed remarkable. Politically its effect was twofold: to draw the dominions closer to Britain and at the same time – since the implementation of plans and the measure of dominion cooperation remained a matter for the determination of their several governments – to make the British government increasingly sensitive to dominion views.

The changing nature of British-dominion relations did not pass altogether unnoticed in the European chancelleries. The German ambassador in London, Prince von Lichnowsky, told the German chancellor in 1914 that the possibility of the tightening of the Anglo–French *Entente* and of its transformation into a definitive military alliance of the kind which both the French and the Russian governments would have welcomed and which the German government feared, might be discounted on a number of grounds, one of them being that the dominions would not approve of it. The source of his information was the Foreign Office, where it was pointed out to him that 'most continental critics forgot entirely that not England alone, but also the entire British world Empire had a word to say in military and naval matters, and that the British cabinet had to pay much consideration to the wishes and needs of the dominions.' The German ambassador did not himself question the correctness of this Foreign Office view but confined himself to the comment that further use might be made of it.[17]

When war came on 4 August 1914 it was not the diversity but the unity of the Empire that was apparent. King George V declared war on behalf of the whole Empire on the advice of the cabinet of the United Kingdom. In theory, therefore, on this issue of supreme national moment the status of the dominions remained subordinate. But in practice this was only partially so since, as foreshadowed, the dominions (unlike India or the Crown colonies) determined the extent of their own participation. This qualification implicit in self-government was important. It meant that practice was continuing to make inroads upon theory. Those inroads were to be driven deeper in the course of the war, though from the outset and throughout within the context of an impressive unity. Immediately on the outbreak of war there was coordination on the basis of pre-war planning, with dominion navies placed at once under Admiralty control and dominion expeditionary forces recruited, trained and sent overseas, with their officers to serve under British supreme command and strategic direction. Outside the continent of Africa the war proved, as widely forecast, to be one of naval and military concentration, with the outcome to be determined in the North Sea and the continent of Europe including its near-east borderlands.[18] This concentration increased the closeness of Anglo-dominion cooperation and the sense of solidarity in a common cause.

Great Britain and the overseas dominions fought in the first as in the second world war from first to last. The challenge and the sacrifices of war sharpened their sense of separate identities and strengthened their feelings of nationality. The war memorials to be found throughout the length and breadth of the dominions; the Room of Remembrance in the Peace Tower high over the Parliament buildings in Ottawa with its record, on which few can look unmoved, of Canadian contributions to victory on the Western Front 1914–18; the Anzac memorial at Port Said, visited by countless Australians and New Zealanders until destroyed by the Egyptians in 1956; the memorial to the million dead of the British Empire on a pillar in the shadows of an aisle in the Cathedral of Nôtre Dame in Paris; all bear witness to the losses of the dominions on battlefields thousands of miles from home. These losses have been set out statistically, though not altogether precisely as citizens of the dominions or of the United Kingdom by no means invariably served in their own national units. But with such qualifications in mind, the record shows that of the 6,704,416 men – 22.11 per cent of the adult male population – who enlisted in the British Isles, 704,803 lost their lives; of the 458,218 Canadians who served overseas, 56,639 lost their lives; of the 331,814 Australians who served overseas 59,330 lost their lives; of the 112,223 New Zealanders who served overseas 16,711 lost their lives; of the estimated 76,184 South Africans who served outside

South Africa 7,121 lost their lives. The dominion forces that served overseas, or in the case of South Africa outside South Africa, accounted for 13.48 per cent of the male population of Canada; 13.43 per cent of the male European population of Australia; 19.35 per cent of the European male population of New Zealand and 11.12 per cent of the European male population of South Africa. There were contingents from Newfoundland among colonies of settlement, and combatant troops from West and East Africa and other parts of the colonial Empire. There was also, in a category all its own, the Indian Army in the ranks of which there enlisted nearly one and a half million volunteers, of whom over 62,000 lost their lives.[19] And while the cause was common, each dominion had memories of its own – the Australians and New Zealanders of the landings at Gallipoli, the Canadians of Passchendaele and Vimy Ridge, the South Africans of the early seizure of German South-West and later of the more protracted gentlemanly campaigning of General Smuts against the Germans under General von Lettow Vörbeck in East Africa. These were harsh and heroic experiences that served at once to strengthen the bonds of nationhood and to enrich each national treasure-house of memories.

   Within the dominions, war was at once a unifying and dividing force. In 1914 dominion governments and parliaments were at one in their support – majority support in the case of South Africa – for active participation in the war. In New Zealand and Australia this was at no time in doubt or question – the temper of the two dominions being well expressed in the pledge of Andrew Fisher, prime minister of Australia from 17 September 1914 till 27 October 1915 when he was succeeded by W. M. Hughes, that Australia would support Britain 'to the last man and the last shilling'. In Canada the German invasion of Belgium was deemed to have been decisive in enlisting French–Canadian sympathy for the Allied cause and thus ensuring a unanimous vote in the House of Commons for the government's war measures, while in South Africa the government, of which the former commandant-general of the Boer forces in the South African war, Botha, was head, sent a cabled message to London announcing its willingness 'to employ the defence force of the Union for the performance of the duties entrusted to the imperial troops in South Africa' and so to release these troops for service elsewhere. The British government, in accepting the offer, enquired further whether the South African government would desire and feel themselves able to seize strategic areas in German South-West Africa and in so doing to perform 'a great and urgent imperial service'. The Union government answered, as Botha had forecast to Lloyd George in 1911, in the affirmative. In so doing they divided Afrikaner opinion.

South Africa's participation in the war was approved by a large majority in the House of Assembly. But what mattered was less the size of the majority than the intensity of the feelings of the minority. They were expressed constitutionally by General Hertzog. He acquiesced in the fact that South Africa was legally at war because of the king's declaration on behalf of the whole Empire but urged that the Union's belligerency should be passive. Some among his fellow Afrikaners felt however that South Africa's involvement in an Empire's war demanded forceful protest, while many others (especially in the Orange Free State, who did not themselves necessarily feel impelled to take so grave a step) nevertheless were understanding of those who did so. Their sympathies were heightened to the point of open antagonism to the government firstly by the shooting, on 15 September 1914, of General de la Rey after nightfall while on his way to the western Transvaal to urge opposition to the government's attack on German South-West Africa, accidentally – though this was far from universally credited – by a police patrol; and secondly, on the night of 8 December by the death of General Beyers, who was in command of the Union defence forces at the outbreak of war but who, after seeming acquiescence, openly led the protest against the invasion of south-west Africa, left Pretoria and was drowned when his horse was shot under him while he was trying to escape across the Vaal river. The rebels were crushed; if they had not been, there was an offer dated 23 October 1914 from the British government to make available for that purpose 30,000 Australian and New Zealand troops already at sea *en route* for Europe. The offer was kept open until 9 November, when Botha and Smuts were able to rule out the need for assistance, acceptance of which would have been fraught with grave embarrassment.[20] General Botha took personal command of the Union forces in a campaign in South-West Africa which was successfully concluded by July 1915. But the rebellion (though militarily of no great significance), and the personal tragedies associated with it, added to the burden of memories which shadowed all attempts at the final reconciliation of a united Afrikanerdom with the British Commonwealth. The events of 1914, as interpreted by General Hertzog who had no knowledge of the British offer of Australian and New Zealand troops – that remained undisclosed for some fifty years – meant that South Africa enjoyed a free constitution but had an unfree government – one that acted at the behest of imperial authority. So

long as that situation continued, so long in his view and in that of
the Nationalist party he had founded in 1912 and now led, would
there be cause for dissension among Afrikaners. As Botha and
Smuts moved towards the achievement of their destinies as
Commonwealth statesmen there remained – drawing sustenance
from unhappy circumstances and nurtured by General Hertzog's
hand – the conviction that responsibility for the division of Afrikanerdom was to be attributed not to those who had rebelled
against the participation in an Empire's war but rather to those who
had sought first reconciliation with that Empire and then involved
South Africa in an imperial war. In so doing they had shown
themselves, so nationalists alleged, to be 'lackeys of imperialism'
and 'traitors' to the Afrikaner people.

In the dominions other than South Africa the long extended war
with its heavy casualties produced severe political strains. Notable
among them were the conscription crises of 1916–18. Conscription
was enforced in Britain for the first time under the National Service
Act of January 1916. That example was followed in New Zealand.
Opinion in Australia however was deeply divided, there being
strong objections to it, voiced by many spokesmen of unorganised
labour as well as by the organised unions and also by the
Irish–Australians with Archbishop Mannix as their spokesman.
The issue was submitted to the electorate in a referendum in
September 1916, in which conscription was rejected by a narrow
majority. Of the Australian soldiers overseas 72,000 voted for and
59,000 voted against conscription.[21] A second referendum produced no different result.

In Canada the conscription crisis of 1917 revealed not social but
cultural division. While there had been agreement from the outset
among English- and French-speaking Canadians about participation in the war, the emphasis was different. This was reflected in
the utterances of the political leaders of the Liberal and Conservative parties even at the outbreak of war when Sir Robert Borden
gave unquestioned and immediate backing to the mother country
while Sir Wilfrid Laurier, in full accord on the major issue,
underlined once again that it was for 'the Canadian people, the
Canadian parliament and the Canadian government alone to
decide'.[22] In June 1917 Borden introduced a Conscription bill into
the Canadian Parliament. Laurier opposed it. He believed that
conscription would do more harm than good, that it would divide
the country on cultural grounds and that it would hand over
Quebec to the extremists. The Liberal party split. Some supported
Laurier, others the prime minister's efforts to form a union

government pledged to conscription as part of an all-out war effort. There followed a general election in December 1917, fought in an atmosphere of high emotion, which strained national unity almost to breaking point. The outcome was a clear verdict in favour of conscription, the Union government securing 153 seats against 82 for the Opposition Liberals. Yet no less than sixty of the Opposition members were returned by Quebec constituencies. The dominion had divided along its line of cultural cleavage and as a result the confederation was subjected to a test which was thought by many to threaten its survival. There was then 'introduced into Canadian life', Professor Lower has commented, 'a degree of bitterness that surely has seldom been equalled in countries calling themselves nations'.[23] Conscription was enacted but not vigorously enforced in Quebec, where even qualified attempts to do so resulted in resistance or riots. The objection of French-speaking Canada to conscription was passionate and sincere; the grievance of English-speaking Canada authentic. Of the four hundred thousand Canadian soldiers overseas in 1917 it was estimated that less than thirty thousand were French Canadians.[24]

The position of dominion governments in the earlier years of the first world war was not altogether enviable. Their countries were at war, their forces were fighting in distant theatres of operations, they were responsible for their recruitment and their equipment, they determined as they thought best the extent and the manner of their country's participation in the war including the use of its manpower and resources, but they had control neither of the higher direction of the war itself nor of the policies that might determine its duration and its ending, nor indeed in all cases of the intended deployment of their forces – neither the Australian nor the New Zealand governments for example having been made aware of the offer and possible diversion of their troops to assist the South African government. If on the part of dominion governments there was acceptance of necessary and practical limits of their authority in respect of the command and higher direction of the war, there was marked and increasing restiveness at the lack of consultation or even of information from London on the part of Canada, Australia and New Zealand. Early in 1915 it prompted Sir Robert Borden to go to London in the hope of securing fuller knowledge of events and policies, while in October of the same year Andrew Fisher resigned his prime ministership, influenced by domestic political factors, but also in order to serve as Australian high commissioner in London with the same object in mind.

Borden's visit to London, while serving some immediate purposes, effected no lasting improvement in respect of consultation. On 1 November 1915 he found it necessary to cable the Canadian high commissioner in London, Sir George Perley, asking him to tell the colonial secretary, Andrew Bonar Law, that the Canadian government would appreciate fuller and more exact information from time to time respecting the conduct of the war and proposed military operations

> ... AS TO WHICH LITTLE OR NO INFORMATION VOUCHSAFED. WE THOROUGHLY REALISE NECESSITY CENTRAL CONTROL OF EMPIRE ARMIES BUT GOVERNMENTS OF OVERSEAS DOMINIONS HAVE LARGE RESPONSIBILITIES TO THEIR PEOPLE FOR CONDUCT OF WAR, AND WE DEEM OURSELVES ENTITLED TO FULLER INFORMATION AND TO CONSULTATION RESPECTING GENERAL POLICY IN WAR OPERATIONS.

When the high commissioner conveyed the message to Bonar Law, the colonial secretary explained that while the British government had been only too delighted to put the Canadian prime minister in possession of all the information available to the cabinet when Sir Robert Borden had been in London, it was much more difficult to keep in touch with him once he was back in his own country. In principle Bonar Law allowed that the Canadian government was entitled to be consulted and to have some share in the direction of a war effort in which Canada was playing so big a part. But, he continued:

> I am, however, not able to see any way in which this could be practically done. I wish, therefore, that you would communicate my view to Sir Robert Borden, telling him how gladly we would do it if it is practicable and at the same time I should like you to repeat to him what I said to you – that if no scheme is practicable then it is very undesirable that the question should be raised.[25]

Borden commented with some asperity and more justice that the colonial secretary's letter was not especially illuminating and had left the matter precisely where it was before he had raised it. He then proceeded to restate the grounds of his complaint:

> During the past four months since my return from Great Britain, the Canadian government (except for an occasional telegram from you or Sir Max Aitken) have had just what information could be gleaned from the daily press and no more. As to consultation, plans of campaign have been made and unmade,

measures adopted and apparently abandoned and generally speaking steps of the most important and even vital character have been taken, postponed or rejected without the slightest consultation with the authorities of this dominion.

It can hardly be expected that we shall put 400,000 or 500,000 men in the field and willingly accept the position of having no more voice and receiving no more consideration than if we were toy automata. Any person cherishing such an expectation harbours an unfortunate and even dangerous delusion. Is this war being waged by the United Kingdom alone or is it a war waged by the whole Empire? If I am correct in supposing that the second hypothesis must be accepted then why do the statesmen of the British Isles arrogate to themselves solely the methods by which it shall be carried on in the various spheres of warlike activity and the steps which shall be taken to assure victory and a lasting peace?

It is for them to suggest the method and not for us. If there is no available method and if we are expected to continue in the role of automata the whole situation must be reconsidered.[26]

In 1916 a more formidable dominion controversialist, in the person of W. M. Hughes, set out for London. On his way he called at Ottawa and reached an understanding with Sir Robert Borden about dominion aims which was of first importance. Once in London Hughes showed that he was no respecter of persons in high positions, least of all of Asquith, and had no inhibiting sensitivity about proclaiming publicly his views about what was needed for the effective direction of the Empire's war. He was in all invited to attend two sessions of the War Council and two of the War Cabinet and at the first of these on 9 March, two days after his arrival, he was placed at the prime minister's right hand. The two principal matters that came up for discussion, although indirectly affecting the dominions, were within the exclusive jurisdiction of Britain. Hughes, so he recalled, spoke on them 'as I would have done had the problems arisen before the Commonwealth cabinet' and supported the minority on each occasion. He reflected later that

Mr Asquith was not so enamoured of the reception of what no doubt appeared to him as a most courteous gesture towards the dominions as to make him eager to issue regular invitations and thus crystallise into an institution that which he could only regard as a most unfortunate experiment . . . So other invitations came

along – at spacious intervals intended to make it clear that one
must regard what he had done as an act of courtesy rather than
an established practice. The dominion representative attended
when he was invited. When he was not, he just hung around or
went through the country making speeches.[27]

The second was Hughes's practice. But when due allowance is
made for the forthright tactics of this passionate and pugnacious
controversialist, the fact remains that dominion leaders were far
from satisfied with the overall direction of war policy and more
particularly in respect of their own participation in it; they were
interested not in the occasional courtesies but in formal acknowledgment of what they deemed to be their due share of responsibility. The attendance of an individual prime minister at a cabinet
meeting was an arrangement welcome so far as it went but it
satisfied neither the Australian nor general dominion demand for
continuing participation in the direction of an imperial war. As the
Report of the Imperial War Conference 1917 later recorded, the
feeling continued to grow that 'in view of the ever-increasing part
played by the dominions in the war . . . it was necessary that their
governments should not only be informed as fully as was possible of
the situation, but that, as far as was practicable they should
participate, on a basis of complete equality, in the deliberations
which determined the main outlines of imperial policy'. How was
this feeling to be satisfied? Lloyd George in his first speech to the
House of Commons as prime minister on 19 December 1916
(acting, it would seem, on Milner's advice) took the first significant
step by announcing that the dominions were to be invited to meet at
an Imperial Conference in the Spring of 1917.[28]

The Conference, which met in March that year, was a successor
Conference to the Imperial Conference of 1911, and it has gone
down to history as the Imperial War Conference. The Conference
had little to do with the conduct of the war. Its proceedings are
remembered chiefly because of one debate on the future constitution of the Empire. It took place in the light of a new departure in
the conduct of British-dominion relations for which L. S. Amery
has claimed the credit. When, on 19 December 1916, he heard
Lloyd George's announcement in the House about the forthcoming Imperial Conference the thought occurred to him, why
should not the representatives from the dominions be asked 'to join
the war cabinet itself and so assert their full equality and their right
to be at the heart of things in deciding the conduct of the war?'[29] In
cabinet, Milner gave his influential backing, the idea was adopted

and Lloyd George invited dominion governments to take part in 'a series of special and continuous meetings of the war cabinet in order to consider urgent questions affecting the prosecution of the war ...' According to Hankey, who was much amused by the wording, the new War Cabinet 'have not a notion what they are to discuss', while Bonar Law commented, 'When they are here, you will wish to goodness you could get rid of them.'[30] The first at the time no doubt was true; the second proved, some interludes apart, ill-founded. In any event the course was now set. There was to be an imperial war cabinet – the name was of Hankey's devising[31] – in addition to an Imperial War Conference. It was arranged that they should sit on alternate days, the prime minister presiding over the cabinet, the colonial secretary over the Conference. Responsibilities were to be divided so that the Conference would be left with its traditional rôle of reviewing imperial relations, while the imperial war cabinet was to be concerned with the conduct of the war and the defining of peace aims in their imperial aspects.

The imperial war cabinet met for the first time on 20 March 1917 and was served by the cabinet secretariat established by Lloyd George on his accession to office in December 1916.[32] The original intention had been to confine its membership to dominion prime ministers, allowing them to bring ministerial colleagues only on occasion and as required, but this aim was not realised. There was a coalition government in New Zealand with W. F. Massey as prime minister and Sir Joseph Ward as his principal partner-colleague – a sort of political Siamese twins, Hankey termed them. Ward insisted upon coequality of status with Massey in the imperial war cabinet as the price of continued coalition in New Zealand. Concession followed, and with concession to New Zealand there had of necessity to be concessions to the other dominions. In addition to the dominions India was represented by the secretary of state assisted by three assessors, two of them Indians the maharajah of Bikaner and Sir S. P. Sinha nominated by the secretary of state and present in recognition of India's outstanding services in the war. The imperial war cabinet thus became not the compact body Lloyd George had originally contemplated but a comparatively large gathering. As a result, to avoid the British ministers being outnumbered the prime minister felt compelled to increase the British war cabinet from five to eight among whom, however, from June 1917 was General Smuts, a member of the South African Parliament. Moreover (so Hankey recalled) Lloyd George, while deciding that 'the whole caboodle' of dominion ministers must be asked, 'was very bored'.[33] More important, the size of the imperial war cabinet led to the delegation both in 1917 and 1918 of much of its business to subcommittees. The most important of these was the subcommittee of prime ministers set up in June 1918 while the imperial war cabinet was meeting for its second session to consider the critical situation on the Western Front. It met between 21 June 16 August.[34]

The imperial war cabinet captured the imagination of governments and of most of those preoccupied with problems of imperial relations. Sir Robert Borden – hitherto so critical of lack of information and consultation with the dominions on major issues of policy – sensed its potentially far-reaching implications. Addressing the Empire Parliamentary Association in 1917 while the imperial war cabinet was still in session, he observed that for the first time in the Empire's history there were sitting in London two cabinets, both properly constituted and both exercising well-defined powers. The prime minister of the United Kingdom presided over each of them. One was designated the war cabinet; the other the imperial war cabinet, and each had its distinct sphere of responsibility and jurisdiction. Borden noted especially that in the imperial war cabinet prime ministers and other representatives of dominions met with the prime minister and ministers of the United Kingdom cabinet as equals. Ministers of six nations sat around the council board, all of them responsible to their respective Parliaments and to the people of the countries which they represented. Each dominion, Borden felt, had its voice upon questions of common concern and of the highest importance as the deliberations proceeded; and each preserved unimpaired its perfect autonomy, its self-government and the responsibility of its own ministers to their own electorate.[35] Lloyd George was no less enthusiastic. He told the House of Commons on 17 May 1917 that members of the imperial war cabinet were unanimous that the new procedure had been of such service that it ought not to be allowed to fall into desuetude. He had himself proposed at the concluding session that meetings of an imperial war cabinet should be held annually and that the cabinet should consist of the prime minister of each of the dominions (or some specially accredited alternate possessed of equal authority) and of a representative of the Indian people to be appointed by the government of India. This proposal, generally approved, opened the way for further meetings of the imperial war cabinet in 1918. Lloyd George also laid some emphasis on the fact that dominion leaders, through their membership of the imperial war cabinet, would be able 'to obtain full information about all aspects of imperial affairs and to determine by consultation together the policy of the Empire in its most vital aspects, without infringing in any degree the autonomy which its parts at present enjoy'.[36]

There is little doubt that many of those most closely associated with the work of the imperial war cabinet thought of it (particularly after its second session in 1918) as an innovation that had grown out of the necessities of war but one which in some form would survive the immediate occasion of its coming into being. It was the full and formal imperial war cabinet that attracted the attention of the public but the sub-committee of prime ministers constituted in 1918, though technically subordinate to the larger body and reporting to them when time allowed, were compelled by force of circumstances to take decisions 'every time they met' on matters that 'would brook no delay'. Had the war continued, the trend towards a concentration of authority in the prime ministers' hands might have continued.[37] But in any case there were institutional problems deriving from the very nature of the cabinet (or its sub-committees) apt to be overlooked or discounted by some enthusiastic contemporaries.

One characteristic of the imperial war cabinet was that in the established meaning of the term it was not a cabinet at all. The ministers who composed it were neither collectively responsible to nor members of a single Parliament, and accordingly two of the classic conventions of cabinet government were not observed. Amery, a principal architect and eulogist of the imperial war cabinet, while conceding that it had no collective responsibility to a single representative body argued at the time that a substitute for this might be found in its distributed responsibility to a number of Parliaments. He also later recalled, and with approval, Sir Robert Borden's 'apt phrase' – 'a cabinet of governments rather than of ministers'. In so far (he wrote) as the imperial war cabinet 'worked as a single body of colleagues all concerned with the same end and each contributing to the best of his individual judgement, it deserved the title of cabinet as fully as any cabinet that I have ever attended'.[38] Meriting and being however are by no means always the same thing.

Amery thought of the innovation of the imperial war cabinet not as an end in itself but as the hopeful starting point for further imperial consolidation in purpose and action. From the premise that 'the imperial cabinet is undoubtedly a real cabinet' he proceeded, in a memorandum[39] of some eighteen pages dated June 1918, which was circulated to dominion prime ministers among others, to argue in favour of a continuing imperial cabinet that was small so that it might be personal and intimate; that was responsible; and that was continuous. Yet only the first of these conditions could be satisfied without posing fundamental questions about the nature both of the cabinet and of imperial relations. If there were to be an imperial cabinet that was responsible, to whom and for what was it to be responsible? Amery, it would seem from his memorandum, contemplated the disentangling of imperial from United Kingdom interests with responsibility for the former lying to all the parliaments of the Empire. He conceived that the principle of equality of status and responsibility as between Britain and the dominions really postulated that a department, such as the Foreign Office and its various agencies abroad, serving imperial purposes should be jointly controlled and financed by a contribution shared between Britain and the dominions, with the shadowy figure of an imperial minister of finance to deal with the consequential problems of imperial financial cooperation. And as for continuity in session, that was possible only if dominion prime ministers or their representatives were to remain more or less permanently in London. If they did so, what authority would they carry with their colleagues at home? How closely in touch would they remain with dominion public opinion? Amery suggested, at least as a part answer, that the imperial cabinet system should have as a necessary complement something in the nature of a sounding-board; some arena in which policy could be openly expounded and discussed and so reach the press and public of the Empire. 'The Imperial Conference,' he noted hopefully, 'expanded into a Conference of Parliaments, would exactly fill this need.' Dominion experiences of war presaged developments in quite other directions but historically it is interesting – even ironic – to recall how the appearance and to some extent the reality of concentration of power in the imperial war cabinet encouraged thoughts of the possibilities of developing post-war centralisation of Empire.

However Amery's spacious reflections be regarded, the problem that inspired them was real enough. The dominions at the imperial war cabinet were moving towards a measure of control in war and foreign policy. How was this in fact to be exercised? Was there to be an area of joint British-dominion responsibility? Austen Chamberlain, reflecting on this, as a result of some observations of W. M. Hughes at a meeting of the imperial war cabinet in July 1918, felt the matter was essentially one not for Britain but for the dominions to resolve. He did not question the perfect justice of the dominions' claim to be regarded as sister nations in free and willing cooperation with the United Kingdom but he did wonder how this cooperation was to be carried on.

> Even in war-time [he noted] when the most momentous issues arise from day to day and have to be rapidly decided, it is not possible for the prime ministers of the sister nations to be present at our deliberations for more than a few weeks in the year. In peace time they may find that their own electorates and Parliaments become impatient even of such short absences. How then can touch best be maintained during that large portion of the year when the personal presence of all the prime ministers in London is not possible, and how can the dominion governments be given their due influence in the decisions of the Empire's policy?

If and when there were dominion representatives in London, an imperial cabinet might meet weekly or as often as required, whether in war or in peace.

> The real problem [he continued] I think is how these dominion representatives are to be chosen and how it can be secured that they shall possess the mind and confidence of the government which they represent sufficiently to be of real assistance in council, or in other words, under what circumstances and in what measure a dominion government would be content that such a representative should take decisions in its name.

Austen Chamberlain posed with cogency and precision the question to which dominion statesmen were unable to find an answer that was acceptable and satisfying to them. So long as that was so, notions of joint control and joint responsiblity, exercised through an imperial war cabinet or otherwise, fell to the ground. The remarkable thing is how slow many British and some dominion statesmen were to become reconciled to these facts of imperial political life.

The opportunities and the perplexities inherent in a changing dominion/United Kingdom relationship alike became apparent when victory was won. Lloyd George's original invitation to the dominion prime ministers to come to London for an Imperial War Conference and to take part in the meetings of an enlarged war cabinet had referred not only to urgent questions affecting the prosecution of the war but also to the possible conditions of peace. Both were in fact discussed during the sessions of the imperial war cabinet in 1917 and again in August 1918. Later that year the collapse of the Central Powers necessitated an urgent summons to the dominion prime ministers (other than W. M. Hughes of Australia who with commendable foresight had remained) to return to London so as to take part in discussions about peace terms at meetings of the imperial war cabinet, which began what proved to be its last session on 20 November. Already there had been indications, notably from Hughes, of dominion concern about the rôle in peace-making that might or might not be allotted to their representatives. Thus on 29 October 1918 Sir Robert Borden, of whom it has been remarked[40] that he had entered the war a devout imperialist, but ended it a determined nationalist, largely because of intractable problems of consultation, communication and confidence, of which he himself had experience at a high political level and awareness of that of others in respect of practical military cooperation, sent a secret, private and personal message to Lloyd George saying that there was need for serious consideration of the question of the representation of the dominions in the peace negotiations.

> The press and people of this country [he observed] take it for granted that Canada will be represented at the Peace Confer-ence. I appreciate possible difficulties as to representation of the dominions but I hope you will keep in mind that certainly a very unfortunate impression would be created and possibly a danger-ous feeling might be aroused if these difficulties are not overcome by some solution which will meet the national spirit of the Canadian people. We discussed the subject today in Council and I found among my colleagues a striking insistence which doubtless is indicative of the general opinion entertained in this country. In a word they feel that new conditions must be met by new precedents.

On 4 December Hankey had a meeting with Borden – 'he was full of grievances and rather formidable' Hankey recalled, being resentful about not being told of the allied decision to bring the Kaiser to trial (of which he strongly disapproved) complaining of irregular procedure and oversight about Canada's representation at the Peace Conference and telling him he had not come to take part in light comedy. Borden's principal point was that Canada had come into the War on the broadest grounds, and had claim to representation for that reason, but would be affronted by a suggestion that she should be entitled to representation on questions on which she was specially affected. There were none.[41]

Throughout, Lloyd George was receptive and sympathetic to dominion representations and particular concerns as well as persuasive and there was discussion about them in the imperial war cabinet proceeding on the initial assumption that only five places could be secured for the British Empire at the Peace Conference. If that assumption proved correct, it meant the adoption in some form or another of a panel system under which representation of the British Empire at the Peace Conference would be selected from day to day from a panel made up of representatives of the United Kingdom and the dominions. This was bound to be a constricting arrangement for both. Accordingly, the members of the imperial war cabinet agreed that they should press not only for a British Empire representation of five according to the panel system but also for separate representation for each dominion similar to that accorded to smaller Allied powers. These proposals were discussed with the principal Allied powers; though received with initial coolness they were finally accepted. As a result the dominions and India secured dual representation, first, as occasion required, on the British Empire panel – which in practice allowed of a substantial meeting of Canada's position as set out by Borden – and then separately as belligerent powers with special interests entitled to send two plenipotentiary delegates to Paris. In the first capacity Britain and the dominions formed the British Empire Delegation which was regarded as an extension of the imperial war cabinet, meeting in Paris for the particular purpose of agreeing a common policy on the terms of peace, and as such was served by Sir Maurice Hankey as secretary and by the secretariat of the war cabinet reinforced by dominion personnel. In the second capacity each dominion decided upon its own representation.

What were the implications of dual dominion representation, and how effective did it prove? Dr Loring Christie, the legal adviser to the Canadian prime minister, essayed an answer in a Memorandum summarising the development of the status of Canada as an international person at the Paris Peace Conference. He felt that the dominions gained by their dual status. As members of the British Empire delegation they received the confidential papers of the Conference such as the minutes of the Council of Ten and the Council of Five, denied to other smaller powers, and as a result were able in their own individual capacities to watch and check the proceedings more effectively. The dominions also secured through membership of the British Empire delegation a more significant rôle on committees and commissions than would have otherwise been the case. Dominion ministers were, for example, nominated to and acted for the British Empire on the principal inter-Allied commissions of the Peace Conference, and all the dominion prime ministers took part in the Council of Ten when the disposition of the German colonies was being discussed and decided. Since the Peace Treaty was largely drafted by commissions of the Peace Conference in the first instance, dominion representation on them was correspondingly important. Moreover, as Christie recorded: 'Every Commission report, every aspect, every section of the Conditions of Peace was first considered in meetings of the British Empire delegation (whose personnel was the same as that of the imperial war cabinet) before the assent of the British Empire was given.' In view of this, in view of the attendance of dominion prime ministers from time to time at the Council of Ten and of the prime minister of Canada's participation on a number of occasions in the work of the Council of Four and the Council of Five, Christie concluded that the dominions' participation in the making of peace had been very substantial.[42] If a longer retrospect suggests an altogether more sceptical opinion it is nevertheless worth recording that on the British side Amery reached much the same conclusion as Christie. The dominions, Amery thought, by virtue of their membership of the British Empire Delegation and their association in it with the representatives of one of the 'Big Four' were able to exercise a continuous influence on the negotiations and were 'in a quite different position from the ordinary run of secondary powers whose delegates hung about, picking up such stray crumbs of information about their own fate as might be vouchsafed to them'.[43]

The influence of Australia, New Zealand and South Africa was certainly significant in respect of the disposition of the former German colonies and the extension of the Mandates' system to the Pacific and Africa. They were all interested parties. Australia at the outset pressed vigorously for the outright annexation of the former German possessions in the Pacific. Hankey, who had already had experience of the problems of providing the 'extraordinarily nice drafting [required] to reconcile Borden, who doesn't want to grab territory, and Botha, Smuts and Hughes who do' is on record as having 'invented' with the aid of Smuts and J. G. Latham, an Australian Legal Adviser, 'the device of the "Class C" League of Nations mandates whereby territories whose people were regarded as too sparse and "remote from the centres of civilization" for self-government should be "administered under the laws of the mandatory" '. After protracted disputation, in the face of 'overwhelming odds', W. M. Hughes reluctantly abandoned his annexationist demand, on the understanding that the 'C' class mandate granted would be 'the equivalent of a 999 years' lease as compared with freehold'. For reasons of security there could never be an open door to Asiatic immigration. 'There should be', as Hughes later phrased it, 'a barred and closed door with Australia as the guardian of the door.'[44] South Africa was equally resolved to secure – and obtained – comparable control over south-west Africa. From the dominions the evidence of a revival or stirring of the expansionist spirit was as pronounced as that of the enlightenment that might be thought implicit in notions of intra-imperial equality founded in national freedom. In so far as the latter found expression at Versailles it was through the voice of General Smuts, the second delegate for South Africa, who used all his gifts of persuasion and his personal prestige in a vain endeavour to modify the harshness of the peace terms imposed upon the defeated enemy.[45]

The form of status accorded to the dominions at the Peace Conference carried one possible theoretic liability. When the treaty came to be signed the dominion plenipotentiaries appended their signatures, 'for Canada', 'for Australia', as the case might be, under the signatures of the plenipotentiaries from the United Kingdom, who signed for the British Empire as a whole. While on the one hand therefore it might be asserted that the dominion signatures represented recognition of the dominions as international persons, it could be argued on the other hand that they were formal or even superfluous.[46] This was an ambiguity some at least of the dominions were resolved in due course to remove. In the meantime they had established their individual right whether or not to accede to the treaty and had simultaneously secured (again not without some misgiving on the part of other powers) membership and representation in the Assembly and Council of the new League of Nations in all respects the same as that of other members. Technically they became members of the League as signatories of the treaty and no distinction was made in this respect between them and other signatory members. The dominions, Christie cautiously concluded in his memorandum 'have asserted a sovereign status of some sort and have for some purposes entered the family of nations. There were at Paris, and will be, anomalies . . .' That was certainly true; but whatever the anomalies about the status of the dominions in the present, it was clear after 1919 that each was moving towards the goal of separate sovereignty, internationally recognised.

In the one debate of lasting moment at the Imperial War

Conference 1917 the dominion representatives had considered the future of imperial relations. The language was for the most part hopeful but not complacent. They gloried in the nationhood of the dominions. They spoke constantly of equality. 'I believe,' said Sir Robert Borden, 'that the dominions fully realise the ideal of an imperial Commonwealth of United Nations . . .'. They were really bound together by the tie of common allegiance, by like institutions and ideals of democracy, and by like purposes.

> We are [said General Smuts] the only group of nations that has ever successfully existed. People talk about a league of nations and international government, but the only successful experiment in international government that has ever been made is the British Empire, founded on principles which appeal to the highest political ideals of mankind.

But this was not sufficiently recognised in the constitution of the Empire. General Smuts proceeded:

> Too much, if I may say so of the old ideas still clings to the new organism which is growing. I think that although in practice there is great freedom, yet in actual theory the status of the dominions is of a subject character. Whatever we may say, and whatever we may think, we are subject Provinces of Great Britain. That is the actual theory of the constitution . . .

It was a theory that in his view could not and should not survive. The young nations were growing into great powers; they would require readjustment of relations on a basis of equality but such readjustment was not the appointed task of the Imperial War Conference of 1917. The Conference approved a Resolution (Resolution 9) recommending that this should be the chief responsibility of the first Imperial Conference to assemble after the end of the war.[47] But by the time that Conference met in 1921 something of the warm glow of common conviction had departed from dominion representatives, while the British government had reason to be more preoccupied with the opening of negotiations for a dominion settlement in Ireland and other immediate issues than with a review of relations with existing dominions. 'We do not want', Milner had told the Prime Minister in October 1920, shortly before his resignation as Colonial Secretary, 'a "constitutional" or other "conference" . . . between the Mother-country and the Dominions. That may have to come some day but it is too soon. . . . What we do want is . . . to discuss and settle on the basis of our existing institutions the various practical and urgent problems which affect the Dominions as well as the Mother-country . . . That is to say, we want very soon a meeting of what we once called the Imperial War Cabinet . . . The only essential thing is to get the different PMs together under your Presidency.'[48] Yet the purpose of the 1917 Resolution was not forgotten. General Smuts saw to that. He was not politically in a position to remain passive. He was under constant Nationalist fire in South Africa about his own and his country's subservience to British policy. He did not, comments his biographer, have the option of leaving the question of imperial constitutional relations alone. 'Both his personal history and his political circumstances compelled him to formulate a doctrine, to promulgate a code.'

In 1921, Smuts drafted a memorandum entitled, 'The Constitution of the British Commonwealth' and intended to serve as a basis for the discussion of questions which might come before the Constitutional Conference, recommended by the Imperial War Conference 1917. But the memorandum was not, in fact, circulated to the Imperial Conference 1921, because Smuts wished first to prepare the ground for it in discussion and the proposed Constitutional Conference did not take place. It was not, therefore, an official Conference Paper, which on the shorter term, and not without a helping hand from Hughes, served to diminish its impact.[49] It was, moreover, in any case a highly personal appraisal, steeped in South African background, of the direction in which the Commonwealth should advance, consistent with past development, present position between and within each of the dominions and its own political nature. The language of the memorandum was urgent and its conclusions in some respects remarkable, even if regarded as no more than essays in political prognostication. But its chief interest lies in the light it throws upon the nature of the debate on Commonwealth and Empire, provoked by the cataclysmic experiences of war.

At the outset the tone of Smuts's memorandum was cautionary. 'Delay in the settlement of dominion status is fraught with grave dangers . . . The national temperature of all young countries has been raised by the event of the great war.' Unless dominion status was settled soon, in a way that would satisfy the legitimate aspirations of 'these young nations, we must look', he argued, 'for separatist movements in the Commonwealth. Such movements already exist, notably in South Africa, but potentially in several other dominions also.' The only way to deal with them was 'to forestall them and to make them unnecessary by the most generous satisfaction of the dominion sense of nationhood and statehood. The warning against always being too late with a proper solution, of which Ireland is an example to the whole Commonwealth, is one which we can ignore only at our own peril.' The root of the problem lay in the conflict between law and usage.

In principle Smuts conceded that the existence of dominion equality was to be inferred from dominion signatures to the peace treaties in 1919 and their membership of the League of Nations. But that equality did not exist in law. Law, therefore, ought to be brought into harmony with practice. It was true that as things stood, any attempt of the Parliament of the United Kingdom to legislate for a dominion would be unconventional even revolutionary. But clearly it was legal. Could, enquired Smuts, action in conformity with existing law be then regarded as 'revolutionary'? Therein lay the paradox. A simple solution would be to end the legislative sovereignty of Parliament at Westminster in respect of the dominions. Smuts did not favour it. It would be a negative step; it was better to leave such theoretic sovereignty alone as 'a sort of symbolic reminder of the historic unity of the Commonwealth'. The positive and constructive course would be to assure the legislative sovereignty of dominion Parliaments and to give them the power, which they did not possess, of legislating with extra-territorial effect. All dominions should have the power to amend their own constitutions. The Colonial Laws Validity Act, 1865, which laid down that any dominion legislation in conflict with British statute law was to the extent of such repugnancy null and void, should be repealed. Given the necessary authority, particularly to amend their own constitutions in every case, the dominions could decide for themselves whether or not for example they should abolish appeals to the judicial committee of the Privy Council in cases where appeals were still admitted.

Smuts then turned to the field of foreign affairs. Here too he detected continuing anomalies. The dominions had acquired international status and received international recognition in 1919 but practice had not been correspondingly changed. In effect the Foreign Office still continued to control the relations between the dominions and foreign countries. There was in fact little consultation between the British and dominion governments in such matters beyond the sending of occasional summaries of the international situation. True there had been important advances. The dominions could now advise the king to appoint dominion ministers to foreign countries. It was also now recognised by convention that the dominions could not be bound by treaties they had not signed. But practice was unsettled and foreigners were confused. They found it

> difficult to grasp the difference between legal theory and constitutional practice in the Empire and to see how the law of the constitution is moulded and finally abrogated by the practice of the constitution, and how, without a change of the law, a British colony becomes in constitutional fact an independent state. These abstruse matters might be cleared up in some formal way which would show the true nature of dominion status as distinct from legal archaisms.

How should it be done? Here too Smuts had his proposals. They were remarkable chiefly for the measure of continuing centralisation which he was ready to contemplate.

Dominion governments, Smuts suggested, should become coordinate governments of the king with full equality of status. This would mean 1. that they should

> cease to be placed under the Colonial Office or any other British Department, 2. that the Dominion government should have direct access to the king who will act on their advice without the interposition of the British government or a secretary of state, 3. that the governor-general should become viceroy simply and solely and only represent the sovereign in his dominion executive and not also the British government.

The second – direct dominion access to the sovereign – was all important to Smuts. In his view it would represent the crucial step from which all else would follow. It would necessarily have to be laid down that the king in his conduct as a dominion sovereign would act only on the advice of his dominion government. Since the king in practice resided in England this would mean the residence in England of a dominion minister of the Crown with direct access to the sovereign. But (argued Smuts) this should not be allowed to impair the intimate relations keeping British and dominion governments in close touch. Machinery would be needed; without it there was the risk they would drift apart. This machinery should comprise three organs of conference for consultation about the policies and common concerns of the Commonwealth. One was to be a 'Commonwealth Congress, or Imperial Conference', held every four years. It was to include not only cabinet ministers but also representatives of Parliamentary oppositions. The second was to be a prime ministers' Meeting, or Conference, in place of the imperial cabinet, which should meet every two years 'to review the foreign and defence or other common policies of the Commonwealth as a whole'. Finally there would be a smaller body, a dominions' Committee, consisting of the prime ministers or their deputies and providing a continuing organisation to ensure continuous consultation. This Committee would be served by a Commonwealth secretariat.

Smuts concluded his analysis with a recommendation that the imperial cabinet should draft a general scheme of future Commonwealth constitutional relations; that the scheme should take the form of resolutions to be submitted to a Constitutional Conference and that these resolutions should provide for legislation by the Parliament at Westminster 1. giving power of constitutional amendment to the dominions, 2. extending their legislative jurisdiction beyond their territorial limits, and 3. abrogating the Colonial Laws Validity Act. There should be further a declaration of rights, as had been suggested by H. Duncan Hall in *The British Commonwealth of Nations*, providing that 1. the British Parliament had no constitutional right of legislation in respect of the dominions, 2. that the Royal Veto was in the same constitutional position in the dominions as in the United Kingdom, 3. that the dominions had direct access to the sovereign without the intervention of any British secretary of state, and 4. that the international status and rights of diplomatic representation of the dominions were unquestioned. Finally Smuts proposed that a new name should mark 'this epoch-making departure'. It should be the British Commonwealth of Nations, for what was no longer an empire but a society of free and equal states. He also thought that there should be some great symbol to mark the equal status of the dominions and their entry among the nations of the world and that the most appropriate might be the adoption, in the case of each dominion, of a distinctive national flag.

The immediate importance of General Smuts's memorandum was less than might have been supposed. There were three reasons for this. The first, already mentioned, was its lack of official status. That meant it was not formally laid before an Imperial Conference nor formally debated. But more substantially, the theme of the memorandum was unacceptable to majority opinion at the Imperial Conference, 1921 and knowledge of its content, if anything hardened opposition to any attempt to reduce the Commonwealth to writing or to the formulation of what Hughes discounted as a 'flamboyant declaration of rights'. Thirdly – and technically and tactically important – the Imperial Conference 1921 was not the constitutional Conference contemplated in Resolution 9 of the Imperial War Conference of 1917. On this point Lloyd George was explicit in issuing invitations to it. Was it part of its responsibility then to prepare for such a Conference? This was a matter that was left to the Conference to decide and it could do so if it seemed desirable, or even necessary, to consider afresh the purposes a constitutional conference might serve. 'It may be that I am very dense', remarked W. M. Hughes, 'but I am totally at a loss to understand what it is this Constitutional Conference proposes to do. Is it that the dominions are seeking new powers, or are desirous of using the powers they already have, or is the Conference to draw up a declaration of rights, to set down in black and white the relations between Britain and the dominions? What is this Conference to do? What is the reason for calling it together?'[50] Hughes thought there was none that justified its assembling. Massey from New Zealand agreed with him. So long as there was a partnership of nations it appeared to Massey to matter little whether it was called a family of nations, a Commonwealth of Nations, or anything else. Nor did the words that might be placed upon paper to define that relationship matter much more. The strength of the Empire rested upon the patriotic sentiments of the British people, by which the New Zealand prime minister meant not only Anglo–Saxons or Europeans but 'the British people right through the Empire, including the native races. You cannot go beyond sentiment.' Arthur Meighen, who represented Canada and was chiefly pre-occupied with discouraging the further extension in time of the Anglo–Japanese alliance, was more inclined to sympathise with such Australasian opinions than any Canadian prime minister of the century. Opposition, reinforced by indifference, sufficed accordingly to ensure the inclusion of a sentence in the Resolutions at the end of the Conference saying that in view of developments since 1917 no advantage was to be gained by holding a Constitutional Conference. While retrospectively therefore it may seem a foregone conclusion that the status of the dominions and their relations with Great Britain should be reviewed and, so far as was possible, defined in terms of convention and of law, this was by no means self-evident even as late as 1921. It was not Hughes, who was well pleased to be able to report to his fellow countrymen on his return that he had soldered up the constitutional tinkers in their own tin can, but Smuts who had reason to feel frustrated when the Imperial Conference dispersed.

Against short-term disregard, however, must be placed long-term reality. General Smuts's memorandum was closer to that reality than any known contemporary document. It expressed succinctly the problems and the possibilities of the British Commonwealth of Nations as it emerged from the first world war. It had an appreciation, which time proved to be well founded, of the dangers particularly of disregard of nascent dominion nationalisms. In itself it provided a programme for the future. 'Smuts's memorandum of June 1921' claims his biographer[51], 'contained by anticipation the Balfour Declaration of 1926 and the entire constitutional achievement from then until the Statute of Westminster of 1931 . . .' Essentially it was a sanguine document. It was infused by a sense of the possibilities before the Commonwealth. 'The tents have been struck, and the great caravan of humanity is once more on the march.' So Smuts had said in 1918 and he at least had no doubt that the Commonwealth was in the vanguard. His greatest misconception, as may be seen from this vantage point in time, lay in his implicit assumption about British imperial power. The British Empire, he told his colleagues later at the Imperial Conference, 'emerged from the war quite the greatest power in the world, and it is only unwisdom or unsound policy that could rob her of that great position'.[51] It was an assumption which did not qualify the politico-psychological arguments for dominion equality with Britain but one which never the less encouraged facile disregard of the possible politico-strategic price of the progressive decentralisation of imperial authority.

7 Ireland: the Dominion Settlement

'I need not enlarge to you on the importance of the Irish question for the Empire as a whole.' Smuts to Lloyd George, June 1921.

The Irish question in the form in which it had dominated the politics of late Victorian England passed into history with the signing of the Anglo–Irish Treaty in the early morning of 6 December 1921. It had a threefold importance in its concluding phases. In English politics the Irish settlement was a principal cause of the break up of Lloyd George's Coalition government and of the subsequent return to traditional party alignments at Westminster. In Irish history it represented the substantial but not the complete failure of English attempts to rule Ireland which had lasted some seven hundred years, the incompleteness deriving from the continuing inclusion of the six plantation counties of the north-east within the United Kingdom. Finally, the Irish question became a landmark in the history of the British Commonwealth of Nations because dominion status was conferred by the treaty for the first time on a country which was not in origin a colony of settlement and had not progressed by stages towards that politico-constitutional relationship with Britain. It is the last alone that has its place in Commonwealth history. But how and why it attained that place, against logic and historical probability, is not to be understood without consideration first of English and then of Irish political attitudes.[1]

The Liberal approach to the solution of Anglo–Irish relations was in full accord with the classical doctrines of mid-nineteenth century Liberal imperialism adapted to a situation that had no close parallel historically or geographically in the British Empire. The essence of the doctrine was consolidation, in this case of union, by timely concession and consequent enlistment of indigenous, national opinion in its support. In 1882 Gladstone himself had attempted – vainly as it proved – to persuade Queen Victoria of the wisdom of pursuing such policies in Ireland by drawing her attention to their earlier success, in the face of much gloomy foreboding, in Canada. By a comparable concession of autonomy Ireland also, he urged, might be reconciled to Britain and to the Empire.[2] The correctness of his conclusion remains a matter of historical speculation. There were three attempts, the first two by Gladstone himself, to apply such traditonal Liberal remedies, in the form of Home Rule, to Ireland. All of them failed. The first Home Rule Bill was defeated by a narrow majority in the House of Commons in 1886; the second passed the House of Commons but was rejected by an overwhelming majority by the House of Lords in 1894; the third, introduced in April 1912, its passage in Parliament and in the country vehemently disputed at every stage by the English Unionist party and their Ulster Unionist allies, pledged by solemn covenant to resist the incorporation of Ulster in a Home or, in the terminology of the day, Rome ruled Ireland, was placed on the Statute Book in October 1914 but together with an Act suspending its operation until after the end of the war and coupled with an assurance of amendment in respect of the Ulster counties. Suspended and to be amended, the Act served most of all to discredit the Irishmen who had followed first Charles Stewart Parnell and then John Redmond in the constitutional parliamentary movement. John Redmond, so it would appear from some of his letters,[3] thought it not impossible that he might be cast in the rôle of an Irish Botha, and by 1912 many Liberals, elated by the success of their South African policies, shared his hope that it might be so. But the events of 1914 ensured that there would be no Irish Botha.

The defeat of Home Rule stemmed from roots growing deep in English domestic politics. After 1886 it was not the parties of reform, whether Liberal or Labour, but the Unionist, or Conservative, party that was the major force in English politics. In the ninety odd years that have since elapsed that party has been in office either on its own, or in coalitions in which it has been the dominant partner, rather more than sixty. In the shorter period between the introduction of the first Home Rule Bill and the Anglo–Irish settlement, the balance between Unionists and Liberals was somewhat in favour of the Liberals in terms of time, but in the decisive years in Anglo–Irish history, 1886 and 1920–1, the Unionists and their allies possessed a parliamentary majority, while in the prewar struggle over the third Home Rule Bill they were sufficiently strong to frustrate Liberal purposes. This fact of Unionist dominance – especially at critical moments – needs re-statement if only because historical interest is apt to be drawn disproportionately to Liberal or Labour administrations. This is not surprising. It is more exciting to read or write about change and reform than about conservation. Yet it can be misleading, as it has been in the historiography of Anglo–Irish relations. If classical Liberal notions were never applied to Ireland, Unionist policy was fully tested.

At this point it is well to look more closely at the common Liberal assumption that it was more important that Gladstone should have proposed a Home Rule Bill in 1886 than that Joseph Chamberlain should have killed it. Is the assumption well founded? Might it not be argued that the rejection of Home Rule by the Radicals in association with Tories and dissident Whigs was the event that was crucial in its consequences for the next half century? It had meant in the first place that the establishment, in terms of the traditional landed interest and propertied classes, was reinforced by radical lower middle-class and working-class votes, which were important and at times possibly decisive electorally. But it had also a further, long-term significance. The cause that united left with right, deriving from common opposition to Home Rule, was maintenance of the union. Their association accordingly brought into existence a party generally pragmatic in its outlook but of political necessity rigid and ideological on the issue which had brought it into being.

'Jack Cade' may have vanished, as Professor Thornton[4] has remarked of the archetypal radical-unionist Joseph Chamberlain, 'behind orchid and eyeglass, taking his Radicalism with him'. But his Unionism always retained its pristine importance. The Conservative Party became the Unionist Party and the change of name symbolised a modification, at the least, in character. Adaptable as the party might be in its response to changing interests in other fields, implicit in its very being was one unchanging element – support for the union. In this respect it was a party depriving itself, from 1886 to 1921, of its customary freedom of political manoeuvre. Its attitude to Ireland could not change in response to changing circumstances (as, for example, it was to do a generation later – with dramatic consequences – in respect of Africa) because of the manner in which Home Rule was defeated in 1886. Unionism was a party dogma and was in effect written into its constitution. And it was this party, tied to dogma in this one particular, that with the aid of its in-built majority in the House of Lords negatively or positively determined British policies in Ireland between 1886 and 1905; and which, down to 1921, was generally able to call up sufficient reserves of establishment influence or electoral strength to block all but the most resolute of

Liberal reformers, in a period in which Liberal reformers were not generally remarkable for their resolution on Irish issues.

Was Unionist policy towards Ireland in these years then a study in political negation? The answer is qualified. Its unchanging premise was a negation – no Home Rule – from which there derived certainly a broad but by no means necessarily a detailed conclusion. Herein lay the area of debate and discussion within the party. Home Rule rejected, what was to replace it? Coercion? Or conversion? In essence those were the alternatives. Four-fifths of the Irish electorate supported Home Rule. Home Rule was not to be conceded. Were the Irish then to be coerced in perpetuity into acceptance, or at the least acquiescence in union? Or was there some other way by which they might be persuaded to abandon the Home Rule dead end? The second, it is not to be doubted, was the hope of all except a die-hard (but possibly realistic) minority. Arthur James Balfour supplied the necessary conceptual foundation for it. 'He is', noted Sir Henry Lucy[5] when Balfour first made some mark in the House of Commons in 1880, 'a pleasing specimen of the highest form of the culture and good breeding which stand to the credit of Cambridge University.' But he was also something more – 'a pretty speaker, with a neat turn for saying nasty things',[6] and as Sir Henry had occasion to note in 1890, in him was to be 'recognised the most perfect living example of the mailed hand under the velvet glove'.[7]

Balfour's analysis of the Irish question possessed a broad imperial interest. In his opinion what went at the time by the comprehensive name of Parnellism was a superficial and dangerously misconceived political expression of ills which were real. Those ills were social and economic. They were endemic in the Irish social system, especially the land system. They were deep-seated, hard to alleviate, but given persistence, time and above all a sense of common British party purpose, not beyond remedy. Such political consensus, in the Balfourian exegesis, should be forthcoming if only by reason of British self-interest, or to be more precise of the interests of the British propertied classes. For while the outward manifestations of Parnellism were political, its inward dangers were in equal measure social. The exploitation of agrarian distress for political purposes had resulted in an assault upon the rights of property in Ireland where they were most vulnerable and Balfour, like Salisbury and many others besides and before him, argued that the undermining of property rights in one part of the United Kingdom would by necessary consequence open the way to their impairment in others. On this reasoning, which (it will be noted) had little force or application in respect of distant colonies, the right course was to remedy Irish grievances, relieve Irish social distress, foster industries and the welfare of the Irish people and so not merely maintain, but strengthen through new contentment, the union and incidentally, but significantly, re-insure the rights of property throughout the United Kingdom. The phrase was 'killing Home Rule with kindness'. The kindness, however, on the Unionist premise, was a pre-condition of the killing. But therein lay – as Balfour was to find – a familiar and inexorable dilemma. The moment of reform is always difficult, sometimes dangerous, for an autocratic régime. Hitherto (Balfour had said at the outset of his chief secretaryship in 1887) English governments had 'either been all for repression or all for reform. I am for both: repression as stern as Cromwell; reform as thorough as Mr Parnell or anyone else can desire.'[8] He sought, in other words, to avert the risks associated with reform by 'resolution' in government. The price however was that the resolution counterbalanced or outbalanced the psychological effects of reforms. 'Bloody Balfour', 'the man of Mitchelstown', was not associated in the Irish mind with 'kindness'. That was a handicap for the chief secretary and, more important, for the policy he propounded, which was never overcome.

Balfour, however, did not stand alone. There were twenty years of Unionist rule between 1886 and 1905, broken only by a three-year interlude of uncertain Liberal administration. In the chief secretary's office, A. J. Balfour was followed by his brother, Gerald (who first applied the phrase 'killing with kindness' to Home Rule) and then by George Wyndham – an attractive, gifted personality and a romantic Tory, of whom it was said that Sir Walter Scott was 'his only outpost in the modern world'.[9] Yet, for all his gifts Wyndham lacked one thing, as important to politicians as Napoleon deemed it to be for generals – luck.[10]

He came to office resolved to settle the land question. It is not much of an exaggeration to say he settled it. The foundation provided by a Land Conference under Lord Dunraven's chairmanship was used to frame an Act that encouraged landlords to sell and tenants to buy, the inducement for both being provided by a substantial Exchequer grant. Wyndham however was not content to think of the Land Act as an end. It was a means – a means, as his biographer has written, 'of euthanasia for Home Rule'.[11] There was an element (or possibly a double element according to the point of view) of illusion here. Even Liberals, by no means convinced of the reality of Irish nationalism, argued that if nationalism derived from social oppression, where was the assurance that it would end with it? And if Irish nationalism was in itself not a derivative but an absolute, then there was no possible foundation for the notions Wyndham entertained.

Wyndham himself soon had reason for doubt. He had appointed, as happened on a number of occasions in Irish administration under the union, an eminent imperial administrator, Sir Antony MacDonnell (lieutenant-governor of the United Provinces who was, however, also an Irishman and a Catholic with Home Rule sympathies) under-secretary at the Irish Office. Balfour's keen political nostrils scented the whiff of danger. But Wyndham, less perspicacious and relaxing abroad after the passage of the Land Act, inadvertently overlooked the extent (of which he was, albeit a little casually, informed)[12] of the under-secretary's commitment to a modest programme of political and administrative devolution for Ireland. There were first indignant rumblings and then angry protests from within the Unionist Party at this supposed official commitment to some small loosening of the sacred bonds of union. MacDonnell survived the storm but Wyndham resigned. In effect the Unionist experiment in killing Home Rule with kindness was ended. It had had its successes, notably the 1903 Land Act, on the road to final failure. Far from being killed, Home Rule was showing every sign of re-invigoration. Nor was it a question of Home Rule alone; it was self-evidently the larger question of Irish nationalism. Salisbury, Balfour, George Wyndham, all alike had denied the reality of its existence. That was an article of their Unionist faith. How much longer could the party subscribe to it?

Out of office from December 1905 until the formation of the first wartime coalition in 1915, the Unionist Party moved (though not so rapidly as is retrospectively apt to be supposed) towards an extreme position, or perhaps more accurately towards an extreme attitude, for it could be argued that Unionist insistence upon the union and nothing but the union was in itself the extreme fundamentalist position. But at least – so long as Balfour was leader of the party – it spoke the language of reason and not of violence. There could be no compromise about the union, but were there not ways in which concessions might be made to Irish sentiment consistent with that fundamental purpose? Indications were not lacking that this was a possibility, which had all the appearance of a last chance and which was about to be more seriously weighed. No one can read English Unionist discussion about future Irish Policy at this time without sensing behind the polemics a mood of deepening perplexity.

In 1906 there appeared F. S. Oliver's *Life of Alexander Hamilton*. It enjoyed great success – except with historians; it had far-reaching influence. Its theme, in biographical form, was the making of the American federation. Oliver believed with George Washington that 'influence is not government' and the moral he drew from the early experience of the United States was the need for authority to ensure the triumph of centripetal over centrifugal forces. Some years later he sought to apply the lessons to the Britisn Isles. In 1910 he published a series of letters under the title *Federalism and Home Rule*, the argument of which was that while 'the union of the United Kingdom is a great thing, and to impair that would be to lose all', that union was not necessarily inconsistent with federalism or even conceivably – certain conditions being fulfilled – with Home Rule. In further pamphlets, *The Alternative to Civil War* (1913) and *What Federalism is Not* (1914) Oliver elaborated his views. In so far as federalism or Home Rule were consistent with devolution of authority, as distinct from division, he was prepared to favour them. He believed that a delegation of powers from Westminster to the four national units in the British Isles on a permanent basis would at once preserve the union and might be made a part of a larger plan for the federation of the whole of the British Empire, the 'grand federal idea' on which Oliver and his colleagues in *The Round Table* had set their sights. It was all a dream. Irishmen were even more opposed to the federation of the British Isles than Canadians and South Africans were to the federation of Empire. But in each case the reason was the same. They were aware that such a federation would not lead, and was not intended to lead, to recognition of their several and separate political identities, but to their merging with and ultimate submergence in a larger whole. At root therefore, behind the forms, the phrases and the idealism of the Round Tablers, the gulf between imperialism and nationalism lay unbridged. Oliver's conception of Home Rule was limited to a delegation of power to all four national units in the British Isles, leaving unimpaired 'the union of these Islands', which as he wrote and as Stephen Gwynn[13] who later edited his letters noted, was to men of his views 'by its nature, sacramental'. In that context federalism implied, not as Oliver suggested 'a new departure' for Unionism, but superficial rearrangement of the forms of union to make it more palatable to Irish nationalists.

In 1913, in the same year in which Oliver wrote of federalism, A. J. Balfour, now dispossessed of the leadership of the party by Andrew Bonar Law, reflected, also in pamphlet form, upon *Nationality and Home Rule*. His approach was closer to political realities. He conceded that there was an Irish problem. He argued that it lay neither in the existing parliamentary system nor in the existing financial system, both of which indeed he claimed were more favourable to Ireland than to Britain. The land system was reformed, the administrative system was being reformed. Where then was the justification for Home Rule?

> It lies in the fact [noted Balfour] that the Irish Nationalist Party claim that Ireland, *on the ground of a separate nationality*, possesses inherent rights which cannot be satisfied by the fairest and fullest share of the parliamentary institutions of the United Kingdom. What satisfies Scotland cannot satisfy them, and ought not to satisfy them. It would be treason to Ireland.

Balfour then proceeded to probe the foundations of Irish nationality and concluded that neither in respect of Irish institutions nor of Irish culture nor of Irish descent or civilisation was there sufficient ground for the separate nationalism implicit in Home Rule. The explanation for that was to be found 'in the tragic coincidences of Irish history'. In them, Irish nationalism originated and from them it derived its anti-British tradition. How should British statesmen respond? To Balfour there were only two alternatives. The first was maintenance of the union and the keeping of Ireland in full political communion with England and Scotland. The second was to give her complete autonomy. That was 'a counsel of despair'. Yet, Balfour noted, it was apparently suited to the disease. It gave nationalist Ireland what it professed to desire. In that respect it was at least a solution of the Irish nationalist problem. But what of Home Rule? It offered the middle course but it solved no problem whatsoever. Financially, administratively and constitutionally, he argued, it was at once indefensible and unworkable. His own answer was time, time in which to give the measures enacted by the Unionist administration a chance to have their remedial and beneficial effects. And to those who argued that 'Irish patriotism, in its exclusive and more or less hostile form, is destined to be eternal', he replied that they should think in logic not of Home Rule but of separation.

By 1913 Balfour possessed influence but no longer enjoyed power within the party. That rested in the improbable hands of Bona Law, a pugnacious pessimist elected to the leadership because he was known to be politically a first-class fighting man. On the ground that the Parliament Act of 1911 by curbing the powers of the House of Lords had upset the balance of the constitution, Bonar Law felt warranted in urging the party of 'law and order' to take all steps to resist Home Rule. The Liberal government was, he declaimed at Blenheim on 27 July 1912, 'a Revolutionary Committee' which had seized by fraud upon despotic power. The Unionists accordingly would no longer be restrained by the bonds which would influence their action in any ordinary political struggle. They would use whatever means seemed most likely to be effective. Under Bonar Law's leadership the English Unionist Party committed themselves, even to the point of threatened violence, to the support of the Ulster Unionist cause. Yet Ulster was not an end in itself to the majority of English Unionists, even if Bonar Law's own position on this point (possibly by reason of his Ulster descent) remained personal and distinctive.[14] It was a means to an end and that end was the preservation of the union and thereby of the integrity of the Empire. The imperial interest thus reinforced, in a way that has been insufficiently recognised, domestic opposition to Home Rule. It moved imperial administrators, soldiers, and even statesmen not otherwise interested in Irish affairs to action. Many of them had at most qualified faith in democratic processes.

Lord Milner provided the outstanding example. By temperament and by reason of his pro-consular experiences in South Africa he had nothing but contempt for the British parliamentary system. He felt 'only loathing for the way things were done in England, in the political sphere' and despised English politics. He hated the pressure of parliamentary necessities, he disdained the whims of a 'rotten public opinion', and if in South Africa he had made sacrifices they were not 'for this effete and dislocated Body Politic'. In the supposed interests of Empire and without regard for British parliamentary tradition, Milner (as A. M. Gollin in his *Proconsul in Politics* first made plain) used his remarkable administrative gifts for the organisation of opposition to Home Rule in Great Britain, chiefly through the Union Defence League, securing by 1914 close on two million signatures for the British covenant. He also sought, and apparently succeeded, in securing substantial financial backing for measures which he was only too ready to contemplate but from which even the Ulster leadership under Sir Edward Carson and James Craig shrank. Of all the Unionist leaders Milner 'was the least anxious to seek a compromise solution to the Ulster problem'.[15] As for the English Unionist leaders, Milner himself noted that they preferred to talk rather than to enter into any definite plan for ridding themselves, by other than constitutional means, of the 'horrible nightmare' of a Home Rule into acceptance of which Ulster might have to be coerced. If these leaders are remembered for the great lengths to which they went, there were even greater being urged upon them.

In the last phase of Unionist opposition to Home Rule, poised as it was on the brink of violence, there were at least three identifiable elements in Unionism. There were first the Irish Unionists (whose attitudes and assumptions by no means always coincided with those of their English allies) themselves subdivided between the Ulster and southern Unionists; secondly there was the main body of English Unionists who thought of Home Rule chiefly as an issue in domestic politics; and finally there were the imperialists, accustomed to autocratic rule, some though not all of them with Milner on the extreme right, little interested in Anglo–Irish politics for their own sake but thinking of the unity of the British Isles as an essential condition of the unity and therefore of the greatness of the British Empire. Bound together by one supreme and testing issue, this was the formidable combination before which Liberals weakened and the cause of Irish constitutional nationalism succumbed.

For Unionism the Easter Rising, 1916, was the moment of truth. Unionists had declined to credit the authenticity of Irish nationalism. That was not for them a matter of political opinion but something that had become in effect close to an article of political faith. The rising, immediately for some but in the longer run for almost all, destroyed the conviction on which it rested. Irish nationalism came to be recognised for what it was. In time this introduced a new element of realism. Arthur Balfour had already argued, as we have seen, that there was no halfway house between union and separation. In that important respect at least he was at one with Sinn Féin. The two extremes were agreed in discounting the possibility of a *via media* if in nothing else. After 1916, Home Rule discarded and discredited, they were left face to face. The outcome, almost inevitably, was violent. Not until 1921 was the Unionist dilemma resolved – with the abandonment of union. Henceforward, British Conservative (no longer Unionist) statesmen, freed from their ideological burden, returned to pragmatic paths and for the most part showed a steady resolve, as Baldwin remarked in the 1930s, that there should not be another Ireland in India or anywhere else. If it be true that Unionist fundamentalism, lending countenance to threats and preparations for armed resistance in Ulster to Home Rule in the years before the first world war, bore a heavy – possibly a decisive – responsibility for creating a situation in which a violent resolution of the Irish question became probable, it has also to be remarked that with the qualified exception of Cyprus the leadership of the party was not again immobilised by credal conviction on a national issue on 'the wrong side of history', as its last essay in decolonisation in Rhodesia Zimbabwe strikingly testified. That was one part of the legacy of the Irish question to Empire and Commonwealth. There were others.

While British and more especially Unionist attitudes to Irish self-government were not merely distinguishable but at significant periods sharply contrasted with their response to demands for colonial or dominion self-government, so too the Irish claims were couched – even by constitutional nationalists – in terms different from those commonly used in the colonies or dominions of European settlement. These differences suggested that while the Irish enjoyed less freedom they were likely, despite the modesty of their immediate claims, in the long run to demand more than their colonial counterparts. Even their constitutional leaders talked not of concessions to be granted but of rights to be acknowledged. They deemed themselves to be the spokesmen not of colonists but of an ancient people. They referred to the Irish race and to the Irish nation. No man, said Parnell in words later inscribed around the plinth of his statue in O'Connell Street, can fix a boundary to the march of a nation. In moments of foreboding, British states-men of all parties feared that this might be precisely true.

While Home Rule was championed by one of the great English parties as a means of strengthening the union by timely but carefully circumscribed concession, no British party or statesman advocated colonial or dominion status for Ireland. Nor did the members of the Irish Parliamentary Party, with the qualified exception of John Redmond, ordinarily think along such lines – despite their pointed references in the debates on the Common-wealth of Australia and South Africa Bills, to the liberties still denied to Irishmen but to be extended to Australians and South Africans; Tim Healy on the former occasion not missing the opportunity of taunting 'the Right Hon. Gentleman, the colonial secretary' with an enquiry as to why it was that he 'and all his friends, who took so large a part in endeavouring to defeat the [second] Home Rule Bill, do not think it necessary upon this occasion to move any of the Amendments which they considered were so absolutely vital seven years ago', and with a suggestion that it might be because an Irishman was not to 'be trusted with Home Rule unless he has first been transported'.[16] At a fundamental level however both British and Irish leaders could neither overlook nor discount the differences between Ireland and the dominions. The Irish were not, even if some of their leaders were, of settler stock; they felt rather as Europeans and, even the constitutionalists among them, were mindful of the revolutionary, nationalist currents that filled their sails. Those revolutionary forces were anti-British and in the main anti-monarchical even before they became dogmatically republican. For those reasons alone the goal of British settler communities overseas could hardly be the goal of Irish nationalism. Yet the question seemingly remained at least debatable until 1916 whether despite such identifiable and natural differences the Irish might not be reconciled to partnership within the Empire on the basis of responsible government. After all, in immediate purposes and broad objectives there was much in common between Ireland and the dominions and it might be the course of wisdom not to seek to probe the secrets of a more or less remote future. In Canada, Australia, New Zealand and in English-speaking South Africa the colonists had sought domestic self-government in the first instance: they had then pressed for its bounds to be extended into areas of government hitherto reserved to the imperial authority; and ultimately they were to seek its reinterpretation and redefinition in terms of national autonomy. It is true that although, so to speak, they wanted more, they did not aspire to something different, But neither, it may be (such certainly was the Gladstonian-Asquithian presumption), did the Irish before 1916. The Parnellite claim was not for separation here and now but for the restoration of an Irish Parliament with adequate political and fiscal authority (including a right to levy tariffs), and with the passage of time and under Redmond's leadership that demand was not enlarged but diminished. No dominion in 1912 would have tolerated limitations upon its powers of domestic self-government of the kind embodied in the Third Home Rule Bill and yet the bill was warmly welcomed in spirit by the Irish constitutional party leadership. Furthermore, the aim of Sinn Féin, founded by Arthur Griffith in repudiation of constitutional methods and in the disillusioned temper of Irish politics that followed the fall of Parnell, while revolutionary in the sense that it involved the rejection of the authority of the British parliament – an authority in Griffith's view without legal foundation, having been 'usurped' in 1800 – was also conservative and traditionalist in its professed purpose of substituting for the single crown of the United Kingdom an Anglo–Irish dual monarchy on the Austro–Hungarian model of 1867.[17] This was something which despite its continental and revolutionary – as distinct from Commonwealth evolutionary – conceptual origins would hardly have chilled the blood of that staunch and very British conservative Canadian, Sir John A. Macdonald, with his dreams of a vast kingdom in North America associated forever with the British Crown.

It is however quite wrong to suppose the Irish at any time before 1921 rejected dominion status. They were not offered it. The British parties were united in excluding them from it. The division between the parties was on Home Rule – something altogether more limited. But in 1914, when the hour of final frustration for the Irish Parliamentary party had struck, popular revulsion against the humiliating ineffectiveness of constitutional methods opened the way psychologically for the revival of a revolutionary nationalism relying upon physical force and a blood sacrifice to win independence. It received its classic expression in Pádraic Pearse's graveside oration for O'Donovan Rossa, the venerable Fenian, at Glasnevin in 1915:

> Life springs from death: and from the graves of patriot men and women spring living nations. The defenders of this realm have worked well in secret and in the open. They think that they have pacified Ireland. They think that they have purchased half of us and intimidated the other half. They think that they have foreseen everything, think that they have provided against everything; but the fools, the fools, the fools! – they have left us our Fenian dead, and while Ireland holds these graves, Ireland unfree shall never be at peace.[18]

Here was the spirit that was behind the Easter Rising 1916 and that inspired the Proclamation of the republic, 'in the name of God and of the dead generations'. The timing, at the crisis of a Great War, ensured maximum impact and demand for retribution. A Durham with a gesture of 'prodigal clemency' (see p. 41) might best have served longer-term British interests – but in Dublin Castle there was no Durham, only a discredited Chief Secretary, an isolated Viceroy and politically insensitive soldiers who assumed control. Executions followed, 'few but corroding' in Churchill's words,[19] which served in time only to harden the temper and extend the area of revolt. They also changed the nature of the political debate. It was no longer, except in form, about the concession by Britain of Home Rule to Ireland, but about the relationship nationalist Ireland might be prepared or compelled to accept with Britain and the Empire.

At the Sinn Féin Árd-fheis, 1917, Arthur Griffith's concept of a dual monarchy was discarded, an incidental casualty, so to speak, of deepening Anglo–Irish antagonism, and a new constitution was adopted, stating that Sinn Féin aimed at securing 'the international recognition of Ireland as an independent Irish republic' and that, having achieved that status, 'the Irish people may by referendum choose their own form of government'. But all the emphasis was on republican achievement, not on the ultimate (and soon largely to be forgotten) libertarian goal. It was for a republic that the martyrs of 1916 had died; it was, in Fintan Lalor's phrase, 'the banner that floats nearest to the sky'. It was under this banner that the Irish revolt gathered momentum.

In the post-war general election, the results of which were declared on 28 December 1918, Sinn Féin republican candidates captured seventy-three seats; the Unionists twenty-six (chiefly in their north-eastern strongholds), and the constitutional nationalists a miserable remnant of six. Twenty-four of the thirty-two counties of Ireland had returned none but republican members. The republican majority convened an Assembly of Ireland (*Dáil Éireann*), to be composed of all elected members and to act as an independent Constituent Assembly of the Irish nation. At its first meeting on 21 January 1919 the establishment of the Irish republic was ratified, the independence of Ireland declared and the elected representatives of the Irish people alone vested with authority to make laws binding on the people.[20] Further, and in accord with Griffith's programme, a Sinn Féin administration was established, technically at least responsible to the *Dáil*, which during the succeeding years of guerilla warfare operated side by side with the disintegrating machinery of British controlled government from Dublin Castle. Behind the conflict of arms there existed a conflict of ideas, no longer only in the form of political abstractions but clothed now in partial reality.

The ideological conflict, susceptible in itself of no easy solution, developed immediately in passionate intensity, partly because of the nature of the Anglo–Irish conflict 1919–21, but at a deeper level – because with 1916 the spirit of compromise departed from Anglo–Irish relations. W. B. Yeats had clothed a moment of history, weighty with consequence, in poetic immortality:

> 'O but we talked at large before
> The sixteen men were shot,
> But who can talk of give and take,
> What should be and what not
> While those dead men are loitering there
> To stir the boiling pot?'

More prosaically but altogether realistically an Australian historian later wrote of the 'dreadful tyranny of the dead' that hung thereafter over Irishmen who thought of or engaged in negotiation with England. But even this was not the whole truth. Behind 1916 lay a revolutionary tradition which had claimed many martyrs down the centuries. The 'tyranny' (if that remains *le mot juste*) was of more than the dead of 1916; it was also of those who had died before them creating and confirming a tradition which itself, as Pearse's words by the graveside of O'Donovan Rossa themselves signified, inspired the Easter Rising. When the time came for negotiation with England, the Irish approach was conditioned immediately by memories of 1916 but in historic perspective by this tradition to which Easter 1916 provided an actual and a symbolic climax.[21]

Had dominion status and membership of the British Commonwealth of Nations, conceived and developed elsewhere in terms of compromise, anything to offer against a background and in a situation such as this? The Irish had risen in revolt not to establish an Irish republic at some distant date but to secure recognition for a polity already claimed to be in existence – the republic, in the Irish view (first stated in 1916 and re-stated in the Declaration of Dáil Éireann in January 1919) deriving *de jure* existence from the indefeasible national right of the people to determine a nation's destiny. This was a concept which by its nature did not admit of compromise. It was also a concept altogether alien to the Commonwealth tradition, with its notion of ultimate authority residing in the Crown in Parliament and to be delegated only by legislative enactment or Order in Council. The surprising thing remains not that a dominion status settlement in Ireland proved to be a source of controversy but that one was ever made at any rate for a partitioned Ireland, that is to say with an Ireland from which the natural supporters of that status were excluded. The surprise is the greater because of the British reaction to armed protest in Ireland. It was not in favour of concessions on dominion, let alone on national lines. What the Unionists had disputed in the face of constitutional pressure before the war, the Coalition government, Unionist-dominated, seemed equally prepared, between 1919–21, to deny to physical force.

Under the Government of Ireland Act 1920, Ireland was partitioned. The north-eastern counties, where before 1914 the Unionist majority had enrolled in an Ulster Volunteer Force to resist Home Rule for all-Ireland, accepted the regional Home Rule embodied in the Act as a means whereby they might order their affairs apart from the rest of Ireland and united with Great Britain. Elsewhere in Ireland Home Rule and partition were uncompromisingly repudiated. Force was met with force. Winston Churchill recorded that by the end of 1920 there were two alternatives before the Coalition government; 'war with the utmost violence or peace with the utmost patience'.[22] With the recruitment and deployment of the Black and Tans and the Auxiliary Police, to outward appearance, Lloyd George had committed himself to the former. But where was it intended to lead? And against whom was the violence directed? The answer to the first question was the restoration of law and order. It was implicit in the official response to the second. Force was directed against Sinn Féin, designated as an illegal and unrepresentative terrorist organisation. Its illegality under British proclamation was indisputable but even in a British context its unrepresentative character seemed questionable. Sinn Féin candidates had swept the twenty-six counties in the general election of 1918. They had assembled to legislate for Ireland as *Dáil Eireann* in January 1919. The *Dáil* was banned, its members proscribed. But could that be given as evidence that they did not represent popular opinion? Such indeed was the theory. Force was being employed, in Lloyd George's phrase, against 'a small nest of assassins'. It was a theory that allowed rational justification for acquiescence in the supposed insistence of Unionists within the Coalition government that the union should be maintained at all costs. It was one which also provided rather flimsy moral cover for a policy of authorised reprisals. It was a 'murder gang' that was to be rounded up. 'We have murder by the throat', declared Lloyd George at the Guildhall Banquet in November 1920. The British government would not rest, boasted Sir Hamar Greenwood, chief secretary for Ireland, 'till we have knocked the last revolver from the last assassin's hand'. With King George V, as with many of his subjects, this language carried no great conviction. When (also in November 1920) Greenwood assured the king's private secretary that 'everywhere the move is upward towards improvement', the king felt obliged to question the correctness of his diagnosis and to complain of his oversanguine representation of the course of events.[23] In succeeding months public opinion in Britain and in the dominions overseas showed signs of increasing dismay. 'If the British Commonwealth can only be preserved by such means', declared the *Round Table*[24] 'it would become a negation of the principle for which it has stood.' In the early summer of 1921 Lloyd George, under pressure, abruptly changed course. He abandoned almost overnight the policy of violence and substituted one of negotiation. 'No British government in modern times', commented Winston Churchill, 'has ever appeared to make so complete and sudden a reversal of policy.'[25] In May the whole power of the state and all the influence of the Coalition were being used to 'hunt down the murder gang'; in June the goal was a 'lasting reconciliation with the Irish people'. That reversal was symbolised in an invitation of 24 June from Lloyd George to Eamon de Valera, described in a face-saving formula as 'the chosen leader of the great majority in Southern Ireland', to a conference in London. From this initiative there followed a truce dating from noon on 11 July.

Why the reversal in British policy? Recent enquiries have focused on two points, both implicit in what is written above. The first is that prognostications of military success, not only had not been fulfilled, but showed no prospect of being fulfilled. And why? Because in the judgment of the historian of *The British Campaign in Ireland 1919–1921*,[26] 'the Republican guerilla campaign proved too determined, too resilient, and too resourceful to be put down by the military force which was employed against it'. This was not simply a question of numbers, or lack of them: it was also a matter of lack of clarity in purpose which in turn led to confusion in the use of means and, calamitous from the British point of view, to divided responsibility and with it, strained relations between military and police, accentuating the demoralisation of a force locally recruited and sensitive to the swing in local sentiment. The IRA had not, on Michael Collins' authority, won the war, they had not driven the enemy out of Ireland. But they had ensured that there would be no timely success for the British forces, that is to say no decisive success, in time to be acceptable to British and Commonwealth opinion, wearied and affronted as it had become by the brutalities of the long-drawn-out struggle. And that brings one to the second explanation that is offered. ' . . . it was the revolt of the British conscience, not the defeat of the British army that obliged Lloyd George to seek terms of peace and settlement with Sinn Féin.' Revolt there certainly was, but it was delayed. An early victory and it would not have sufficed to determine policy. And as it was, it was a revolt against methods much more than against aims. Dr Boyce, a principal proponent of this view, himself allows that had there been a final breakdown in the Treaty talks in December 1921, 'no desire for peace by Great Britain was compelling enough to overcome her unwillingness to admit the Irish claim to complete indepen- dence'.[27] This suggests, and surely rightly, that the influence of public opinion was not an absolute, but was conditioned first by the military situation and then by the nature of any compromise settlement that might be envisaged. It was at this point that a third factor assumed importance, namely the known existence of a relationship tested by experience, acceptable and indeed likely to be welcome to public opinion in Britain, if not to the dominant party in the House of Commons, and while unlikely to commend itself, none the less sufficiently flexible as to be unlikely to be rejected out of hand by the Sinn Féin leadership, whose position also risked erosion from a public opinion desirous of peace. That relationship was dominion status. It held out a prospect that beckoned the Cabinet forward on a course of negotiation, especially as an Imperial Conference was about to foregather.

On the British side the basis of negotiation almost imperceptibly became dominion status for Ireland. Lloyd George made that much clear from the outset in official pronouncements, in speeches and – with carefully contrived dramatic effects – at his first meeting with de Valera. It was in the cabinet room at 10 Downing Street on 14 July 1921. Lloyd George's secretary had never seen him so excited as he was just before the meeting. He had a big map of the British Empire hung up on the wall, 'with its great blotches of red all over it', and his secretary commented to him that he was 'bringing up all his guns!' When prime minister and 'chosen leader' met, Lloyd George, with studied deliberation, pointed to the chairs around the table at which dominion leaders sat at the Imperial Conference – there was Meighen's, representative of English and French Canadians united in one dominion; there was Massey's from New Zealand; there was Australia's Billy Hughes; there was Smuts', with the general symbolising in person the reconciliation of Boer and Briton in a sisterhood of free nations. Then Lloyd George looked long and fixedly at the remaining chair. De Valera later recalled that he sensed that he was expected to ask for whom it was reserved. He declined to do so. So Lloyd George was left to tell him it was for Ireland. 'All we ask you to do,' he said, 'is to take your place in this sisterhood of free nations.' It was an open and (it may be thought) a handsome invitation. If however the Irish did not accept it, if they persisted in thoughts of a republic rather than a dominion, then Lloyd George – despite or perhaps because of advice received from the Secretary of State for War the preceding month to the effect that the situation of the military forces in Ireland was anything but satisfactory and that there was a position of stalemate which might last into the winter, 'a time of decisive advantage to the rebels' – told de Valera of the troops that would soon be coming home from Mesopotamia and the 'trouble-spots' of Empire and looked anxiously to the dreadful consequences that would follow.[28] In its bare essentials, then, Lloyd George's offer was dominion status, with Irish rejection of it meaning renewed

warfare on an intensified scale. From this position Lloyd George
never departed in the course of his subsequent correspondence
with de Valera or in the protracted negotiations in London which
culminated in the signature of the treaty in the early hours of 6
December 1921.

Under the terms of the treaty, Ireland became a dominion. In a
document of many ambiguities there was at least no ambiguity on
that point. The first Article stated that Ireland should have the
same constitutional status in the community of Nations known as
the British Empire as the Dominion of Canada, the Commonwealth of Australia, the Dominion of New Zealand and the Union
of South Africa. The second and third Articles of the treaty defined
the Irish position more closely by saying that her relation to the
imperial Parliament and government should be that of the
Dominion of Canada, and that the governor-general should be
appointed in like manner as Canadian governors-general. The
fourth Article prescribing the terms of the Oath, which Lord
Birkenhead (regrettably enough) may *not* have described as 'the
greatest piece of prevarication in history', made particular reference to Irish membership of the group of nations forming the
British Commonwealth of Nations, the description thereby acquir-
ing official documentary status for the first time. But while the
provisions of the treaty left no room for doubt about the fact that
the Irish Free State was to be a dominion, they invited two larger
questions – why dominion status for Ireland? and what in fact was a
dominion?

Why was dominion status extended to Ireland? There is a simple
answer. It was imposed by the British. Certainly from the outset of
the negotiations dominion status was (with qualifications) the
favoured British solution. On 20 July Lloyd George expressed his
hope that 'the Irish people may find as worthy and as complete an
expression of their political and spiritual ideals within the Empire
as any of the numerous and varied nations united in allegiance to
His Majesty's Throne'.[29] It is true that the dominion status which he
then contemplated was a qualified dominion status. It permitted,
among other things, no protective tariffs. De Valera rightly
commented that 'the principle of the pact' was not 'easy to
determine'. But it was not unqualified dominion status that de
Valera sought. It was not dominion status at all. Accordingly the
removal in subsequent negotiation of the more important of the
limitations, including those on Irish fiscal autonomy, in no way
altered the fact that it was the solution favoured by the British. It
was finally accepted by the Irish plenipotentiaries in London

following upon an ultimatum – the word was Churchill's – and on
pain of a resumption of immediate and terrible war – the phrase
was de Valera's. Is the simple answer then a sufficient one, namely
that dominion status was indeed imposed by the British? Not really;
it is misleading in so far as such a view implies that dominion status
was altogether objectionable to the Irish and altogether acceptable
to the British. It was neither.

The problem central to the whole issue was indicated in Lloyd
George's question to de Valera at the climax of their exchanges by
correspondence seeking to find an agreed basis of negotiations –
how might the association of Ireland with the community of
nations known as the British Empire best be reconciled with Irish
national aspirations? The answer, in the Irish view, was not by
dominion status. On this, so far as existing knowledge goes, the Dáil
cabinet in the summer of 1921 were unanimous. Their demand
was for a republic, externally associated if need be, and by way of
reasonable concession, with the British Commonwealth. And it was
with suggestions to the same end that they sought to counter British
proposals for dominion status. In respect of form the two ideas
were incompatible. Republican status implicit in external association was inconsistent with dominion status. In one sense this was
all-important. Lloyd George and de Valera, however much they
might differ on lesser matters, agreed on what was fundamental.
For both men it was the symbols of sovereignty that signified most.
But their agreement ended there; Lloyd George never failing,
during the long correspondence that preceded the negotiations, in
his insistence that the monarchical symbolism of the Crown must be
the essential feature of any settlement, and de Valera resolved that
the republic should not be sacrificed. It is true that de Valera did
not phrase it in quite that way. What he said was that Ireland's right
to choose for herself 'the path she shall take to realise her own
destiny must be accepted as indefeasible'. But the meaning was
clear. The exercise of that right at the time meant in fact a republic.
In this conflict the British view prevailed, or was imposed, with
dominion status. It was the Crown not the republic that was
embodied in the treaty and later, in a form as diluted as its
draftsmen could devise, in the constitution of the Irish Free State.
This presence of the Crown in the constitution, with its necessary
corollary of an Oath of Allegiance, was a distinguishing feature
common to all dominions of dominion status. Inevitably it was this
feature that attracted attention and resentment in nationalist
Ireland. It symbolised the nature of the settlement. Whether it was
in fact the most important feature of the settlement is a matter on

which Irishmen were, and long remained, deeply divided.

There was in any case more to dominion status than the symbolism of the monarchy. There was the expanding, though still debatable, area of freedom. At the Imperial Conference held in the summer of 1921, dominion statesmen, who showed themselves much concerned to ensure a peaceful settlement of the Irish question while, deliberately, as we have seen, avoiding the undertaking of an essay in Commonwealth constitution-making, none the less had occasion to pronounce upon the present extent and possible future enlargement of their autonomy. They were well aware, and were reminded by W. M. Hughes, that while they had entered the first world war as British colonies, they ended it as separate signatories to the peace treaties at Versailles and as foundation members of the new international organisation, the League of Nations. Two among them, Canada and South Africa, were seeking to secure for themselves a wider independence in international affairs so that they might, for example, assume international obligations or not assume them, as their own parliaments and governments saw fit, enter treaties or not enter into them as their own governments decided and generally to be in no way obliged to follow British foreign policies. It is true that the growing practice of equality was still counterbalanced by a surviving theory of subordination. But might not theory under dominion pressure increased, as it would be, by the coming into existence of an Irish dominion, soon be brought in line with practice? It is true also that there was the fear, strongly voiced by President de Valera and by Erskine Childers, lest in the case of Ireland geographical propinquity would mean a diminution of dominion powers. But, against that, would the overseas dominions readily acquiesce in any such curtailment? In sum, however these things might be regarded, was there not at least a prospect that, in terms of independence, Irish national aspirations might be reconciled with membership of the community of nations known as the British Commonwealth through dominion status? Certainly it did not concede republican symbolism, but it did provide at least a good deal of the substance of what Sinn Féin had been fighting for. There were accordingly assets in respect of power and practice to offset liabilities in respect of constitutional form. With dominion status Ireland at least would pass altogether beyond the constricting limits of Home Rule.

If the argument be accepted that dominion status was not without advantages to the Irish, it was assuredly not without objections for the British. They were voiced in different forms at different stages. 'We must accept the fact of Irish Nationality', wrote Lord Hugh Cecil to the Irish Committee of the Cabinet in October 1918. 'It is regrettable, it is unhistorical; in view of Ulster's feeling it is even absurd. But it is a fact; ... Nationalism connotes independence. Would anything short of independence do? Dominion Home Rule seems to me from the British point of view worse than independence. It leaves Ireland still a burden, still a vexation, probably still discontented and disloyal, and therefore as dangerous as though independent' – all of which led Lord Hugh to favour not independence but provincial devolution within the Union. Others, less idiosyncratic in their reasoning, shared Lord Hugh's misgivings, the Prime Minister by no means least among them. Dominion Home Rule, he warned his colleagues as late as 12 May 1921, 'is a phrase'. But once agree to negotiate on the basis of it, where do you end? 'If we refused to give what New Zealand etc have – ' people would say why break off negotiations on that? 'If we said we must have control over the Western seaports, they'd say, "That's not Dominion Home Rule".' So where, from the British point of view would dominion status take them? Could they be confident it would be consistent with the preservation of their vital interests? It was in the view of the Prime Minister at the outset and of the great body of Unionists throughout the negotiations, that the risk should not be taken, the more so since the Irish in any case did not want dominion status other than with unity, and would feel no loyalty towards it. As Edward Grigg, then one of Lloyd George's advisers on Irish policy, anxiously speculated what might be the effect of granting dominion status upon the other dominions?

In overall perspective it was substantially the case that what was specially attractive about dominion status to the Irish side, namely the prospect of expanding freedom, was precisely what was most objectionable about it to critics of a dominion settlement on the British side. If Lloyd George's approach to dominion status for Ireland was unusually devious here was one important reason for it. He remained the Liberal leader of a Coalition cabinet dependent on the support of a great Unionist majority for survival in office. This majority may not have been made up (as was alleged after the 1918 election and widely publicised by J. M. Keynes) of a lot of hard-faced men who looked as if they had done well out of the war, but at any rate it was made up of men for the most part hostile and in some few cases almost pathologically hostile to the ideal of a self-governing Ireland in any guise. They talked about Lloyd George as 'the great little man who had won the war' but he was also the prisoner of the Coalition, a prisoner who more than once, so

Tom Jones has recorded, thought of escape by resignation. How was he to persuade Unionists to accept a dominion status which many of them, like Lord Hugh Cecil, feared might be worse than independence.[30] When Asquith first among British statesmen, in 1919, formally proposed dominion status for Ireland, the proposal was received by Unionists with a storm of protest. That was partly because of the intensity of their campaign against the former Liberal leader but chiefly because of what they feared would be the consequences. Bonar Law, leader of the Unionist Party in the Coalition and well remembered for his pre-war assault on the third Home Rule Bill, gave the most telling reason for this. The connection of the dominions with the Empire, he warned the House of Commons in 1920, depended upon themselves. If they 'chose tomorrow', he said, 'to say "We will no longer make a part of the British Empire" we would not try to force them'.[31] Dominion status for Ireland therefore might and probably would mean first secession then an independent republic. Should it not on that ground alone be resisted root and branch? Lloyd George gave every appearance of doing so. Further dominion status proposals from Asquith elicited from him the comment 'was ever such lunacy proposed by anybody?' That was in October 1920. In July 1921, however, he warmly commended dominion status of a kind to de Valera. This time the suggestion had come (immediately at least) not from a British but from a Commonwealth source. That in itself by widening the perspective eased Lloyd George's position.

On 13 June 1921 General Smuts, in England for the Imperial Conference, lunched with King George V at Windsor Castle. He found the king 'anxiously preoccupied'[32] about the speech he was shortly to deliver at the opening of the Northern Ireland Parliament. No draft had been submitted to the King by the Irish Office though reputedly 'a blood-thirsty document' had been composed. General Smuts suggested something altogether different. He prepared a draft of which he sent one copy to the king and another with a covering letter to Lloyd George. In the letter he spoke of the Irish situation as 'an unmeasured calamity' and 'a negation of all the principles of government which we have professed as the basis of Empire, and it must more and more tend to poison both our Empire relations and our foreign relations'. He suggested that the king's speech in Belfast should contain a promise of dominion status for Ireland, a promise which he felt sure would have the support of the dominion prime ministers then gathering in London. But, he warned 'such a declaration would not be a mere kite, but would have to be adopted by you as your policy...'

Neither Balfour nor Austen Chamberlain liked, so Tom Jones (who as Cabinet Secretary in attendance at almost all meetings on Irish policy, has left a fascinating account of these events) records 'what they called the "gush" of Smuts' draft', sensing that behind it all there lurked 'the innuendo of oppression'.[33] Lloyd George, who alone could tender advice to the king, was not prepared to endorse Smuts' recommendation with the result that no promise of dominion status was made. But the king's speech contained an anxious and moving plea for peace and understanding and it was shortly thereafter that negotiations were opened. Nor is it to be doubted that General Smuts had given new point and urgency to the idea of dominion status for Ireland. Indeed, in a little more than a month after his conversation with the king, Lloyd George formally submitted proposals for an Irish settlement on a dominion basis. And even if that offer was hedged about with reservations and qualifications, as indeed it was, from the British point of view the offer was decisive. It was one to which the majority of the Coalition's supporters were instinctively opposed. Their hearts had been with the prime minister when he denounced dominion status as insanity; against him when he recommended it as a basis of settlement. Yet in England there was one thing greatly in its favour.

Dominion status was an experiment that had been tried elsewhere and had succeeded. The union of the English and French in the dominion of Canada continued to be thought of as a major triumph of English statesmanship overseas, whilst fresh in the minds of Lloyd George, Austen Chamberlain and Winston Churchill was the success of the policy of trust and reconciliation which brought into being the Union of South Africa. Austen Chamberlain, leader of the Unionist party at the time (because of Bonar Law's temporary withdrawal through illness), said explicitly in defence of an Irish dominion settlement, that it was the success of Liberal policies in South Africa in bringing a South African dominion into existence which more than anything else persuaded him to break with his party's and his family's tradition.[34] In England it is always much easier to take a revolutionary step if it can be said at the same time 'we have travelled this road before'. But in Ireland the advance was to be by untrodden ways.

That might not have mattered quite so much but for one thing. Dominion status lacked precision being traditionally conceived of not as something possessing final form at any given point in time but as something in process of continuing development. In negotiation this was an undoubted liability. Uncertainties implicit in the status served greatly to accentuate mistrust and suspicion, the British coming to regard President de Valera as a 'visionary' likely to see mountains where they saw only molehills, while the Irish thought of Lloyd George as a master of political dexterity – not to say duplicity – who used the liberal-imperial vocabulary of Gladstone to further the purposes of Castlereagh. Yet at root the problem was more than personal. It was not easy to state concisely and with precision especially at that juncture in time, what dominion status for Ireland would involve.

In the House of Commons debate on the Treaty, Lloyd George asked himself, 'what does dominion status mean?' But he did not answer it. He talked instead, and by no means unreasonably, of the dangers of definition, of limiting development by too many finalities, of introducing rigidities alien to British constitutional thinking. He was prepared to say what dominion status did not mean. But not what it did. The treaty itself was no more helpful. It defined dominion status by analogy, that is, by saying that the status of the Irish Free State would be that of the other dominions, which it listed by name, and more particularly that of Canada. The British prime minister was prepared to go no further. Nor were the dominions themselves well placed to do so. When the Irish tried, as some of them did, to look at dominion status through the eyes of the dominions, there were unhelpful obscurities in what they could discern.

In one sense it was very timely that the dominions should be debating their own status at an Imperial Conference in the summer of 1921. But the debate, for a prospective but highly sceptical partner, was hardly sufficiently conclusive. There was General Smuts seeking to have dominion status more clearly defined. Certainly he repudiated Empire and championed Commonwealth. But it was part of his argument that the dominions, while they enjoyed a large measure of equality in practice, were subordinate to the United Kingdom in law and constitutional form. Smuts might want the theory brought into line with practice. But the majority did not. Chief among them as we have seen was W. M. Hughes. He contended forthrightly that there was no need to define imperial relations. 'The difference between the status of the dominions now and twenty-five years ago', he said, 'is very great. We were colonies, we became dominions. We have been accorded the status of nations . . . What greater advance is conceivable? What remains to us? We are like so many Alexanders. What other worlds have we to conquer?'[36] The Irish leaders, had they had the opportunity, could have told him of the other worlds they wished to conquer. But would dominion status enable them to do so? At that crucial moment in the summer of 1921 when it was first formally proposed for Ireland, and even more in the *Dáil* debates on the treaty some six months later, it was hard, if only because of this still not only unresolved but deliberately deferred dominion debate, for the Irish or indeed for anyone else to answer that question, for in order to do so it was necessary first to forecast how dominion relations would develop – and how difficult that was can be imagined by asking, for instance, now, what relations between the countries composing the European Common Market are likely to be in the year 2000.

It is now known that the tide of dominion nationalism was flowing too strongly to be checked. 'The fact of Canadian and South African independence', said Michael Collins in the treaty debate in the *Dáil* 'is something real and solid, and will grow in reality and force as time goes on.' That certainly proved to be true. He was right too in saying: 'We have got rid of the word "Empire". For the first time in an official document the former empire is styled "The Community of Nations known as the British Empire".'[37] Kevin O'Higgins, who like most supporters of the treaty did not believe that dominion status was the fulfilment of Ireland's destiny, hoped none the less that what remained would be won by agreement and by peaceful political evolution. That too proved substantially true. Dominion status, despite the fears of some of its critics and (perhaps even more important) despite the forms with which it was still enshrouded, conferred a substantial measure of freedom and opened the way for complete independence. This might have been more generally recognized at the time but for one thing. Kevin O'Higgins put his finger on it when he said that the most objectionable aspect of the treaty was the threat of force that had been used to influence Ireland to a decision to enter what he called 'this miniature league of nations'. He went on: 'It has been called a league of free nations. I admit in practice it is so; but it is unwise and unstatesmanlike to attempt to bind any such league by any ties other than pure voluntary ties ... I quite admit in the case of Ireland the tie is not voluntary ... the status is not equal.'[38] Ireland was forced into a free association. That contradiction, that handicap, laid upon dominion status when Lloyd George foreclosed debate on 5 December 1921 with an ultimatum, clung to it like an old man of the sea, shaken off only when dominion status itself was discarded.

Many particular objections to dominion status were raised in the treaty debate – objections to the subordination that it might mean in respect of the Crown or its representative, the governor-general, or the armed forces or the judiciary. But in fact such limitations upon Irish (or for that matter upon dominion) sovereignty did not survive very long. At the first Imperial Conference at which the Irish played an active part, in 1926, the actual process of redefining Commonwealth relations was begun. In 1931, with the enactment of the statute of Westminster, what remained of the old colonial Empire had been pulled asunder and the Irish minister for External Affairs, Patrick McGilligan, had reason for claiming in the *Dáil* that the Irish had played a large part in doing it. In that sense dominion status gave freedom to achieve freedom. It may not have been the goal but it had opened the way to the goal. The road to the goal was, however, slow and winding and young men brought up in time of revolutionary change generally prefer to travel by faster ways.

But, probing a little further, as the historian should, the problem central to the debate in 1921 appears in another light. How might the association of Ireland with the community of nations known as the British Empire best be reconciled with Irish national aspirations? Canadians and Australians had advanced with satisfaction from colonial to dominion status. This was the road along which they wished to travel. They felt it was a road along which it was natural they should travel. They were countries of settlement. In Ireland there were counties of settlement – in the north-east. In the dominion their inclusion was the natural, their exclusion the illogical thing. For the rest, Ireland was not a country of settlement. It was one of the historic nations of Europe. It was not extra-European but European national symbolism to which it aspired. The republic, not dominion status, was the goal. The point was put with characteristic forthrightness by Austin Stack in the treaty debate. Assuming that under the treaty Ireland would enjoy 'full Canadian powers', 'I for one,' he declared, 'cannot accept from England full Canadian powers, three-quarter Canadian powers, or half Canadian powers. I stand for what is Ireland's right, full independence and nothing short of it.'[39] What was natural and appropriate for the existing dominions would in effect be unnatural and inappropriate at any rate for a partitioned Ireland. The countries that were dominions in 1921 might seek independence, but Ireland was seeking something more as well – independence and recognition of a separate national identity. Dominion status at that time might lead to the one without necessarily including the other. And to that extent dominion status was conceived, and well conceived, but for another situation. And in so far as the British believed that by conceding dominion status to

Ireland she would become a dominion psychologically as well as constitutionally they were mistaken.

And at this point one comes back to a simple but basic fact: dominion status in 1921 was not compatible with republican status. Allegiance to the Crown was then an essential feature of it. That allegiance had to be expressed in the form of an oath. That oath was embodied in the treaty; it was embodied in the constitution and it could not be removed (because of a fundamental status given to the provisions of the treaty by the Constitution Act) without denouncing the treaty and dominion status of which the oath, at British insistence, was an integral part. It was because this was so that de Valera said in the treaty debate: 'I am against the treaty, because it does not do the fundamental thing and bring us peace.' And again he protested: 'I am against this treaty because it does not reconcile Irish national aspirations with association with the British government . . . I am against this treaty because it will not end the centuries of conflict between the two nations of Great Britain and Ireland.' And why? Because the treaty did not recognise, as de Valera claimed external association would have done, the separate, distinct existence of a republic. On the contrary, it gave away republican independence by bringing Ireland as a dominion within the British Empire and more precisely, as he said, by according recognition to the king as the source of executive authority in Ireland. 'Does this Assembly,' he asked, 'think the Irish people have changed so much within the past year or two that they now want . . . to choose the person of the British monarch, whose forces they have been fighting against . . . as their monarch?'[40] And so against the substance (in part still prospective) of freedom there had to be placed the abandonment of the symbolism which expressed national aspirations and the acceptance of another. The distinction between dominion status and external association was sharp rather than broad and that helps to explain why the division that ensued was deep and lasting. There are times when constitutional forms express the things that for many men matter most and this was one of them.

It was because this was so that the debate on dominion status in Ireland – it sounds paradoxical but is nevertheless true – enlarged the experience of the British Commonwealth of Nations and had an interest far beyond its frontiers. The question posed in 1921 might be rephrased to read: How may national, republican aspirations best be reconciled with a monarchical, imperial or commonwealth states system? The suggested answer on the Irish side was external association, something that would possess the substance of dominion status but replace its monarchical with republican forms. In 1921 that solution was deemed impossible of consideration, as politically it then was, by the British negotiators. India, a historic nation of another continent, later posed the same problem, coupled with an explict wish to remain a member-state of the Commonwealth as a republic. Profiting by Irish experience with which many leading members of the Indian constituent assembly were fully familiar, the problem of republican India's relations with the Commonwealth was resolved in 1949; the formula by which India acknowledged the king as Head of the Commonwealth being virtually identical with the formula proposed by President de Valera for the same purpose in Document No. 2 in 1922. The Commonwealth henceforward allowed complete constitutional as well as political equality, its member states being monarchical or republican as they themselves desired. But by the time the Commonwealth had found an answer the Irish had lost interest in the question.

Notes

CHAPTER 1

1 W. S. Churchill, *My African Journey*, London, 1908 (as reprinted 1962), pp. 3 and 144.
2 George Bennett, *The Concept of Empire, Burke to Attlee* 1774–1947 (2nd ed.), London, 1962, is a notably well and evenly balanced selection to which the criticisms that follow in no way apply.
3 Hansard, *Parliamentary Debates* (Commons), Third Series, vol. xix, col. 536.
4 Earl of Ronaldshay, *The Life of Lord Curzon* (3 vols), London, 1928, vol. 2, p. 230; Philip Woodruff, *The Men Who Ruled India* (2 vols), London, 1953–4, vol. 2, p. 199, also alludes to the incident. The quotation which follows is from a speech at Birmingham on 11 December 1907, reprinted in Bennett, *The Concept of Empire*, pp. 354–7.
5 W. F. Monypenny and G. E. Buckle, *The Life of Disraeli* (6 vols), London, 1910–29, vol. 5, pp. 194–6; and Hansard, *Parl. Deb.* (Lords), vol. ccxxxix, col. 777.
6 *The Annual Register* 1886, p. 181.
7 Merriman Papers, Cape Town Public Library.
8 As stated in the records in Rhodes's cottage at Muizenberg.
9 E.g. F. H. Underhill in his admirable *The British Commonwealth*, Durham, North Carolina, 1956, covering the period from the Durham Report onward never mentioned Rhodes.
10 See however an interesting and speculative consideration of it by D. A. Low, 'Lion Rampant', *Journal of Commonwealth Political Studies* (1964), vol. ii, no. 3, pp. 235–52. This later formed chap. 1 of *Lion Rampant: Essays in the Study of British Imperialism*, London, 1973.
11 A. P. Newton, *A Hundred Years of the British Empire*, London, 1940, pp. 240–1.
12 Sir Kenneth Roberts-Wray, *Commonwealth and Colonial Law*, London, 1966, pp. 98–116, provides an authoritative analysis of the acquisition of colonies; J. M. Ward, *Empire in the Antipodes, The British in Australasia* 1840–1860, London, 1966, pp. 53–4, summarises the facts on New Zealand and for illustration of the Nizam's views, see N. Mansergh and Penderel Moon (eds) *Constitutional Relations between Britain and India. The Transfer of Power 1942–7*, London, 1970–, vol. VII, no. 267 and see also no. 262. Vols. I–IV, edited by Mansergh and E. W. R. Lumby.
13 *Cf.* R. Hyam, *Britain's Imperial Century 1815–1914*, London, 1976, pp. 108–9, and W. S. Churchill, *The River War*, first published in 2 vols in 1899 and reprinted in W. S. Churchill, *Frontiers and Wars*, London, 1962, p. 319.
14 *The Cambridge History of the British Empire* (2nd ed.), Cambridge, 1963, vol. 8, p. 516. S. G. Millin, *Rhodes* (new and revised ed.), London, 1952, p. 229; see also Low, 'Lion Rampant', p. 244.

244

15 Monica Hunter, *Reaction to Conquest* (2nd ed.), London, 1961, p. 8.
16 Prakash Tandon, *Punjabi Century, 1857–1947*, London, 1961, pp. 12–3.
17 Low, 'Lion Rampant', p. 237; see J. G. Lockhart and The Hon. C. M. Woodhouse, *Rhodes*, London, 1963, p. 479, for an account of the incident.
18 J. D. Kestell, *Through Shot and Flame*, London, 1903, p. 285; Kestell was chaplain to President Steyn and a joint secretary to the two republican governments.
19 A. G. Gardiner, *The Life of Sir William Harcourt* (2 vols), London, 1923, vol. 1, p. 497.
20 Quoted in S. R. Mehrotra, *India and the Commonwealth*, 1885–1929, London, 1965, p. 47.
21 Sir Michael O'Dwyer, *India as I Knew It, 1885–1925*, London, 1925, chapters 17 and 18, gives an account of what happened and of his reasons as lieutenant-governor of the Punjab for backing Dyer's action, while disapproving of some of his subsequent measures.
22 Jawaharlal Nehru, *An Autobiography*, London, 1936, pp. 43–4 and 190.
23 Jawaharlal Nehru, *The Discovery of India*, Calcutta, 1946, p. 281.
24 The Marquess of Crewe, *Lord Rosebery*, (2 vols), London, 1931, vol. 1, pp. 185–6.
25 Lord Rosebery, *Oliver Cromwell: A Eulogy and an Appreciation*, London, 1900.
26 Quoted by S. R. Mehrotra in 'On the Use of the Term Commonwealth', *Journal of Commonwealth Political Studies*, vol. 2, no. 1 (November 1963), p. 9.
27 *Fabianism and the Empire*, A Manifesto by the Fabian Society, London, 1900; quotations from p. 1, pp. 8 and 32, pp. 15 and 23, pp. 49–50 note 1.
28 Dr Mehrotra has discovered and recorded many of them in his article.
29 Richard Jebb, *Studies in Colonial Nationalism*, London, 1905, p. 1.
30 Merriman Papers, 24 June 1909.
31 See W. K. Hancock, *Survey of British Commonwealth Affairs* (2 vols), London, 1937, vol. 1, p. 53 note 2.
32 *Minutes of Proceedings of Imperial War Conference*, 1917, Cd. 8566, p. 5.
33 *Ibid.*, p. 40–1.
34 *Ibid.*, p. 47; also J. C. Smuts, *War-Time Speeches*, London, 1917, pp. 13–9.
35 As reprinted in W. K. Hancock and Jean van der Poel, *Selections from the Smuts Papers* (4 vols), Cambridge, 1966, vol. 3, pp. 510–1; see also Smuts, *War-Time Speeches*, pp. 25–38, for an amended version.
36 *Minutes Imp. War Conf.*, Cd. 9177, p. 18.
37 Hancock and Van der Poel, *Selections from the Smuts Papers*, vol. 3, p. 518.
38 Gladstone Papers, Ms. 44632, ff. 36–45 and 111–3. I am indebted to Dr D. G. Hoskin for first drawing this fact to my attention. Gladstone also had before him extracts from the constitution of the United States.
39 Campbell-Bannerman Papers, B.M., Ms. 41243, f. 62.
40 Hancock and Van der Poel, *Selections from the Smuts Papers*, vol. 2, p. 374, letter dated 8 January 1908, and pp. 417–8, letter dated (?) March 1908; and Merriman Papers, 26 October 1908 for constitutional commentaries.
41 See Mansergh and Lumby (eds), *The Transfer of Power*, vol. 1, no. 60, p. 112 and N. Mansergh, *Documents and Speeches on British Commonwealth Affairs 1931–1952*, (2 vols), London, 1953, vol. 2, p. 685.
   R. J. Moore, *Churchill, Cripps and India 1939–1945*, Oxford, 1979, pp. 45–6 makes it clear that Agatha Harrison of the India Conciliation Group had floated the idea of a Cripps visit to India in December 1941.
42 Quoted by S. R. Mehrotra, 'Imperial Federation and India, 1868–1917',

Journal of Commonwealth Political Studies, vol. 1, no. 1 (November 1961), p. 33.

43 N. H. Carrier and J. R. Jeffery, *External Migration: A Study of the Available Statistics, 1815–1950*, HMSO, London, 1953, p. 33. For Irish emigration see O. MacDonagh, 'Irish Emigration to the United States of America and the British Colonies During the Famine', in R. Dudley Edwards and T. Desmond Williams, *The Great Famine*, Dublin, 1956, especially appendix, p. 388.

44 CAB. 32. E-6. The paper was prepared for the Imperial Conference, 1921.

45 L. S. Amery, *My Political Life* (3 vols), London, 1953, vol. 2, pp. 385 and 389–90.

46 Hancock, *Survey*, vol. 1, pp. 60–1.

47 Roberts-Wray, *Commonwealth and Colonial Law*, p. 9; see generally pp. 7–14 for a discussion of this and other precedents.

48 *Parl. Deb.* (Commons), 1949. vol. 464, col. 643–4.

CHAPTER 2

1 It is often spoken of as unique but this is not so. On the other side of the St Lawrence (to go no further) there is also a common memorial to General Murray and the Marquis de Lévis.

2 G. W. Pierson, *Tocqueville and Beaumont in America*, New York, 1938, pp. 319–24; the sketch of the obelisk faces p. 320.

3 Hansard, *Parl. Deb.* (Commons), 16 January 1838, vol. xl, col. 41.

4 *Ibid.*, col. 309–10. A representative selection of extracts from this debate is reprinted in George Bennett, *The Concept of Empire* (2nd ed.), London, 1962, pp. 115–24.

5 The flavour of Mackenzie's thinking is best recaptured in his own speeches and writings, full as they were of anger, protest and indignation against what he deemed injustice. They are reprinted in Margaret Fairley's collection of his *Selected Writings 1824–1837*, Toronto, 1960. Mackenzie also wrote his own narrative of *The late rebellion – exhibiting the only true account of what took place at the memorable seige of Toronto, in the month of December 1837*, Toronto, 1937.

6 Helen Taft Manning, *The Revolt of French Canada*, 1800–1835, London, 1962, supplies the background to the revolt and an account of Papineau's earlier ideas and career. For a more general analysis see D. G. Creighton, *Dominion of the North*, Cambridge, Mass., 1944, chapter 5.

7 Pierson, *Tocqueville and Beaumont in America*, pp. 319–24.

8 D. G. Creighton, *John A. Macdonald*, 2 vols., Toronto, 1952 and 1955, vol. 1, *The Young Politician*, p. 52.

9 Sir Charles Lucas (ed.), *Lord Durham's Report, on the Affairs of British North America* (3 vols), Oxford, 1912 vol. 2, pp. 77–8; in abridgement Sir R. Coupland, *The Durham Report*, Oxford 1945.

10 Lucas, op. cit., pp. 72–3.

11 The phrase had been in current use among reformers in Upper Canada for some time before Lord Durham's mission but it had lacked definition and any accepted meaning; see Chester New, *Lord Durham's Mission to Canada*, Ottawa, 1963; The Carleton Library no. 8, pp. 28–41.

12 Lucas (ed.), op. cit., vol. 2, pp. 279–80.

13 *Ibid.*, p. 282.

14 *Cambridge History of the British Empire* (2nd ed.), Cambridge, 1963, vol. 2,

chapter 10: J. R. M. Butler, 'Colonial Self-Government, 1838–1852', pp. 342–3.

15 Lucas (ed.), op. cit., vol. 2, p. 16.
16 *Ibid.*, p. 70.
17 Charles Buller, *Sketch of Lord Durham's Mission to Canada in 1838*, reprinted in Lucas (ed.), *Lord Durham's Report*, vol. 3, p. 340; see also Chester New, *Lord Durham's Mission to Canada*, p. 50.
18 Lucas (ed.), op. cit., vol. 2, p. 288.
19 J. M. de Moine, *Quebec Past and Present*, pp. 277–80.
20 Only one wing of the château had survived and as it was too small to accommodate the high commissioner and his retinue he took up residence in the Quebec Parliament Buildings which were themselves burned down in 1854. Lord Durham '*en fit raser les ruines*' of the château; see Literary and Historical Society of Quebec, *Transactions 1880–1*, Quebec, 1881. *Notes sur le Château St Louis*. Préparées par E. Gagnon.
21 Creighton, *John A. Macdonald*, vol. 1, pp. 54–5.
22 *Ibid.*, p. 59.
23 Buller, op. cit.; Lucas (ed.), op. cit., vol. 3, p. 370.
24 *The Union Act, 1840*, 3 and 4 Vict. C. 35; and see also Creighton, *Dominion of the North*, p. 250.
25 Quoted in C. A. Bodelsen, *Studies in Mid-Victorian Imperialism*, New York, 1935, p. 18 note 1.
26 *Selections from the speeches of John, First Earl Russell 1817 to 1841 and from Dispatches 1859 to 1865* (2 vols), London, 1870, vol. 2, pp. 66–9; reprinted in A. B. Keith, *Selected Speeches and Documents on British Colonial Policy 1763–1917*, (2 vols), vol. 1, pp. 173–8.
27 J. S. Mill, *Representative Government*, first published London, 1861; reprinted London Everyman Edition, 1910, in *Utilitarianism, Liberty and Representative Government*, p. 377.
28 Lucas (ed.), op. cit.; in abridgement, Coupland, op. cit.; Chester New, op. cit., pp. 53–8 and 161.
29 J. S. Mill, *Autobiography*.
30 For radical reappraisal see G. W. Martin, *The Durham Report and British Policy*, London, 1972, and his essay in R. Hyam and G. W. Martin, *Reappraisals in British Imperial History*, London, 1975, entitled perhaps misleadingly, *The Influence of the Durham Report*, since the theme is its comparative lack of influence at the time and subsequently. For other recent commentaries see P. Burroughs, *The Colonial Reformers and Canada 1830–1849*, Toronto, 1969, and *The Canadian Crisis 1828–1841*, London, 1972, the latter comprising extracts from speeches and documents by colonial reformers. See also J. M. Ward, *Colonial Self-Government*, London, 1976.
31 D. G. Creighton, *Dominion of the North*, p. 247.
32 *Ibid.*, p. 246.
33 Sir H. Maxwell (ed.), *The Creevey Papers*, London, 1905, p. 374.
34 See above, p. 27.
35 *Cf.* Bodelsen, op. cit., chapter 1.
36 Douglas Pike, *Paradise of Dissent, South Australia 1829–57*, London, 1957, examines critically Wakefield's actual rôle in the founding of the colony.
37 *Responsible Government for Colonies*, London, 1840; reprinted in E. M. Wrong, *Charles Buller and Responsible Government*, Oxford, 1926. See also Paul Knaplund in *James Stephen and the British Colonial System, 1813–1847*, Madison,

1953, for a reappraisal of Buller's indictment of Stephen.

38 Hansard, *Parl. Deb.* (Commons), 23 January 1838, vol. xl, coll. 384–6.

39 R. B. Pugh, 'The Colonial Office', *The Cambridge History of the British Empire*, vol. 3, chapter 19, p. 723.

40 *Parl. Deb.* (Commons), 6 March 1838, vol. xli, coll. 476–83.

41 Sir Arthur G. Doughty, *The Elgin-Grey Papers, 1846–1852* (4 vols.), Ottawa, 1937, vol. 1, pp. 351–2.

42 Quoted *The Cambridge History of the British Empire*, vol. 2, p. 680.

43 D. G. Creighton, 'The Victorians and the Empire', *The Canadian Historical Review* (1938), vol. xix, p. 144.

44 Bodelsen, op. cit., p. 59.

45 'Agenda for the Study of British Imperial Economy, 1850–1950' *Journal of Economic History* (1953), vol. xiii, no. 3, p. 257.

46 Creighton, 'The Victorians and the Empire', p. 141.

47 Doughty, op. cit., vol. 1, p. 448.

48 Creighton, *Dominion of the North*, pp. 256–7.

49 Creighton, 'The Victorians and the Empire', p. 144.

50 John Gallagher and Ronald Robinson, 'The Imperialism of Free Trade', *Economic History Review* (1953), vol. vi, no. 1, pp. 1–15; see also vol. xiv (April 1962) for a critique by O. G. MacDonagh, 'The Anti-Imperialism of Free Trade'. The phrase 'informal empire' to describe the expansion of Britain's financial and commercial power and indirect control beyond the limits of imperial sovereignty is said to have been first used by Professor C. R. Fay in *Imperial Economy and its Place in the Foundation of Economic Doctrine 1600–1932*, Oxford, 1934; see R. W. Winks, *The Historiography of the British Empire-Commonwealth*, Duke, 1966, p. 58.

51 Earl Grey, *The Colonial Policy of Lord John Russell's Administration* (2 vols), London, 1853, vol. 1, pp. 17–18.

52 G. S. Graham, 'A Canadian Declaration of Independence', *The Listener*, 5 November 1959.

53 The Memorial and the dispatches are reprinted in Keith, *Selected Speeches and Documents*, vol. 2, pp. 51–83.

54 See A. R. M. Lower, *Colony to Nation* (4th ed. revised), Toronto, 1964, pp. 281–9 and 379–80.

55 Quoted in Donald Creighton, *The Road to Confederation*, Toronto, 1964, p. 37.

56 *Ibid.*, pp. 136–40.

57 Public Archives of Canada, Series G, vol. 221A, 7 September 1866. Quoted in W. Menzies Whitelaw, 'Reconstructing the Quebec Conference', *The Canadian Historical Review* (1938), vol. xix, p. 137.

58 *The Quebec Resolutions* are reprinted in Keith, *Selected Speeches and Documents*, vol. 1, pp. 245–63.

59 P. B. Waite (ed.), *The Confederation Debates in the Province of Canada, 1865*, The Carleton Library, no. 2, Ottawa 1963, p. 57.

60 *Le Monde*, 26 July 1967, p. 6, col. 1.

61 Quoted Pierson, op. cit., pp. 343–4.

62 Waite (ed.), *The Confederation Debates*, p. 49.

63 Quoted by Alexander Brady in *The Transfer of Institutions*, W. B. Hamilton (ed.), Duke, 1964, chapter 3, 'Canada and the Model of Westminster,' p. 68. Professor Brady's analysis, pp. 59–80, in concise and illuminating.

64 André Siegfried, *The Race Question in Canada*, London, 1907, p. 133.

65 Keith, *Selected Speeches and Documents*, vol. 1, p. 292. The reference is given to

Keith on grounds of convenience. Macdonald's speeches are however also and
more extensively reproduced in Waite (ed.), *The Confederation Debates*, pp.
39–48, 130–1, 134–5, 139–46 and 155–7.
66 Keith, *Selected Speeches and Documents*, vol. 1, p. 292.
67 On this point see A. Brady's *Democracy in the Dominions* (3rd ed.), Toronto,
1958, pp. 44–9.
68 *Cf.* K. C. Wheare, *Federal Government* (3rd ed.), London, 1953, pp. 19–21.
69 Borden Papers: The papers of Sir Robert Laird Borden in the National
Archives, Ottawa.
70 30 and 31 Vict. c. 3. See vol. 2, p. 33.
71 Creighton, *Macdonald*, vol. 1, p. 464.
72 Hansard, *Parl. Deb.* (Commons), 28 February 1867, vol. clxxxv, col. 1184.
73 Creighton, *The Road to Confederation*, pp. 421–2.
74 *Ibid.*, pp. 423–4.
75 Creighton, *Dominion of the North*, pp. 312–3.
76 British North America (No. 2) Act (12, 13, and 14 Geo VI, Ch. 81) reprinted in
Mansergh, *Documents and Speeches*, vol. 1, pp. 90–1.

CHAPTER 3

1 W. K. Hancock, *Smuts* (2 vols), Cambridge 1962 and 1968, vol. 1, *The Sanguine
Years 1870–1919*, pp. 108–10; see also Alan Paton, *Hofmeyr*, Cape Town,
1964, p. 73; T. R. H. Davenport's *South Africa – A Modern History*, London,
1977, which illustrates at once the potentialities and the problems of recording
the development of a multi-cultural, multi-racial polity; M. Wilson and L. M.
Thompson (eds), *The Oxford History of South Africa*, vol. 2, 1870–1960, Oxford,
1971.
2 *Cf.* C. W. de Kiewiet, *British Colonial Policy and the South African Republics,
1848–1872*, London, 1929, pp. 2–3, on concepts of South African history, and
the same author's *A History of South Africa, Social and Economic*, Oxford, 1941,
pp. 47–8 on the nature of its problems.
3 W. K. Hancock and Jean van der Poel, *Selections from the Smuts Papers* (4 vols),
Cambridge, 1966, vol. 1, p. 117.
4 James Bryce, *Impressions of South Africa*, London, 1897, p. 571.
5 A. F. Hattersley, 'Slavery at the Cape', *The Cambridge History of the British
Empire*, vol. 8, pp. 272–7.
6 G. McC. Theal, *History of South Africa South of the Zambesi, 1843–54*, Cape
Town, 1926–7, pp. 90–115; *The Cambridge History of the British Empire*, pp.
324–6, and E. A. Walker, *The Great Trek*, London, 1934.
7 The routes of the Voortrekkers were graphically set out in an exhibition at the
Cape Archives in 1964.
8 See J. S. Galbraith, *Reluctant Empire: British Policy on the South African Frontier,
1843–54*, California, 1963, and also a review of it by E. A. Walker in *The
Historical Journal*, vol. viii, no. 1 (1965), pp. 145–7.
9 I am indebted to Dr Ernst Kohl of the *Deutsche Afrika-Gesellschaft* for drawing
my attention to this point. The original text is reproduced in G. W. Eybers,
Select Constitutional Documents illustrating South African History, 1795–1910,
London, 1918, p. 364.
10 For what is claimed to be the only authentic record of the discovery given by

Jacobs in his old age, see Eric Rosenthal, *River of Diamonds*, Cape Town, 1957, pp. 10–12.

11 Hedley A. Chilvers, *The Story of de Beers*, London, 1939, pp. 6–7.

12 Two important studies have been made of British policy in South Africa at this time. The first was C. W. de Kiewiet, *The Imperial Factor in South Africa*, Cambridge, 1937, and the second Dr C. F. Goodfellow's *The Policy of South African Confederation, 1870–1881*, Cape Town, 1967. Dr Goodfellow's study also includes (in chapter 2) an account of Earl Grey's embryonic scheme in the 1850s and an appraisal of its bearing on Carnarvon's later proposals.

13 G. McC. Theal, *History of South Africa, 1873–1884* (2 vols), London, 1919, vol 1, p. 271.

14 It was the subject of a study by Sir R. Coupland, *Zulu Battle Piece: Isandhlwana*, London, 1948.

15 Hansard, *Parl. Deb.* (Lords), vol. cclxxxvi, coll. 7–8.

16 James Bryce, *Impressions of South Africa* (third ed.), London, 1899, pp. xxi–xxiii.

17 J. S. Marais, *The Fall of Kruger's Republic*, Oxford, 1961, p. 1.

18 *Cf.* Alan Paton, *Hofmeyr*, pp. 7 and 158; 'Onze Jan' was a cousin of J. H. Hofmeyr, the subject of Paton's biography.

19 H. Marshall Hole, *The Making of Rhodesia*, London, 1926, p. 17–8.

20 A. G. Gardiner, *Pillars of Society*, London, 1913, pp. 12–5.

21 *German Diplomatic Documents, 1871–1914* (4 vols), selected and translated by E. T. S. Dugdale, London, 1928, vol. 3, p. 114.

22 There is uncertainty about when and how Rhodes' substantial contribution was paid; see C. C. O'Brien, *Parnell and his Party*, Oxford, 1957, p. 266 note 4.

23 Marais, op. cit., p. 88.

24 A memorial volume, with photographs of the president, commemorating the first journey on the Delagoa Bay line, is preserved in Kruger's home, now a museum, in Pretoria. B. L. Reid, *The Lives of Roger Casement*, New Haven, 1976, pp. 22–3.

25 John Buchan, *Memory Hold-the-Door*, London, 1940, p. 99.

26 Marais, op. cit, p. 89.

27 J. L. Garvin, *The Life of Joseph Chamberlain* (3 vols), London, 1932–4, vol. 3, pp. 71–2.

28 The history of it has been written by Jean van der Poel, *The Jameson Raid*, Cape Town, 1951, and Elizabeth Pakenham, *Jameson's Raid*, London, 1960; see also Ethel Drus, 'A Report on the Papers of Joseph Chamberlain relating to the Jameson Raid and the Inquiry', *Bulletin of the Institute of Historical Research*, vol. xxv (1952), and 'The Question of Imperial Complicity in the Jameson Raid', *English Historical Review*, vol. lxviii (Oct. 1953).

29 Alfred Austin, *Jameson's Ride*; understandably this poem was not reprinted in later volumes of Austin's collected poems.

30 Garvin, *The Life of Joseph Chamberlain*, vol. 3, p. 78.

31 Pakenham in *Jameson's Raid* presents the case for Chamberlain; Van der Poel in *The Jameson Raid* and Marais in *The Fall of Kruger's Republic* the case against him. Professor Marais', indictment set out in chapter 4 is summarised pp. 94–5; it appears, given the lack of evidence on certain points, as conclusive as may be.

32 N. Rich and M. H. Fisher (eds), *The Holstein Papers* (4 vols), Cambridge, 1955–63, vol. 1, pp. 162–3.

33 A photograph in the museum at Dar es Salaam, where the colonel commanded

German forces during 1893–5, makes the description plausible.

34 Dugdale, *German Diplomatic Documents 1871–1914*, vol. 2, p. 287.

35 E. Pakenham, *Jameson's Raid*, p. 96.

36 R. C. K. Ensor, *England 1870–1914*, Oxford, 1936, p. 246, and Marais, op. cit, pp. 210–2.

37 See C. Headlam (ed.), *The Milner Papers, South Africa 1897–1899* (2 vols), London, 1931–3, vol. 1, p. 212, and also Marais, op. cit., pp. 200–2, for an account of the electoral campaign.

38 Quoted by Marais, op. cit., p. 196.

39 Headlam (ed.), op. cit., vol. 1, pp. 221–2.

40 Marais, op. cit., p. 298 note 1.

41 Headlam (ed.), op. cit., vol. 1, pp. 349–53.

42 Ensor, op. cit., p. 250–1.

43 For an account, especially of Smuts's rôle before and during the Bloemfontein conference see W. K. Hancock, *Smuts*, vol. 1, chapter 5.

44 *Ibid.*, p. 99.

45 Headlam (ed.), op. cit., vol. 1, pp. 407–15; for an account of the conference see chapter 15.

46 T. Pakenham, *The Boer War*, London, 1979, pp. 100–1.

47 *Fabianism and the Empire*, London, 1900, p. 13.

48 This is the title of the first chapter of Professor G. H. Le May's *British Supremacy in South Africa, 1899–1907*, Oxford, 1965. The quotations that follow are from p. 36. See also p. 89 and generally chapters 3 and 4.

49 T. Pakenham, op. cit., p. 571, in his graphic account of the occasion and course of the war, supplies a needed corrective to the notion that feelings of mutual esteem among leaders on either side were generally shared by other ranks.

50 The record is set out in *The Peace Negotiations*, Rev. J. D. Kestell (secretary to the Orange Free State government) and D. E. Van Velden (secretary to the government of the South African republic), London, 1912. See p. 59.

51 *Ibid.*, pp. 76–7.

52 *Ibid.*, pp. 79–87.

53 *Ibid.*, p. 91.

54 Merriman Papers, Cape Town Public Library.

55 The argument set out in the following pages is more fully developed in N. Mansergh, *South Africa 1906–1961: The Price of Magnanimity*, London, 1962.

56 Lord Riddell, *More Pages from My Diary, 1908–1914*, London, 1934, p. 144; see also Randolph Churchill, *Churchill*, London, 1967, vol. 2, pp. 144–56, and R. Hyam, *Elgin and Churchill at the Colonial Office, 1905–1908*, London, 1968, pp. 103–36, for a detailed analysis of the circumstances surrounding the decision to restore self-government.

57 'The Myth of the Magnanimous Gesture' in Hyam and Martin, *Reappraisals*.

58 R. B. McCallum, *Asquith*, London, 1936, p. 55 and R. B. McCallum, *The Liberal Party from Earl Grey to Asquith*, London, 1963, p. 151.
For a review of the discussion see J. Wilson, *C. B. A Life of Sir Henry Campbell-Bannerman*, London, 1973, pp. 479–85.

59 Hansard, *Parl. Deb.* (Commons), 1906, vol. clxii, col. 84.

60 This emerges *inter alia* from notes in the Campbell-Bannerman Papers at the British Museum.

61 J. A. Spender, *The Life of Sir Henry Campbell-Bannerman* (2 vols), London, 1923, vol. 2, pp. 237–8.

62 Hancock, op. cit., *The Fields of Force*, vol. 2, 1919–1950, p. 518.

63 Merriman Papers.
64 The first letter is in the Merriman Papers, Smuts to Merriman, 28 Nov. 1906, the second dated 1 August 1907, in Hancock and Van der Poel, op. cit., vol. 2, p. 355.
65 The authoritative account is L. M. Thompson, *The Unification of South Africa, 1902–10*, Oxford, 1960.
66 Quoted *ibid.*, p. 169.
67 C.O. 417/351 ff. 392–3.
68 Le May, *British Supremacy in South Africa*, p. 177.
69 C.O. 291/112.
70 Merriman Papers.
71 *Ibid.*, letter dated 13 March 1906; also reprinted in Hancock and Van der Poel, op. cit., vol. 2, p. 242.
72 *Ibid.*, vol. 2, p. 526; letter to Merriman dated 2 October 1908.
73 *Ibid.*, pp. 440–2; Smuts to Hobson, 13 July 1908.
74 *Ibid.*, pp. 530–2; letter dated 16 December 1908.
75 *Ibid.*, pp. 446–8; letter dated 19 July 1908.
76 Hansard, *Parl. Deb.* (Lords), 1909, vol. 2, col. 767.
77 Headlam (ed.), op. cit., vol. 1, p. 178, and Le May, op. cit., pp. 11–12, where the whole passage is quoted.

CHAPTER 4

1 J. A. Froude, *Oceana, or England and Her Colonies*, London, 1886, p. 82.
2 James Bryce, *Impressions of South Africa*, London, 1899, p. 589.
3 Froude, op. cit., p. 103.
4 André Siegfried, *Democracy in New Zealand*, London, 1914, p. 63.
5 *Ibid.*, pp. 48 and 90.
6 Alan Moorehead, *Cooper's Creek*, London, 1963, Chapter 1.
7 Edward Gibbon Wakefield, *A Letter from Sydney, the Principal Town of Australasia, Together with the Outline of a System of Colonisation*, London, 1829, pp. 201–2.
8 C. W. Dilke, *Greater Britain*, London, 1885, p. 391.
9 N. H. Carrier and J. R. Jeffrey, *External Migration, 1815–1950*, H.M.S.O., 1953, p. 95.
10 Elie Halévy, *A History of the English People in the Nineteenth Century* (new ed., 6 vols), London, 1961, vol. 3, *The Triumph of Reform*, pp. 230–3; A. G. L. Shaw, *Convicts and the Colonies. A Study of Penal Transportation from Great Britain and Ireland to Australia and other parts of the British Empire*, London, 1966, gives in an appendix (pp. 363–8) statistical details about the numbers of convicts, their countries of origin and their Australian destinations on the basis of available records.
11 *A Letter from Sydney* (see note 7 above).
12 *Ibid.*, pp. 169–70.
13 *Cf.* Keith Sinclair, *A History of New Zealand*, 2nd ed. London, 1961, p. 52.
14 Carrier and Jeffrey, *External Migration*, p. 95.
15 In 1951 a department store in Christchurch erected a panoramic representation of the landing of a Victorian family; top-hatted, frock-coated father, mother with bonnet and bustle, followed by a boy and a girl and solid Victorian furniture coming ashore, in celebration of the centenary of the arrival of the

Canterbury settlers 1851. In response to protests that the mother was wearing no wedding ring, an outsize ring was painted in!

16 Quoted in Harold Miller, *New Zealand*, London, 1950, p. 143.
17 F. W. Eggleston, *Reflections of an Australian Liberal*, Melbourne, 1953, chapter 3 and Shaw, *Convicts and the Colonies*, p. 358.
18 E. H. Hargraves, *Australia and its Gold Fields*, London, 1855, pp. 114–6; see also C. M. H. Clark, *Select Documents in Australian History 1851–1900*, Sydney, 1955, pp. 3–4.
19 Quoted in *ibid.*, pp. 5–8.
20 Miller, *New Zealand*, pp. 75–6.
21 Quoted in Clark, *Select Documents*, p. 473.
22 J. M. Ward, *Colonial Self-Government*, London, 1976, p. 328. Professor Ward is concerned to underline the importance of changes in British conventions of government in influencing, or even determining, what was deemed appropriate for British settled colonies.
23 Governor Grey to Earl Grey 3 May 1847, quoted in W. K. Jackson and G. A. Wood, *New Zealand Parliament and Maori Representation*, Institute of Commonwealth studies, Reprint series no. 22. The article is a valuable, concise summary of the question.
24 Keith Sinclair, *The Origins of the Maori Wars*, Wellington, 1957, pp. 85–110.
25 Miller, *New Zealand*, p. 53, and see chapter 5 *passim*.
26 Jackson and Wood, *New Zealand Parliament and Maori Representation*, pp. 387–94.
27 Siegfried, *Democracy in New Zealand*, pp. 350–1.
28 Angus Ross, *New Zealand Aspirations in the Pacific in the Nineteenth Century*, Oxford, 1964, pp. 112–3 and chapter 16 *passim*.
29 *Ibid.*, p. 290.
30 Keith Sinclair, *A History of New Zealand*, p. 165.
31 F. L. W. Wood, *Understanding New Zealand*, New York, 1944, pp. 61–3.
32 Siegfried, *Democracy in New Zealand*, pp. 50–6 and p. 61.
33 James Bryce, *Modern Democracies* (2 vols), London, 1921, vol. 2, *New Zealand*, pp. 300–2, and W. P. Reeves, *The Long White Cloud* (4th ed.), London, 1950, pp. 302–3; see also Siegfried, *Democracy in New Zealand*, pp. x–xi, on Seddon.
34 Siegfried, *Democracy in New Zealand*, pp. 97–9.
35 Keith Sinclair's *William Pember Reeves, New Zealand Fabian*, Oxford, 1965, provides a biographical study.
36 Clark, *Select Documents*, pp. 477–8.
37 Dilke, *Greater Britain*, pp. 285–6.
38 Quoted in M. Clark, *Sources of Australian History* (new ed.), Oxford, 1963, p. 433.
39 Clark, *Select Documents*, p. 475. Dr M. N. Lettice has made a detailed analysis of Anglo–Australian exchanges on the New Hebrides in her unpublished Cambridge dissertation on *Anglo–Australian Relations, 1901–1914, A Study at the Official Level*.
40 Clark, *ibid.*, p. 474–6.
41 J. A. La Nauze, *Alfred Deakin. A Biography* (2 vols), Melbourne, 1965, vol. 1, pp. 158 and 167; chapter 8 contains much important evidence on Deakin's rôle and on the movement to federation.
42 Quoted in A. B. Keith, *Selected Speeches and Documents on British Colonial Policy, 1763–1917* (2 vols), vol. 1, p. 344.
43 L. F. Crisp, *The Parliamentary Government of the Commonwealth of Australia*,

London, 1949, pp. 1–2. This standard work has now gone into its 4th edition, *Australian National Government*, Melbourne, 1978.

44 A. Deakin, *The Federal Story* (2nd edition, edited by J. A. La Nauze), Melbourne, 1963; see also La Nauze, *Deakin*, vol. 1, p. 171 and chapter 8 *passim*.

45 Keith, *Selected Speeches and Documents*, vol. 1, p. 347.

46 *Ibid.*, p. 351.

47 *Ibid.*, p. 361.

48 63 and 64 Vict. c. 12.

49 La Nauze, *Deakin*, vol. 1, p. 190 and chapter 9 *passim*.

50 *Cf*. K. C. Wheare, *The Constitutional Structure of the Commonwealth*, Oxford, 1960, pp. 50–2.

51 Geoffrey Sawer, *Australian Government Today* (new and revised ed.), Melbourne, 1964, pp. 26–7.

52 Crisp, op. cit., pp. 224–6.

53 *Ibid.*, p. 236.

54 For a summary of events and their implications, see H. V. Hodson, 'The Constitutional Consequences of Mr. Whitlam' in *The Round Table*, April. 1976, pp. 135–44. For accounts by the principal protagonists, see John Kerr, *Matters for Judgment*, Melbourne, 1978, and Gough Whitlam, *The Truth of the Matter*, Melbourne, 1979, and for comments by a former Governor-General see Sir Paul Hasluck, *The Office of Governor-General*, Melbourne, 1979.

55 Kerr, *ibid.*, p. 298.

56 Whitlam, op. cit., p. xi.

57 *Ibid.*, Chapter 8, 'The Ambush', pp. 108–10 and Kerr, op. cit., pp. 358–60.

58 For a table giving date, nature of amendment and outcome of referenda up to 1977, see Crisp, op. cit., 4th edn., pp. 45–8.

59 Bryce, *Modern Democracies*, vol. 2, pp. 178 and 181.

CHAPTER 5

1 J. R. Seeley, *The Expansion of England*, London, 1883, p. 2. D. Wormell, *Sir John Seeley and the Uses of History*, Cambridge, 1980, places the book in the context of Seeley's views on the writing and teaching of history.

2 Seeley, *ibid.*, p. 8.

3 *Ibid.*, p. 14.

4 *Ibid.*, p. 13.

5 *Ibid.*, p. 11.

6 *Ibid.*, p. 16.

7 *Ibid.*, p. 300.

8 *Ibid.*, p. 293.

9 *Ibid.*, p. 46.

10 *Ibid.*, pp. 302–4 and 196.

11 *Ibid.*, p. 16.

12 W. F. Monypenny and G. E. Buckle, *The Life of Disraeli* (6 vols), London, 1910–29, vol. 5, p. 194; also quoted in George Bennett, *The Concept of Empire* (2nd ed.), London, 1962, p. 257; see above, pp. 5–6.

13 Philip Magnus, *Gladstone* (new ed.), London, 1963, p. 264.

14 Seeley, op. cit, pp. 11–12.

15 W. C. B. Tunstall, *The Cambridge History of the British Empire*, vol. 2, *Imperial Defence, 1815–1870*, p. 806; C. P. Stacey, *Canada and the British Army*,

1846–1871, Toronto, 1936, p. 43; also quoted in R. A. Preston, *Canada and 'Imperial Defense,'* Durham N.C., 1967, p. 23.

16 Hansard, *Parl. Deb.* (Commons), vol. cc, col. 1900–3. Reprinted in Bennett, *The Concept of Empire*, pp. 254–5 for Gladstone, and Hansard, *Parl. Deb.* (Commons), vol. clxv, col. 1060, for the Resolution on the Mills Committee.

17 Monypenny and Buckle, *The Life of Disraeli*, vol. 5, p. 193.

18 See D. C. Gordon, *The Dominion Partnership in Imperial Defense, 1870–1914*, Johns Hopkins, 1965, chapter 2 *passim*, and Preston, *Canada and 'Imperial Defense'*, chapter 1. For later developments see *The Cambridge History of the British Empire*, vol. 3, chapter 5 by R. E. Robinson and chapter 7 by W. C. B. Tunstall, *Imperial Defence 1870–1897*.

19 C. W. Dilke, *Greater Britain* (2 vols), London, 1868, vol. 2, p. 151.

20 H. W. Lucy, *A Diary of Two Parliaments* (2 vols), London, 1885–6, vol. 1, p. 419.

21 Magnus, *Gladstone*, p. 261.

22 See Gordon, *The Dominion Partnership*, pp. 62–7, and Preston, *Canada and 'Imperial Defense'*, pp. 91–3 and 131–6, for recent accounts of its work based on the use of the original papers.

23 *Cambridge History of the British Empire*, vol. 3, pp. 220–1.

24 A. Tilney Bassett (ed.), *Gladstone's Speeches*, London, 1916, p. 570.

25 A. J. P. Taylor, *Germany's First Bid for Colonies 1884*–1885, London, 1938, p. 4.

26 See above, p. 50.

27 Reprinted in Bennett, *The Concept of Empire*, p. 262.

28 S. R. Mehrotra, 'Imperial Federation and India, 1868–1917', *Journal of Commonwealth Political Studies*, vol. 1, no. 1.

29 *Proceedings of the Colonial Conference, 1887*, vol. 1 (C. 5091), p. 5. H.C. (1887), lvi., p. 19.

30 Gordon, *The Dominion Partnership*, pp. 91–2; Preston, *Canada and 'Imperial Defense'*, pp. 102–5.

31 C. 7553. *Report by the Right Hon. the Earl of Jersey on the Colonial Conference at Ottawa, with the Proceedings of the Conference and certain Correspondence*, London, August 1894.

32 J. Schull, *Laurier, The First Canadian*, Toronto, 1965, pp. 346–55, gives a graphic account of the celebrations and their impact on Laurier who became both a privy councillor and a knight.

33 C. 8596. *Proceedings of a Conference between the Secretary of State for the Colonies and the Premiers of the Self-Governing Colonies at the Colonial Office*, London, June and July 1897, pp. 5–6.

34 Borden Papers, 35345, and see also Schull, *Laurier, The First Canadian*, p. 356.

35 C. 8596, pp. 7–8 for Chamberlain's speech and pp. 15–18 for the subsequent naval debate.

36 Lady Violet Bonham Carter, *Winston Churchill As I knew Him*, London, 1965, pp. 50–2.

37 Maurice Ollivier (ed.), *The Colonial and Imperial Conferences from 1887 to 1937* (3 vols), Ottawa, 1954, vol. 1, p. 153 and Cd. 1299, p. 4. No report of the 1902 Conference Proceedings was published in London. Papers relating to the Conference were, however, published there in Cd. 1299 and correspondence relating to the proposed publication of the Report of the Proceedings in Cd. 1723.

38 *The Poems of Matthew Arnold 1840–1867*, London, 1913, p. 429, 'Heine's Grave'.

39 Ollivier, *Colonial and Imperial Conferences*, vol. 1, pp. 154–5. Cd. 1299, p. 5.

40 Reprinted in A. B. Keith, *Speeches and Documents on British Colonial Policy 1763–1917* (2 vols), Oxford, 1948, vol. 2, p. 238. See also Gordon, *The Dominion Partnership*, pp. 147–8, for an account of the discussions preceding the drafting of the memorandum.
41 Ollivier, *Colonial and Imperial Conferences*, vol. 1, p. 155.
42 The speeches of Selborne, Laurier and Barton are reprinted in Ollivier, *Colonial and Imperial Conferences*, vol. 1, pp. 161–8; see also Gordon, *The Dominion Partnership*, chapters 7–9, and R. A. Preston, *Canada and 'Imperial Defense'*, pp. 287–307.
43 Canada, *Parliamentary Debates* (Commons), vol. li, col. 72 (5 Feb. 1900).
44 *Ibid.*, vol. lvii, col. 4726 (12 May 1902).
45 Julian Amery, *The Life of Joseph Chamberlain* (4 vols), London, 1951, vol. 4, p. 423. The first three volumes of the biography were written by J. L. Garvin.
46 Ollivier, *Colonial and Imperial Conferences*, vol. 1, p. 156; see generally pp. 155–7.
47 *Survey of British Commonwealth Affairs*, vol. 2, part 1, p. 85.
48 *Ibid.*,
49 *Cf.* Amery, *The Life of Joseph Chamberlain*, vol. 4, p. 525, for Chamberlain's letter on this point to the Duke of Devonshire; see also pp. 400–7 for circumstances in which the duty on corn was imposed, and for Commonwealth Imperial Preference generally see chapter XLVII.
50 For a recent political analysis see Alfred Gollin, *Balfour's Burden: Arthur Balfour and Imperial Preferences*, London, 1965.
51 Richard Jebb, *Studies in Colonial Nationalism*, London, 1905; see especially the Preface and chapters 6 and 7 on 'The South African War' and 'The Colonial Conference, 1902', respectively.
52 Amery, *The Life of Joseph Chamberlain*, vol. 4, p. 435.
53 *Correspondence relating to the Future Organisation of Colonial Conferences*, 1905, Cd. 2785.
54 Cd. 3523. There was an illuminating discussion on the substitution of the term 'dominion' for 'colony' *ibid.*, pp. 78–83.
55 J. A. La Nauze, *Alfred Deakin: A Biography* (2 vols), Melbourne, 1965, vol. 2, p. 500.
56 Cd. 3523, pp. 71–2; see also Deakin's earlier comments pp. 8–10, 26–9, 41–4, 63–5; La Nauze, *ibid.*, vol. 2, chapter 22, for background; J. A. Cross, 'Whitehall and the Commonwealth', *Journal of Commonwealth Political Studies*, vol. 2, no. 3, pp. 190–1, and R. Hyam, The Colonial Office Mind 1900–14 in N. Hillmer and P. Wigley (editors), *The First British Commonwealth*, London, 1980. Dr Hyam comments elsewhere in the chapter on the academic attainments and range of interests of a staff constricted in their field of action, the department not being in the strict sense a department of administration.
57 Cd. 3523, p. 35.
58 *Ibid.*, pp. 37–42.
59 See generally J. A. Cross, *Whitehall and the Commonwealth: British Departmental Organisation for Commonwealth Relations 1900–1966*, London, 1967; for the 1907 reforms see chapter 3.
60 Indian Office Library. Morley Papers MSS. Eur. D. 573/2; Schull, *Laurier*, p. 348, and La Nauze, *Deakin*, vol. 1, p. 203.
61 Cd. 3523, p. vii.
62 CID Paper 161B. *Committee of Imperial Defence: Constitution and Functions*, 27 August 1912 (Cab. 4/5).

63 L. S. Amery, *Thoughts on the Constitution*, Oxford, 1953, p. 146; and Maurice Hankey, *The Supreme Command 1914–1918* (2 vols), London, 1961, vol. 1, pp. 43 and 125.
64 Cd. 3523, pp. 97–9.
65 Cd. 3524, p. 19.
66 *Memorandum on Sea Power and the Principles involved in it,* presented to the Colonial Conference 1902, Cd. 1299, and in amended version Cd. 1597, 1903.
67 Hansard, *Parl. Deb.* (Commons), 17 March 1914; reprinted in Keith, *Speeches and Documents*, p. 354.
68 *Cf.* R. C. K. Ensor, *England 1870–1914*, Oxford, 1936, pp. 412–13, Gordon, *The Dominion Partnership*, chapter 10, and Preston, *Canada and 'Imperial Defense'*, chapter 13, for a detailed account of the 1909 naval crisis and U.K.–dominion discussions.
69 For Canadian views and generally see Borden Papers, 66441–5 for notes on the Liberals and a fleet unit; also 35352–4 for notes on Imperial Defence and for Australian views. See also Hankey, *The Supreme Command,* vol. 1, pp. 125–7, and Gordon, *The Dominion Partnership*, pp. 237–9.
70 Cd. 5741, p. 84.
71 *War Memoirs of David Lloyd George* (new ed., 2 vols), London, 1938, vol. 1, p. 28, and Hankey, *The Supreme Command,* vol. 1, pp. 128–9.
72 Cd. 5745. Also reprinted in Keith, *Speeches and Documents,* vol. 2, pp. 304–7.
73 Keith, *Speeches and Documents*, vol. 2, pp. 308–38.
74 *Ibid.,* p. 353.
75 C.I.D. Paper 81–C. The Representation of the Dominions on the Committee of Imperial Defence, 18 May 1911; also Harcourt's despatch of 10 December 1912 to Governors-General of the dominions in Borden Papers 66218–20, and Hankey, *The Supreme Command*, vol. 1, pp. 130–2. See also S. Roskill, *Hankey – Man of Secrets,* (3 vols), London, 1970–4, vol. 1, pp. 106–7.
76 The relevant memoranda and other particulars as circulated are *inter alia* to be seen in the Laurier Papers, 1907 and 1911, vols 742–44, the Union Archives, Pretoria, and Harcourt's despatch (no. 30) of 20 January 1911 to Viscount Gladstone, governor-general of South Africa.
77 CAB. 37/106 1911, no. 52.
78 Cd. 5745. *Minutes of Proceedings of the Imperial Conference, 1911,* pp. 194–6 in respect of Civil Service exchanges. New Zealand had advanced more limited proposals in 1907, relating only to the staff of the Colonial Office. Elgin had argued that it would serve no useful purpose and indeed that the proposal might be founded on a misapprehension since the C.O. had nothing to do with local administration in the dominions and dealt with business which depended more on principles than local characteristics. Cd. 3523, p. 619 and also Cd. 5746, p. 214 (XII) for summary on 'Interchange of Civil Servants'.
79 *Ibid.,* pp. 55–6.
80 Keith Sinclair, *Imperial Federation. A Study of New Zealand Policy and Opinion 1880–1914*, London, 1955, p. 41–4, J. E. Kendle, *The Round Table Movement and Imperial Union*, Toronto, 1975, p. 93; see also pp. 88–95 and 112–14, and J. Marlowe, *Milner-Apostle of Empire*, London, 1976, pp. 210–12.
81 Cd. 5745, p. 70.
82 *Smuts Papers*, vol. 3, p. 36.
83 Hankey, *The Supreme Command*, p. 130 and chapter 13 *passim*.
84 Cd. 5745, p. 22 and also reprinted in Keith, *Speeches and Documents*, vol. 2, p. 243–4.

258 *Notes*

85 Roskill, op. cit., vol. 1, p. 120.
86 CID Minutes of 119th Meeting, 1 August 1912 (885 B).
87 The Laurier Papers in the National Archives, Ottawa, and more especially the Memoranda on Colonial and Imperial Conferences and on proposals for an Imperial Council in the Borden Papers, National Archives, Ottawa, which provide a valuable retrospective summary in terms of Canadian interests, have been consulted in the writing of this chapter (35344–54 and 65924). The National Archives in Pretoria have also been consulted, especially the correspondence and other records relating to the Imperial Conference, 1911.

CHAPTER 6

1 C. S. Goldman (ed.), *The Empire and the Century*, London, 1905.
2 C. Headlam, *The Milner Papers (South Africa) 1897–1905* (2 vols), London, 1931–3, vol. 2, p. 561. The letter was dated 27 February 1906.
3 S. Gopal, *British Policy in India 1858–1905*, Cambridge, 1965, pp. 180 and 303–4.
4 The story is told in Sir Almeric Fitzroy, *Memoirs* (2 vols), London n.d., vol I, p. 348.
5 R. Hyam, 'Smuts and the Decision of the Liberal Government to Grant Responsible Government to the Transvaal, January and February 1906', in *The Historical Journal*, vol. viii, no. 3 (1965), p. 380–98, emphasises Elgin's role in this issue. His study of *Elgin and Churchill at the Colonial Office 1905–1908*, sets out the evidence for a reassessment of Elgin. See also his chapter 'The Colonial Office Mind 1900–1914' in Hillmer and Wigley (editors), *The First British Commonwealth*, London, 1980.
6 See R. R. James, *Rosebery*, London, 1963, chapter 9, *passim*.
7 See Asquith Papers, Dep. 11. Churchill to Asquith, 14 March 1908.
8 Asquith Papers, Bodleian Library. Box 11, letter dated 14 March 1908.
9 India Office Library, Morley Papers, MSS. Eur. D. 573/2.
10 *Ibid.*, MSS. Eur. D. 573/2 and 573/11.
11 Roy Jenkins, *Asquith*, London, 1964.
12 *List of Cabinet Papers*, PRO, HMSO, London, 1964. Copies are in the Asquith Papers. Photo copies of the full set 1868–1916 are on Cab. 41.
13 See above p. 153.
14 E. T. S. Dugdale (ed.), *German Diplomatic Documents, 1871–1914* (4 vols), London, 1928, vol. 1, 177–8.
15 Maurice Hankey, *The Supreme Command 1914–1918* (2 vols), London, 1961, vol. 1, p. 130.
16 *Ibid.*, pp. 134–5.
17 Dugdale, *German Diplomatic Documents*, vol. 4, pp. 359–60.
18 R. A. Preston, *Canada and 'Imperial Defence'*, Durham N. C., 1967, pp. 462–3.
19 For an account of 'The Empire at War, 1914–1918, see *The Cambridge History of the British Empire*, chapter 16, from which the statistics are taken.
20 I am indebted to Professor N. G. Garson for this disclosure, which is made in his paper 'South Africa in World War I' in Hillmer and Wigley (editors), *The First British Commonwealth*, London, 1980, p. 70. For Botha's message, quoted above, see W. K. Hancock, *Smuts* (2 vols), Cambridge, 1962 and 1968, vol. 1, pp. 379 and 390.
21 L. F. Fitzhardinge, *W. M. Hughes*, (2 vols), Melbourne 1964 and 1979, vol. 11,

The Little Digger 1914–1952, p. 209. See chaps. viii, ix and xiii for full and lively account of the crises.

22 O. D. Skelton, *Life and Letters of Sir Wilfrid Laurier* (2 vols), Toronto, 1921., vol. 2, p. 437.

23 A. R. M. Lower, *Colony to Nation* (4th ed.), Toronto, 1964, p. 466.

24 *C.H.B.E.*, vol. 3, p. 634.

25 Borden Papers, letter of 3 November 1915. For an account of the background generally and more particularly of 'the isolation in which Borden was obliged to conduct the dominion's war effort' and which was by 1915 'almost intolerable' with his visit to London bringing him 'no closer to information on policy', see P. G. Wigley, *Canada and the transition to Commonwealth: British–Canadian Relations, 1917–1926*, Cambridge, 1977, p. 23.

26 Borden Papers, letter of 4 January 1916 to Sir George Perley.

27 W. M. Hughes, *The Splendid Adventure*, London, 1929, chapters 2–4 (see especially pp. 40–1) and Fitzhardinge, op. cit., vol. 11, pp. 95–105. Hughes felt Asquith's cabinet would have got more done with 'fewer clever men and more ordinary ones'.

28 Hansard, *Parliamentary Debates* (Commons), vol. lxxxviii, col. 1355.

29 L. S. Amery, *My Political Life* (2 vols), London, 1953–4, vol. 2, p. 91. See also Lord Long, *Memories*, London, 1923, p. 237, for improvements in communication effected by him as colonial secretary at this time.

30 Cd. 9005, p. 6. S. Roskill, *Hankey. Man of Secrets*, (3 vols), London, 1970–4, vol. I, p. 348.

31 Hankey, *The Supreme Command*, vol. 2, p. 660.

32 Records of the imperial war cabinet were handled by the war cabinet office in the same way as those of the war cabinet and its minutes are classified in a separate series – Imperial War Cabinet Minutes in Cab. 23; *Cf. The Records of the Cabinet Office to 1922*, London, PRO, 1966, pp. 4–5, and also Hankey, *The Supreme Command*, vol. 2, pp. 658–9.

33 Hankey, *ibid*.

34 *Ibid.*, p. 816, and *The Records of the Cabinet Office*, p. 5.

35 Amery, *My Political Life*, vol. 2, pp. 105–7.

36 *Ibid.*, p. 108.

37 Hankey, *The Supreme Command*, vol. 2. p. 816 and Preston, *Canada and 'Imperial Defence'*, pp. 519–22.

38 L. S. Amery, *Thoughts on the Constitution* (2nd ed.), London, 1953, p. 120.

39 Borden Papers.

40 By Desmond Morton in Hillmer and Wigley, op. cit., p. 56.

41 *Ibid.*, On Hughes' role see L. F. Fitzhardinge, *Canadian Historical Review*, June, 1967, vol. xlix, 2, pp. 160–9. Wigley, *Canada and the Transition to Commonwealth* offers an analysis of Borden's developing views, see pp. 68–79. Roskill, op. cit., vol. II, pp. 29–30 for quotation from Hankey.

42 L. C. Christie, *Notes on the Development at the Paris Peace Conference of the Status of Canada as an International Person*, 1 July 1919, Borden Papers.

43 Amery, *My Political Life*, vol. 2, pp. 177–8.

44 Roskill, op. cit., vol. II, pp. 38 and 54. *Official History of Australia in the War of 1914–18*; Ernest Scott, *Australia During the War*, vol. 2, pp. 787 and 796.

45 See Hancock, *Smuts*, vol. 1, chapter 21 and below vol. 2, p. 208.

46 *Cf.* K. C. Wheare's comment in *CHBE*, vol. 3, p. 664.

47 *Minutes of Proceedings of the Imperial Conference*, 1917, Cd. 8566.

48 Quoted in John Marlowe, *Milner. Apostle of Empire*, London, 1976, p. 353.

49 C. O. 886/10. For an account of the circumstances in which the memorandum came to be written, as well as an analysis and appraisal of its content, see Hancock, *Smuts*, vol. 2, pp. 38–49. *Cf.* also C. M. van den Heever, *General J. B. M. Hertzog*, Johannesburg, 1946, p. 212; O. Pirow, *Hertzog*, Cape Town, 1957, p. 103; and H. Duncan Hall, *The American Political Science Review*, December 1953, pp. 1005–6.
50 Cmd. 1474.
51 Hancock, *Smuts*, vol. 2, p. 49.
52 Cmd. 1474.

CHAPTER 7

1 The Anglo–Irish background to the Treaty Settlement is examined in N. Mansergh, *The Irish Question 1840–1921*, London, 1965, and in longer perspective in J. C. Beckett, *The Making of Modern Ireland, 1603–1923*, London, .1966.
2 Philip Guedalla, *The Queen and Mr. Gladstone* (2 vols), London, 1933, vol. 2, p. 177.
3 The Redmond Papers are in the National Library, Dublin.
4 A. P. Thornton, *The Habit of Authority*, London, 1966, p. 291.
5 Sir Henry Lucy, *A Diary of Two Parliaments, 1880–1885*, London, 1886, pp. 84–5.
6 Quoted in Kenneth Young, *Arthur James Balfour*, London, 1963, p. 100.
7 Sir Henry Lucy, *Memories of Eight Parliaments*, London, 1908, pp. 155–7.
8 Quoted in L. P. Curtis, *Coercion and Conciliation in Ireland 1880–1892. A Study in Conservative Unionism*, Princeton, 1963, p. 179. This book provides the authoritative account of A. J. Balfour's Irish administration and the ideas behind it.
9 John Biggs-Davison, *George Wyndham: A Study in Toryism*, London, 1951, p. 236.
10 See Young, *Arthur James Balfour*, p. 139, for a strange forecast of Wyndham's early death.
11 Biggs-Davison, *George Wyndham: A Study in Toryism*, p. 132.
12 *Ibid.*, pp. 152–3.
13 Stephen Gwynn (ed.), *The Anvil of War: Letters between F. S. Oliver and his Brother, 1914–1918*, London, 1936, p. 23.
14 Robert Blake, *The Unknown Prime Minister*, London, 1955, p. 531. The author believed that until the war Ulster was one of the two things Bonar Law really cared about. The other was tariff reform.
15 A. M. Gollin, *Proconsul in Politics: A Study of Lord Milner in opposition and in power*, London, 1964, pp. 45–6 and 193. See generally pp. 184–94.
16 Hansard, *Parl. Deb.* (Commons), lxxxiii, coll. 801–2.
17 Arthur Griffith, *The Resurrection of Hungary: A Parallel for Ireland* (3rd ed.), Dublin, 1918, pp. 89–91.
18 It is reprinted in Dorothy Macardle, *The Irish Republic* (new ed.), New York, 1965, pp. 135–7.
19 W. S. Churchill, *The World Crisis; The Aftermath*, London, 1929, p. 281.
20 Macardle, *The Irish Republic*, chapter 27, and T. D. Williams (ed.), *The Irish Struggle*, London, 1966, chapter 3, 'Sinn Féin Policy and Practice (1916–26)' by Desmond Ryan.

21 W. B. Yeats, *Collected Poems*, London, 1934, p. 205. W. K. Hancock, *Survey of British Commonwealth Affairs* (2 vols), London, 1937–42, vol. 1, p. 99; and D. MacDonagh's essay on 'Plunkett and MacDonagh' in F. X. Martin (ed.), *Leaders and Men of the Easter Rising: Dublin 1916*, London, 1967, pp. 166–7.
22 Churchill, *The World Crisis; The Aftermath*, p. 290.
23 Harold Nicolson, *King George V*, London, 1952, pp. 346–9.
24 *The Round Table*, vol. xi, no. 43 (June 1921), p. 505.
25 Churchill, *The World Crisis; The Aftermath*, p. 290.
26 Charles Townshend, *The British Campaign in Ireland 1919–1921*, Oxford, 1975, p. 202.
27 D. G. Boyce, *Englishmen and Irish Troubles, 1918–1922*, Cambridge, Mass., 1972, pp. 180 and 170.
28 Thomas Jones, *Whitehall Diary*, vol. III, *Ireland 1918–1925*, edited by K. Middlemas, London, 1971, p. 71. For a critical appreciation of the overall military position see Townshend, op. cit., Chaps. V–VII. The arrangements for the meeting are recorded in extracts from Miss Stevenson's diary reprinted in Lord Beaverbrook, *The Decline and Fall of Lloyd George*, London, 1963, pp. 85–6; the account of the interview, at which Miss Stevenson was not present, is as recollected by President de Valera. The differences are only in respect of detail.
29 Cmd. 1470, p. 1.
30 *Whitehall Diary*, vol. III, p. 11; also p. 149. Tom Jones, *Lloyd George*, London, 1951, p. 188–9.
31 Hansard, *Parl. Deb.* (Commons), col. cxxvii, col. 1125.
32 See Nicolson, *King George V*, pp. 349–51, and Hancock, *Smuts*, vol. 2, pp. 51–9, for accounts of this episode.
33 *Whitehall Diary*, vol. III, p. 76.
34 Sir Charles Petrie, *The Life and Letters of the Right Hon. Sir Austen Chamberlain* (2 vols), London, 1939, vol. 2, pp. 166–7.
35 *Whitehall Diary*, vol. III, pp. 82–3.
36 Cmd. 1474, p. 23.
37 *Dáil Éireann*: Debate on the Treaty between Great Britain and Ireland; Session December 1921–January 1922, p. 34.
38 *Ibid.*, pp. 45–6.
39 *Ibid.*, p. 27.
40 *Ibid.*, pp. 24–6.

Index

settler communities and of Irish nationalists, 225–6, 241–2; *see also* migration

Shaw, Professor A. G. L., *Convicts and Colonies*, 117

Shaw, George Bernard, *Fabianism and the Empire*, 22; 93

Sheffield Chamber of Commerce, 58

Shepstone, Sir Theophilus, 81–2

Siegfried, André, *The Race Question in Canada*, 63; *Democracy in New Zealand*, 113, 122, 125–6

Sigcau, 12

Sinha, Sir S. P., 199

Sinn Féin, 224; founded by Arthur Griffith, 226; Árd-fheis (1917), 227–8; election results (1918), first meeting of *Dáil Éireann*, 228; force against, 230; Lloyd George seeks settlement with, 231–2, 235

Smith, Adam, *The Wealth of Nations*, 43, 57

Smith, Professor Goldwin, 6, 53, 56, 97, 102, 183

Smuts, General J. C., 20; and use of term 'British Commonwealth', 21, 24–5, 29–30, 32; on Canadian constitution, 27; *A Century of Wrong*, 70; 84; at Vereeniging (1902), 95–7; his talk with Campbell-Bannerman (1906), 97–8, 100; 'the remaking of South Africa', 101–3; and native franchise, 107–9; 179; quoted, 182; campaign in East Africa, 192; Commonwealth statesman, 194; member of British war cabinet, 199; and disposition of German colonies, 206; protests against harshness of peace terms, 207; and 'the only successful experiment in international government' (1917), 208; memorandum (1921) anticipating Balfour Declaration and Statute of Westminster, 209–14; 232; suggestions for King's speech in Belfast (1921), 237–8; and defining of dominion status, 239

Soames, Christopher (Lord), xii

Solomon, Sir R., 98

South Africa, *see* Africa, South

South Africa Act (1909), 91, 94, 196

South African War, the (1899–1902),

28, 93–7; colonial contributions to, 154, 158; 161; and new thinking about defence, 157, 166; 192

South Australia, 46, 115, 128, 130–3, 152

Spain, 28, 35

Spender, J. A., 98–9

Stack, Austin, 241

Stamp Act, the, memory of, 35

Stephen, Sir James, under-secretary for the colonies, 1836–47, 47, 49

Steyn, President M. T., 14, 102

Sudan, the, 11

Swaziland, 108, 110

Sydney, 117, 127, 130

Talleyrand, C.-M. de, Prince, 183

Tandon, Prakash, *Punjabi Century, 1847–1947*, 13

tariffs, first imposed in Canada (1859), 57–8; colonial preferences and resistance to centralising pressures, 159–62; right to impose, 226, 233

Tarkastad, 77

Tasmania, 128, 131, 133, 152

Taylor, A. J. P., 30; *Germany's First Bid for Colonies 1884*–5, 147

Tilley, S. L., 67

Times, The, 15, 56

Thornton, Professor A. P., *The Habit of Authority*, 217

Tocqueville, Alexis de, 35, 61–2

Toronto, 6

trade, 35, 46; imperialism and the fiscal revolution, 51–4; 56; regulation of colonial trade, first Canadian trading agreement (1854) and first Canadian tariff (1859), 57–8; 62, 67, 71, 127; changes in international pattern of, after 1870, 145–6; resolution on trading preferences (1894), 151–2; and naval protection of (1897), 153; colonial flexibility in trading policies, tariff reform and reciprocal preferences (1902), 159–62; (1907), 166, 175; *see also* free trade

Transkei, the, 109

Transvaal, the, 7, 20, 27, 71; independence recognised (1852), 78; flexible constitution, 79; annexation (1877), battle of Majuba Hill (1881), inde-